POSTWAR ARMORED FIGHTING VEHICLES
1945–PRESENT

THE ESSENTIAL
VEHICLE IDENTIFICATION GUIDE

POSTWAR ARMORED FIGHTING VEHICLES
1945–PRESENT

MICHAEL E. HASKEW

amber
BOOKS

This edition published in 2010 by
Amber Books Ltd
Bradley's Close
74–77 White Lion Street
London N1 9PF
United Kingdom
www.amberbooks.co.uk

Library of Congress Cataloging-in-Publication Data
is available from the Library of Congress

ISBN: 978-1-907446-28-3

Project Editor: Michael Spilling
Design: Hawes Design
Picture Research: Terry Forshaw

Printed in Thailand

Photograph and Illustration Credits

PHOTOGRAPHS:
Art-Tech/Aerospace: 6, 8, 10, 12, 19, 29, 76, 102, 104, 136, 168, 186
Cody Images: 62, 79, 90, 92, 93, 110, 113, 134
U.S. Department of Defense: 9, 138–140 (all), 145, 149–151 (all), 175
U.S. National Archives: 60

ARTWORKS:
All artworks courtesy of Art-Tech/Aerospace except for the following:
Mark Franklin: 148, 165 (bottom), 166 (top), 167 (both), 187 (bottom)
Alcaniz Fresno's S.A.: 47, 48 (top), 49 (both), 64–66 (all), 69–70 (all), 74 (bottom), 118
Oliver Missing: 14, 15 (top), 68 (centre and bottom), 71 (both), 84–85 (all), 119–121 (all),
    123 (both), 125 (both), 127 (bottom), 133 (both), 134

Contents

Introduction

During more than half a century of modern
warfare, military strategists and tacticians have
alternately praised and maligned the armoured
fighting vehicle. With the advent of nuclear
weapons, efficient anti-armour missiles and
mines, it seemed at one time that the day of the
tank had passed. However, armoured vehicle
technology has advanced as well, and the role
of the tank has been redefined to the battlefield
of the twenty-first century and beyond.
Through decades of warfare, the key attributes
of firepower, speed and armour protection have
guided the development and deployment of the
tank. The armoured vehicle itself has been
redesigned, fitted with futuristic equipment and
armament, and integrated into the general battle
plans of nations across the globe.

◀ **On manoeuvres**
US crew onboard their M60A2 Patton medium tank discuss strategy during winter exercises in West
Germany. The M60 series remained in US service for almost 30 years, being replaced as the US Army's
main battle tank by the Abrams M1 in the 1980s.

FOLLOWING THE CATACLYSM of World War II, a reassessment of the role of the tank and armoured fighting vehicle in warfare occurred. The division of labour among armoured forces inevitably gave way to a multi-purpose, powerful and highly mobile vehicle. Rather than the continued production of tanks to fit different functions – the lightly armed and armoured tanks for reconnaissance and rapid movement, medium tanks to engage enemy armour in tank versus tank combat, and heavy tanks to provide direct artillery and infantry support – the concept of the all-purpose, main battle tank emerged. This was typified in the Cold War era by the US Patton series, British-made Centurion and the Soviet-originated T-55 and its numerous upgrades and variants.

Offensive prowess

The effectiveness of the main battle tank has been demonstrated in combat and embodies continuing improvement in multiple aspects of design and tactical capacity. Heavier, more versatile platforms mount specialized turrets housing larger calibre guns capable of firing APFSDS (armour-piercing fin-stabilized discarding sabot) ammunition and, in some cases, anti-tank missiles. Stabilization systems allow main battle tanks to fire on the move with great accuracy, while laser rangefinding and infrared night vision equipment facilitate target acquisition and compensate for atmospheric conditions in a variety of climates and weather conditions. Battlefield management systems allow the tracking of multiple targets simultaneously, assisting in the identification of both friendly and hostile vehicles, while advanced communications equipment coordinate operations on a grand scale. Increasingly powerful engines, such as the conventional diesel or innovative gas turbine types, provide speed, reliability and ease of maintenance.

Defensive demands

Defensive modernization includes the introduction of composite, modular and explosive reactive armour, isolated storage space for ammunition with blast doors to protect crew members and components designed to direct an explosion outwards in the event of penetration of the tank's hull or turret. Warning sensors designed to alert the tank crew to an imminent threat when the vehicle is 'locked on' by enemy laser equipment coordinate with appropriate countermeasures to minimize the likelihood of a direct hit.

Smoke grenade launchers are standard on the modern main battle tank, while machine guns remain a necessity for protection against low-flying aircraft or attacking infantry. NBC (nuclear, biological, chemical) defensive systems allow armoured vehicles to operate in such adverse conditions.

Modern low intensity combat has nevertheless constituted a persistent paradox for the armoured fighting vehicle. The confines of urban warfare often limit the capabilities of the tank during close-in fighting, while rudimentary improvised explosive devices (IED) and land mines remain hazards to even the latest in AFV technology. In response, defensive packages specifically designed for low intensity and urban survivability have been introduced.

New tactics

Along with the ever-improving technology, battlefield tactics have also been refined. Recent battlefield experience has confirmed the tank's ability to create and to exploit a breach in enemy lines, rapidly advance across favorable terrain and hold territory in cooperation with armoured infantry. These highly mobile ground troops ride into battle aboard armoured personnel carriers or infantry

▼ Stryker force

US Army M1126 Stryker ICVs of the Stryker Brigade Combat Team kick up plumes of dust as they conduct a patrol near Mosul, Iraq, 2005. Infantry combat vehicles such as the Stryker provide a highly mobile platform from which to deploy infantry and firepower in reconnaissance operations and counter-insurgency warfare.

KEY TO TACTICAL SYMBOLS USED IN ORGANIZATION CHARTS

Symbol for division or larger		Sig	Signals unit
Symbol for regiment or brigade-sized formation		Hv	Heavy weapons unit
Symbol for battalion or smaller unit		Bat	Battery
		Mot	Motorized infantry unit
Arm	Armoured unit	Art	Artillery unit
Mec	Mechanized unit	Rec	Reconnaissance
Eng	Engineer unit	AA	Anti-aircraft unit
Inf	Infantry unit	SP	Self-propelled gun unit

fighting vehicles designed not only to provide transportation but also to add direct fire support with a variety of weapons from light machine guns to anti-tank missiles, chain guns and high-velocity cannon.

The main battle tank, its accompanying armoured fighting vehicles, self-propelled artillery and other types are destined to play active roles in ground warfare well into the future. As technology is continually refined, these versatile vehicles will serve as primary weapons systems in any armed conflict of great magnitude.

Chapter 1

Cold War Europe, 1947–91

**Before the guns of World War II had fallen silent,
the coalition that eventually defeated the Axis had begun to
fracture. Ideological differences, which had simmered just
below the surface, had come to the fore as sharply
contrasting visions of the post-war world collided. In Europe,
an historic battleground, the lines were again being drawn.
This time, the force of armoured power was destined to
project the will of the military planners who deployed their
tanks only a few kilometres from those of their expected
adversaries. The only sure trump card to an overwhelming
mechanized land force was the potential use
of nuclear weapons.**

◀ **Amphibious manoeuvres**
Polish PT-76 amphibious tanks ford a river during a training exercise. Soviet tactical doctrine emphasized
river crossings and amphibious outflanking manoeuvres.

Early Cold War

Germany lay defeated, and former Allies prepared to confront one another in an atmosphere of mutual distrust. The flashpoint of another world war, it seemed, would be in Europe, where tanks and troops were arrayed in readiness.

WITH THE SOVIET RED ARMY dominant in Eastern Europe, where its tanks had fought the largest armoured clashes in modern military history, and the British and American armies controlling the West, an uneasy peace settled across the continent, while the world watched the ebb and flow of political and military tension.

Acknowledging that the Soviet Union was intent on expanding communism around the world, the United States and Great Britain adopted a policy of containment during the early days of the Cold War. Such policy was predicated on the continued deployment of military assets in close proximity to the Soviets, particularly in Europe where armed confrontation, should it develop, was expected to take place; the predominance of the United States in the Pacific; and the simple fact that the US possessed the atomic bomb, its awesome destructive power demonstrated at Hiroshima and Nagasaki.

The Soviets, on the other hand, had extended their sphere of influence into Eastern Europe not only to spread their communist philosophy, but also to assuage their paranoia concerning another attack against their homeland from the west. Meanwhile, on the continent of Asia a civil war raged in China, and Marxist fervour tinged with nationalism had begun to create unrest in Indochina. Still, the power of the atomic bomb was expected to hold the Soviets in check, and the security of Western Europe was top priority.

By 1950, the United States and Britain were facing financial constraints, and military spending was one of those areas which bore the brunt of budget cuts. The armies of the United States and Great Britain

▼ **German M48**

West German Army tank formations were equipped with M48s at first, until enough Leopard tanks were available for frontline service.

consisted of veteran troops who had fought in World War II; however, the conditions of occupation duty and the inevitable relaxation of wartime readiness had degraded combat efficiency. The US military establishment reorganized its divisional make-up. On paper, a tank battalion and an anti-aircraft battalion were added to each infantry division, and an artillery battery was increased from four guns to six. Anti-tank companies were stricken from regimental rolls, and a tank company added. In practice, however, the needed equipment, men and supplies were not readily available. Military readiness in Europe was more of a notion than a fact.

For the West, the containment doctrine and the use of armour were defensive in nature and undergirded by the threat of nuclear arms should the Soviet Union initiate a military campaign. Containment meant the maintenance of a military ground force in Western Europe, face to face with the Soviet military. War was narrowly averted as early as 1948, when the Soviets blockaded Berlin and a massive American airlift of supplies caused them to finally relax their stranglehold on the German capital.

The year 1949 was indeed a Cold War watershed. The Soviet Union successfully tested its first nuclear device, well ahead of Western time estimates, while the communists of Mao Tse-tung gained control of mainland China. The Western powers established the North Atlantic Treaty Organization with 12 nations pledging that 'an attack against one or more of [these nations] shall be considered an attack against them all'. Obviously aimed at the Soviet Union, the NATO alliance further fuelled Soviet suspicions as to the intent of its former allies. Within months, war had erupted on the Korean peninsula.

A harbinger of things to come occurred on 7 September 1945, during an Allied victory parade in Berlin. Celebrating the defeat of Nazi Germany, infantry units marched first, with the Soviet IX Rifle Corps and Fifth Shock Army, the French 2nd Division, the British 131st Infantry Brigade and the US 82nd Airborne Division stepping out.

A large armoured display then passed in review. First, 32 M24 Chaffee light tanks and 16 M8 armoured cars of the US 705th Armored Battalion rolled forward. They were followed by elements of the French 1st Armoured Division, 24 Comet tanks and 30 armoured cars of the famed British 7th Armoured Division and then 52 brand new IS-3 heavy tanks of the Red Army's 71st Guards Heavy Tank Regiment. Western observers were taken aback by the number of new, modern Soviet tanks. The era of the arms race, posturing and global gamesmanship had begun.

Soviet Union
1947–69

Formed in 1955, the Warsaw Pact was a military alliance of the Soviet Union and its satellite states in Eastern Europe undertaken in response to NATO initiatives.

DIVIDED EAST AND WEST, Germany was considered the likely primary battleground between Red Army and Western land forces should a shooting war begin. The Federal Republic of Germany formally joined NATO on 9 May 1955, and less than a week later the Soviet Union formed the Warsaw Pact. Perhaps the most tangible perceived threat to Soviet security was a rearmed West Germany. With the Red Army the primary Warsaw Pact military force, the armies of Poland, East Germany and Czechoslovakia, which bordered the West, were also expected to supply men and arms, as were other client states to a lesser extent.

Of course, the strength of the Soviet alliance has been questioned from the start, and prime evidence of its tenuous nature was the short-lived Hungarian Revolt of 1956, when the Red Army deployed more than 1100 tanks, which rolled through the streets of Budapest and other Hungarian cities.

Warsaw Pact armoured doctrine of the Cold War years was in large part an extension of those tactics which proved successful in World War II – applying overwhelming force to a localized front, achieving a breakthrough and rapidly exploiting the breach in enemy lines. To complement the proven T-34

▲ **IS-2 Heavy Tank (1944 model)**

Soviet Third Guards Mechanized Army / East Germany, 1950

Designed in response to heavy German armour during World War II, the IS-2 heavy tank entered service with the Red Army in 1943. Soon, the Model 1944 incorporated the D25-T 122mm (4.8in) gun (faster-firing than its predecessor), a double-baffle muzzle brake and better fire control.

Specifications	
Crew: 4	Speed: 37km/h (23mph)
Weight: 46 tonnes (45.27 tons)	Range: 240km (149 miles)
Length: 9.9m (32ft 6in)	Armament: 1 x 122mm (4.8in) D-25T gun, plus 3
Width: 3.09m (10ft 2in)	x 7.62mm (0.3in) DT MGs (1 coaxial, 1 fixed in
Height: 2.73m (8ft 11in)	bow and 1 ball-mounted in turret rear)
Engine: 382.8kW (513hp) V-2 12-cyl diesel	Radio: 10R or 10RK

Soviet Independent Guards Heavy Tank Brigade, 1947

Most of the Soviet armoured formations that faced westwards during the early years of the Cold War were elite Guards units. With more than 60 tanks, the Red Army heavy tank brigade was organized into three armoured regiments and one mechanized infantry regiment that included supporting self-propelled assault guns.

HQ (3 x command vehicles)

1 Regiment (3 x command tanks, 21 x IS-2s)

3 Regiment (3 x command tanks, 21 x IS-2s)

2 Regiment (3 x command tanks, 21 x IS-2s)

Light SP Battery (3 x SU-76M)

Support troops (19 x M3 half-tracks)

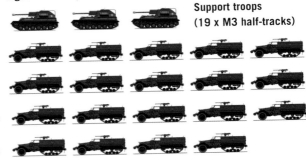

medium tank, the development of heavy tanks such as the IS-2 and IS-3 continued during the 1950s. While several improvements in heavy tank design did not extend beyond the prototype stage, the IS-2 went on to equip the standard Red Army heavy tank regiment of the early Cold War era (each fielded 21); the medium T-34 was deployed in large numbers as well.

In the 1960s, Soviet tank design made a significant leap forward with the T-64, which introduced an automatic loader, eliminating the need for a fourth crewman. The Soviets also refined tactics in the use of

mechanized infantry, designating mechanized rifle divisions as light and heavy. The introduction of the BMP-1, the world's first purpose-built infantry fighting vehicle, and the wheeled BTR-40 and BTR-60 armoured personnel carriers, which had been in service since 1950, facilitated this adjustment.

As the Soviet armoured division's tanks advanced along the main front, the heavy mechanized infantry units were to follow in support, providing cover against enemy infantry and anti-tank units. The light mechanized infantry units were to fan out along the

▲ IS-3 Heavy Tank
Soviet First Guards Tank Army / East Germany, 1952
Nicknamed the 'Pike' due to its distinctively pointed hull, the IS-3 formed the basis for Soviet heavy tank designs of the Cold War era. The turret of the IS-3 was rounded and flattened, resulting in a lower profile while sacrificing space for the crew.

Specifications

Crew: 3	Speed: 40km/h (25mph)
Weight: 45.77 tonnes (45.05 tons)	Range: 185km (115 miles)
Length: 9.85m (32ft 4in)	Armament: 1 x 122mm (4.8in) D-25T gun, plus
Width: 3.09m (10ft 2in)	1 x 12.7mm (0.5in) DshK HMG on AA mount and
Height: 2.45m (8ft)	1 x coaxial 7.62mm (0.3in) DT MG
Engine: 447kW (600hp) V-2-JS V12 diesel	Radio: 10RK

▲ T-10 Heavy Tank
Soviet First Guards Tank Army / East Germany, 1955
In 1948, the Soviet General Tank Directorate ordered a new heavy tank weighing approximately 50.8 tonnes (50 tons). Originally designated the IS-8, the final variant of the 'Josef Stalin' series underwent numerous modifications. With Stalin's death in 1953, the new tank, armed with a 125mm (4.9in) D-25TA gun, was at last named the T-10. Although manufacture ended in 1966, T-10s were not retired from reserve until 1996.

Specifications

Crew: 4	Engine: 522kW (700hp) V12 diesel
Weight: 49,890kg (109,760lb)	Speed: 42km/h (26mph)
Length: 9m (27ft 6in)	Range: 250km (155 miles)
Width: 3.27m (10ft)	Armament: 1 x 122mm (4.8in) gun, plus 2 x
Height: 2.59m (7ft 4.5in)	12.7mm (0.5in) MGs (1 coaxial and 1 AA)
	Radio: n/k

flanks of the advance, securing the main thrust against counterattacks that might threaten the rear of the offensive. In the West, the availability of tactical nuclear weapons to the Warsaw Pact forces was discounted despite the fact that intelligence could not confirm their presence or lack thereof. Conjecture persists as to whether the Soviets were prepared to use nuclear weapons of more than 10 megatons ahead of conventional offensive operations.

During the 1960s, a Soviet modernization programme was under way: the older T-54/55 tank, with its 100mm (3.9in) main weapon, was gradually replaced by the T-62, armed with a 125mm (4.9in) main gun, and subsequently the T-64, while the

BMP-1, BTR-40 and BTR-60 infantry fighting vehicle and armoured personnel carriers provided the rapid mobility necessary for successful operations against NATO forces. Self-propelled artillery, primarily the World War II-vintage SU-76, was organic to the Soviet armoured division as well.

In the autumn of 1962, the United States and the Soviet Union came closer to declared war than at perhaps any other time during the Cold War. The deployment of ballistic missiles to Cuba prompted the US to place its conventional and nuclear assets on high alert. Although war was averted, a telling aspect of the original Soviet commitment to Cuba was the intent to station four motorized regiments, two tank

▲ **T-54A Main Battle Tank**

Soviet Third Shock Army / IX Tank Corps, East Germany, 1956

The T-54/55 was produced in greater numbers than any other tank in history, and its service life extended to nearly half a century. The earliest of Soviet main battle tank designs, the T-54/55 proved relatively easy to modify, and production was not terminated until 1981.

Specifications

Crew: 4	Speed: 48km/h (30mph)
Weight: 36 tonnes (35.42 tons)	Range: 400km (250 miles)
Length (hull): 6.45m (21ft 2in)	Armament: 1 x 100mm (3.9in) D-10T gun, plus
Width: 3.27m (10ft 9in)	1 x 12.7mm (0.5in) DShK AA MG and 2 x
Height: 2.4m (7ft 10in)	7.62mm (0.3in) DT MGs
Engine: 388kW (520bhp) V-54 12-cylinder	Radio: R-113

Specifications

Crew: 2	Speed: (road) 60km/h (37mph); (water) 10km/h
Weight: 9650kg (21,278lb)	(6mph)
Length: 9.54m (31ft 3in)	Range: 530km (330 miles)
Width: 2.5m (8ft 2in)	Armament: 1 x 12.7mm (0.5in) DShKM MG
Height: 2.66m (8ft 8in)	(optional)
Engine: 82kW (110hp) ZIL-123 6-cylinder	

▲ **BAV 485**

Soviet Third Guards Mechanized Army / East Germany, 1957

Similar to the US amphibious DUKW, the BAV 485 amphibious transport vehicle was based on the chassis of the ZiS-151 6X6 truck, which was also used in the BTR-152 armoured personnel carrier. Production began in 1952, and the BAV 485 was modernized and deployed by Warsaw Pact forces into the 1980s.

battalions equipped with T-55s and up to 51,000 troops on the Caribbean island.

Continuing Soviet tank development was evidence of the growing realization among the major powers that the well-defined division of labour among tanks was on the wane. The functions of light, medium and heavy tanks were being consolidated in the main battle tank, a new generation of weapon that would provide the best available combination of armour protection, firepower and mobility.

Soviet Medium Tank Battalion, 1961

By the 1960s, a complement of 32 T-54/55 main battle tanks were organized in two companies to comprise a Red Army medium tank battalion. The T-54/55 was the initial Soviet design to embrace the concept of the main battle tank. The T-54/55 was originally armed with the 100mm (3.9in) D-10T rifled cannon, which was soon upgraded to the D-10T2 with a bore evacuator located near the muzzle.

HQ (1 x T54/55 MBT, 2 x trucks)

1 Company (16 x T-54/55 MBTs)

2 Company (16 x T-54/55 MBTs)

Support Platoon (5 x trucks)

▲ GAZ-46 MAV
Soviet First Guards Tank Army / East Germany, 1965

Patterned after the Ford GPA Seep amphibious vehicle, which had been supplied to the Soviets via Lend-Lease during World War II, the GAZ-46 MAV was intended as a light river-crossing and reconnaissance vehicle. It entered service in the 1950s and has been built under licence from Ford.

Specifications

Crew: 5	Engine: 134kW (180hp) V-B water-cooled petrol
Weight: 11,500kg (25,300lb)	Speed: 75km/h (46.8mph)
Length: 7.35m (42ft 1in)	Range: 405km (253 miles)
Width: 2.69m (8t 9in)	Armament: 40 x 122.4mm (4.82in) rocket-
Height: 2.85m (9ft 4in)	launcher tubes

▲ BM-21 Rocket Launcher
Soviet Eighth Guards Army / East Germany, 1967

The BM-21 Grad (Hail) rocket-launcher system entered service with the Red Army in 1964 and provided tactical fire support for advancing infantry and armoured formations. It had a crew of five, and its complement of 40 122.4mm (4.82in) rockets were initially carried atop the Ural 375D 6X6 truck.

▲ OT-62 Tracked Amphibious Armoured Personnel Carrier
Polish Army / 7th Coastal Defence Division, 1964

Based upon the Soviet-designed BTR-50 amphibious armoured personnel carrier, the OT-62 was capable of transporting 16 soldiers and was built jointly by Poland and Czechoslovakia under licence. Development began in 1958, and the first OT-62 entered service four years later.

NATO – France
1949–66

French armoured vehicle development was interrupted during World War II but regained its impetus rapidly after liberation. Within two years, French designers were developing the prototypes of several tanks.

EVEN DURING GERMAN OCCUPATION, French engineers had conducted a clandestine programme of armoured vehicle design, and by 1946 the *Atelier de Construction de Rueil* (ARL) had produced the ARL-44, a 54-tonne (53-ton) tank mounting a 90mm (3.5in) cannon. In 1953, the 503rd Tank Regiment of the French Army took possession of a few of these, but only 10 per cent of the initially ordered 600 were ever completed. Nevertheless, the French heeded the lessons of armoured combat during World War II and issued requirements for a new generation of armoured fighting vehicles.

The AMX-50 programme, named for the *Atelier de Construction* d'Issy-les-Moulineaux, where it was designed, incorporated a 90mm (3.5in) cannon along with features of successful tanks fielded during World War II and innovative design elements such as an oscillating turret that simplified the laying of the gun and the positioning of the hull in action. However, post-war financial constraints and the delivery of nearly 900 American-built M47 Patton tanks spelled the end of the AMX-50 programme. Meanwhile, the

light, airmobile AMX-13, armed initially with a 75mm (2.9in) gun and oscillating turret, entered production in 1952. The AMX-13 was produced steadily during the next quarter of a century and exported to over 25 countries.

French armaments manufacturers fully expected that West Germany would be allowed to rearm during the 1950s and promoted the production of a light tank which could be sold to the Germans. However, by 1956 a cooperative effort among several European nations endeavoured to come up with a suitable medium tank design to complement the British and American tanks that were deployed on the continent. With French and German designers in the lead, specifications were set forth in early 1957. Differing political and military priorities among the nations thwarted the cooperative effort, and French president Charles de Gaulle eventually withdrew his country from active participation in the NATO military organization in 1966.

In the same year, production of the French AMX-30, as the subsequent independent development project was designated, began in earnest. With the AMX-30, the French opted for a conventional turret and a 105mm (4.1in) rifled gun, and its designers decidedly favoured mobility over armour protection. At the same time as they developed the AMX-13 and AMX-30, the French designed numerous self-propelled artillery pieces and light armoured vehicles.

◀ **French MBT**
Around 3500 AMX-30 main battle tanks were built for France and for export.

▲ MK61 SP Gun

French Army / II Corps, Germany, 1957

The 105mm (4.1in) MK61 self-propelled howitzer was a variant of the AMX-13 light tank, constructed with its enclosed turret atop the AMX-13 chassis. Developed concurrently with the AMX-13, it was eventually supplanted by the 155mm (6.1in) GCT self-propelled gun.

Specifications

Crew: 5

Weight (approx): 16,500kg (36,382lb)

Length: 6.4m (30ft)

Width: 2.65m (8ft 3.3in)

Height: 2.7m (8ft 10.3in)

Engine: 186.4kW (250hp) SOFAM 8Gxb,
  8-cylinder petrol

Speed: 60km/h (37.3mph)

Range: 350km (217.5 miles)

Armament: 1 x 105mm (4.1in) gun, plus
  2 x 7.5mm (0.295in) MGs

Radio: n/k

◀ Panhard AML H-60 Light Armoured Car

French Army / 2nd Armoured Division, Germany, 1965

The Panhard AML H-60 armoured car was developed during the 1950s to replace the ageing British Daimler Ferret armoured cars in service with the post-war French Army. Carrying a 60mm (2.4in) breech-loading mortar and light machine guns, the vehicle entered service in 1960.

Specifications

Crew: 3

Weight: 5.5 tonnes (5.41 tons)

Length: 3.79m (12ft 5.2in)

Width: 1.97m (6ft 5.5in)

Height: 2.07m (6ft 9.5in)

Engine: 67.2kW (90hp) Panhard Model 4 HD
  4-cylinder petrol or 73kW (98hp)

Peugeot XD 3T, 4-cylinder diesel

Speed: 90km/h (56mph)

Range: 600km (373 miles)

Armament: 1 x 60mm (2.4in) low-recoil gun, plus
  1 x 7.62mm (0.3in) MG

Radio: n/k

Specifications

Crew: 4

Weight: 13,500kg (29,800lb)

Length (gun forwards): 6.15m (20ft 2in)

Width: 2.42m (7ft 11in)

Height: 2.32m (7ft 7in)

Engine: 149kW (200hp) Panhard 12-cylinder
  petrol

Speed: 105km/h (65mph)

Range: 600km (370 miles)

Armament: 1 x 75mm (2.9in) or 1 x 90mm
  (3.5in) gun, plus 2 x 7.5mm (0.295in) or
  7.72mm (0.303in) MGs

Radio: n/k

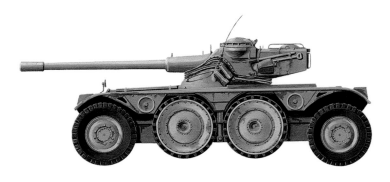

▲ Panhard EBR/FR-11 Armoured Car

French Army / I Corps, Germany, 1963

Actually designed prior to World War II, the Panhard EBR did not go into production until after the war ended. More than 1200 were produced after 1954. Heavily armed with 90mm (3.5in) or 75mm (2.9in) cannon and machine guns, the vehicle was deployed in Europe and in former French colonies.

▲ **Canon de 155 mm Mk F3 Automoteur**

French Army / II Corps, Germany, 1964

Constructed on a modified AMX-13 light tank chassis, the Mk F3 155mm (6.1in) self-propelled gun is the smallest of its kind ever produced. Designed in the early 1950s as a replacement for older US-made M41 self-propelled guns, the Mk F3 entered service with the French Army a decade later.

Specifications	
Crew: 2	Engine: 186kW (250hp) SOFAM 8Gxb 8-cylinder
Weight: 17,410kg (38,304lb)	petrol
Length: 6.22m (20ft 5in)	Speed: 60km/h (37mph)
Width: 2.72m (8ft 11in)	Range: 300km (185 miles)
Height: 2.085m (6ft 10in)	Armament: 1 x 155mm (6.1in) gun

NATO – West Germany
1955–69

With the creation of the Federal Republic of Germany, the pro-Western nation's rearmament was only a matter of time, and the *Bundeswehr* would soon embark on the design and deployment of its own armour.

SIX YEARS AFTER IT WAS CONSTITUTED AS A NATION, West Germany joined NATO and began a programme of rebuilding its armed forces. The direct German alignment with NATO was not without reservations. German leaders were well aware that their country would become the front line in the event of armed conflict with the Soviet Union. Therefore, it was critical to them that a NATO force commitment was substantial enough to defend against an attack by Warsaw Pact armies. In response, NATO adopted a forward defence strategy, which involved locating its forces quite near the national boundaries with the Warsaw Pact countries.

As West Germany rearmed, the US supplied M47 and M48 Patton tanks to the *Deutsches Heer,* or army. The Germans judged these tanks as rapidly becoming obsolescent, and by autumn 1956 German designers had embarked on a programme to develop their own world-class tank. The Leopard programme was under way when Germany and France entered into a joint

venture to develop a common tank, known as the Europa Panzer, in the summer of 1957. While progress was made and prototypes were tested, the effort eventually failed, and both nations chose to pursue their tank development based on perceived priorities.

Production of the Leopard 1 began in 1965, and nearly 6500 of all variants were built. Emphasizing speed rather than armour protection, the tank was lighter than most of its contemporaries. Originally designated the Standard Panzer, the Leopard 1 bore some resemblance to the tanks of its lineage, namely the Tigers and Panthers of World War II, but was essentially a modern tank of 1960s design mounting the British Royal Ordnance 105mm (4.1in) L7A3 L/52 rifled gun. During the 1960s and 1970s, the Leopard 1 was exported to several countries.

By 1960, the Germans had also begun work on a new purpose-built infantry fighting vehicle. The Marder, however, did not make its debut until the early 1970s, and until that time the *Schützenpanzer lang* HS.30, also known as the *Schützenpanzer* 12-3, was the principal such vehicle deployed by West German armoured formations.

From the outset, the Germans had disagreed with US doctrine that armoured personnel carriers were to serve only as 'battle taxis' to deliver infantrymen to the combat zone. US soldiers, transported in their M113s, were expected to dismount and fight. Only after practical experience in Vietnam demonstrated the value of the infantry fighting vehicle did this philosophy begin to change. In fact, battlefield conversions of many M113s were carried out to add firepower.

German designers considered the experience of their Panzergrenadiers, or armoured infantry, during World War II and decided to arm the *Schützenpanzer* 12-3 with a 20mm (0.79in) L/86 HS 820 autocannon

and a 7.62mm (0.3in) machine gun for use against enemy infantry. Up to five combat soldiers could be transported inside the vehicle and engage the enemy from inside or outside the troop compartment. The vehicle-borne troops were trained to work together and in coordination with tanks. Still, some German Panzergrenadier brigades incorporated truck and M113 transportation with the *Schützenpanzer* 12-3.

Although several German armoured divisions were constituted in the 1950s, field deployment departed from the pentagonal division structure of several NATO countries. Initially, armoured and infantry brigades were expected to form battle groups or task forces. Depending on the nature of the mission, additional armoured or infantry battalions could be added to this flexible structure as needed.

Specifications

Crew: 3 + 5
Weight: 14,600kg (32,200lb)
Length: 5.56m (18ft 3in)
Width: 2.25m (7ft 4in)
Height: 1.85m (6ft 1in)
Engine: 175kW (235hp) Rolls-Royce 8-cylinder petrol
Speed: 51km/h (32mph)
Range: 270km (170 miles)
Armament: 1 x 106mm (4.17in) M40A1 recoilless rifle, plus 1 x 20mm (0.79in) HS 820 autocannon

▲ **SPz lang LGS M40A1**

German Army / 10th Armoured Division / Mechanized Infantry Battalion 112, Germany, 1960

An infantry fighting vehicle developed in Germany during the 1950s, the SPz lang HS30 SP Gun was also produced in an anti-tank variant that mounted the 106mm (4.17in) M40A1 recoilless rifle along with the 20mm (0.79in) L/86 HS 820 autocannon. Another variant mounted an 81mm (3.2in) or 120mm (4.7in) mortar.

Specifications

Crew: 4	8-cylinder diesel
Weight (approx): 25,700kg (55,669lb)	Speed: 70km/h (43.5mph)
Length: 6.238m (20ft 5.6in)	Range: 400km (248.5 miles)
Width: 2.98m (9ft 9.3in)	Armament: 1 x 90mm (3.5in) gun, plus
Height: 2.085m (6ft 10in)	2 x 7.62mm (0.3in) MGs
Engine: 372.9kW (500hp) Daimler-Benz MB837	Radio: n/k

▲ **Jagdpanzer Kanone (JPK)**

German Army / 5th Armoured Division, Germany, 1968

Equipped with a 90mm (3.5in) main gun similar to that of the American M47 Patton tank, the light *Jagdpanzer Kanone* tank destroyer was deployed to German units in the mid-1960s and later exported to Belgium. Its lack of a turret limited traverse capabilities.

Specifications

Crew: 4

Weight: 39,912kg (87,808lb)

Length: 9.543m (31ft 4in)

Width: 3.25m (10ft 8in)

Height: 2.613m (8ft 7in)

Engine: 619kW (830hp) MTU 10-cylinder diesel

Speed: 65km/h (40.4mph)

Range: 600km (373 miles)

Armament: 1 x 105mm (4.1in) gun, plus 2 x
7.62mm (0.3in) MGs (1 coaxial and 1 anti-
aircraft) and 4 x smoke dischargers

Radio: n/k

▲ **Leopard 1 Main Battle Tank**

German Army / 1st Armoured Division / 1st Tank Battalion, Germany, 1969

The product of a lengthy development phase that had begun in the mid-1950s, the Leopard 1 main battle tank was the principal weapon of its kind deployed by the German Army for more than 20 years. Its main weapon was the British 105mm (4.1in) Royal Ordnance L7A3 L/52 rifled gun.

NATO – United Kingdom
1949–69

The British presence on the continent of Europe continued following the end of World War II, its infantry and armoured divisions constituting an occupation force in Germany, which soon became a major component of NATO defence.

AT THE END OF WORLD WAR II, Britain had been wracked by six years of war. Despite its commitment overseas to a slowly disintegrating empire, a financially strapped nation nevertheless recognized its obligation to participate in the defence of Western Europe against potential Soviet aggression. The British Army of the Rhine (BAOR) was subsequently established, and during the Cold War its strength ebbed and flowed from 25,000 to more than 60,000 troops. Economic constraints fostered the curtailment of men and equipment on the continent during the late 1940s, and at one time only the famed 7th Armoured and 2nd Infantry Divisions were present.

In 1950, the 6th and 11th Armoured Divisions arrived, and the four units formed the I British Corps, operating from bases in Lower Saxony and North Rhine Westphalia. Three infantry brigades

were dedicated to anti-tank operations, while the three armoured divisions each consisted of three tank brigades, plus supporting motorized infantry, artillery and other ancillary formations.

The primary British tank of the early Cold War period was the Centurion, the product of a design effort undertaken in 1943 but not yet quite in production as World War II in Europe ended in the spring of 1945. The Centurion had originally been conceived as a counter to heavy German armour, which had taken a toll on the lighter M4 Sherman tanks supplied by the US and on the British tank designs deployed during the war.

The Centurion borrowed the basic suspension of the Comet tank, its predecessor, which remained in service with the British Army of the Rhine until the late 1950s. Its production began in November 1945; however, it was soon evident that the 76mm

(3in/17-pounder) and then the 84mm (3.3in/20-pounder) main cannon needed improvement. In 1953, the Centurion Mk 7 variant with a 105mm (4.1in) L7 main gun was placed in production, and this was to become the most prominent of the 24 Centurion configurations, including a variety of support vehicles, to see service.

While the Centurion successfully embodied the initial British endeavour into development of the main battle tank, another project, the Conqueror, was proceeding in the closing days of World War II.

Conceived in response to the heavy Soviet IS-2 and IS-3 tanks, the Conqueror may, in its own right, be considered a main battle tank. However, mounting an American-designed L1 120mm (4.7in) rifled gun, it was envisioned by some tacticians as a longer-range fire support system for the advancing Centurion. Both the Conqueror and the Centurion were components of the post-war effort to develop the 'universal tank'. As the Centurion progressed, the Conqueror waned, and fewer than 200 were built before production ceased in 1959.

▲ Charioteer Tank Destroyer
British Army of the Rhine / 7th Armoured Division, Germany, 1956

Designed during the 1950s to augment the firepower of British Army units deployed with NATO forces in Germany, the Charioteer tank destroyer mounted the Royal Ordnance QF 84mm (3.3in/20-pounder) gun atop the modified chassis of the World War II-vintage Cromwell tank.

Specifications	
Crew: 4	Mks 1–3 12-cylinder petrol
Weight: 28,958kg (63,842lb)	Speed: 52km/h (32.30mph)
Length: 8.8m (28ft 10.4in)	Range: 240km (149 miles)
Width: 3.1m (10ft 2in)	Armament: 1 x 84mm (3.3in/20pdr) gun, plus
Height: 2.6m (8ft 6in)	1 x 7.62mm (0.3in) coaxial MG
Engine: 450kW (600hp) Rolls-Royce Meteor	Radio: n/k

▲ Conqueror Heavy Tank
British Army of the Rhine / 7th Armoured Division, Germany, 1964

The heavy Conqueror was designed concurrently with the better known Centurion main battle tank and considered primarily as long-range fire support for the latter. Shortly after the Conqueror entered production, the concept of the heavy tank was eclipsed by a refined 'universal tank' emphasis.

Specifications	
Crew: 4	Speed: 34km/h (21.3mph)
Weight: 64,858kg (142,688lb)	Range: 155km (95 miles)
Length (gun forward): 11.58m (38ft)	Armament: 1 x 120mm (4.7in) rifled gun, plus
Width: 3.99m (13ft 1in)	1 x 7.62mm (0.3in) coaxial MG
Height: 3.35m (11ft)	Radio: n/k
Engine: 604kW (810hp) 12-cylinder petrol	

NATO armoured doctrine during the Cold War generally rested upon containment of a Warsaw Pact breach in the forward defensive positions of Western forces. The threat of tactical nuclear weapons, which might decimate an attacking Soviet formation, was considered a primary component of grand strategy and a counter to the overwhelming Warsaw Pact superiority in numbers. British armoured and mechanized infantry units would expect to slow a Soviet onslaught; however, prolonged combat would prove problematic. As the focus of British tank development shifted from Nazi Germany to the Warsaw Pact, the Centurion was upgraded to include heavier armour, advanced fire control systems and defences against nuclear, biological and chemical weapons.

During the early years of the Cold War, the Bren Gun Carrier, or Universal Carrier, which traced its origins to the 1920s, was widely used by British forces. Although it was the most highly produced vehicle of its kind in history, the versatile Universal Carrier had become obsolescent by the mid-1950s. In 1962, the FV 430 series was introduced, encompassing a variety of armoured vehicles serving as command, repair, ambulance and troop carrier platforms. The FV 432 armoured personnel carrier was capable of transporting up to 10 combat-ready infantrymen and was armed with a single 7.62mm (0.3in) machine gun. Its configuration complemented the prevailing NATO doctrine that infantry should dismount from 'battle taxi' transport to engage in combat.

▶ **Saladin Armoured Car**
British Army of the Rhine / 11th Armoured Division, Germany, 1967
The six-wheeled armoured car variant of the Alvis FV600 series of armoured fighting vehicles, the FV601 Saladin was designed in the late 1940s but did not enter service until 1958. Mounting a 76mm (3in) gun, it was originally intended to replace the ageing Daimler armoured car.

Specifications
Crew: 3
Weight: 11,500kg (25,300lb)
Length: 5.284m (17ft 4in)
Width: 2.54m (8ft 4in)
Height: 2.93m (9ft 7.3in)
Engine: 127kW (170hp) 8-cylinder petrol
Speed: 72km/h (45mph)
Range: 400km (250 miles)
Armament: 1 x 76mm (3in) gun, plus 2 x 7.62mm (0.3in) MGs (1 coaxial and 1 AA)
Radio: n/k

Specifications
Crew: 4
Weight: 16,494kg (36,288lb)
Length: 5.84m (19ft 2in)
Width: 2.641m (8ft 8in)
Height: 2.489m (8ft 2in)
Engine: 179kW (240hp) Rolls-Royce 6-cylinder diesel
Speed: 47.5km/h (30mph)
Range: 390km (240 miles)
Armament: 1 x 105mm (4.1in) gun, plus 1 x 7.62mm (0.3in) anti-aircraft MG and 3 x smoke dischargers
Radio: n/k

▲ **Abbot SP Gun**
British Army of the Rhine / 6th Armoured Division, Germany, 1969
Beginning in the late 1960s, the Abbot self-propelled gun was deployed to units of the Royal Artillery serving with NATO. Mounting a 105mm (4.1in) L13A1 gun, the Abbot featured an enclosed, fully rotating turret atop the modified chassis of the FV430 armoured fighting vehicle.

NATO – United States
1949–69

From the outset of the Cold War, the United States was to assume a leading role in the development of NATO and the defence of Western Europe against the forces of the Warsaw Pact.

BY THE END OF THE 1940s, the US nuclear weapons monopoly had, for all practical purposes, disappeared. The Soviet Union had detonated a nuclear device, and the potential for a strategic exchange of catastrophic proportions appeared to be increasing. At the tactical level, the US and its NATO allies relied upon the strength of short-range nuclear weapons systems as a deterrent to Soviet aggression. Armoured and infantry forces would attempt to contain any offensive thrust.

During the mid-1950s, the 'forward defence' strategy developed, reassuring the West German government that its territory would be defended as close to the borders of the Warsaw Pact nations as possible. Among the first of the US divisions deployed along the tense frontier between the two alliances was the 3rd Armoured, which defended the strategically vital Fulda Gap, east of the German city of Frankfurt, a likely avenue of advance for any Soviet armoured offensive.

In October 1950, the role of US forces in Europe was changed from constabulary to combat-ready, and four divisions were committed. The pentomic structure of US divisional organization was reevaluated on several occasions and revolved around the flexible infantry brigade, which controlled two or three battle groups. Each brigade included infantry, armour and artillery as needed.

In the early 1960s, the doctrine of flexible response led to another reorganization of the US Army. Subsequently, the US armoured division consisted of six tank and five mechanized infantry battalions, while infantry divisions included two tank battalions supporting eight infantry battalions. US armoured battalions consisted of three companies, each with three platoons of five tanks, while two tanks were assigned to the company headquarters.

The US supplied the majority of equipment to the NATO forces during the early years of the Cold War. These included initially the M4 Sherman and M24

Specifications	
Crew: 5	Speed: 48km/h (30mph)
Weight: 41,860kg (92,301lb)	Range: 161km (100 miles)
Length: 8.61m (28ft 3in)	Armament: 1 x 90mm (3.5in) M3 gun; 1 x
Width: 3.51m (11ft 6in)	12.7mm (0.5in) AA HMG; 2 x 7.62mm (0.3in)
Height: 2.77m (9ft 1in)	MGs (1 coaxial, 1 ball-mounted in hull front)
Engine: 373kW (500hp) Ford GAF V8 petrol	Radio: SCR508/528

▲ **M26 Pershing Heavy Tank**
US Army / 1st Infantry Division, Germany, 1948
With its 90mm (3.5in) M3 gun, the M26 Pershing was the heaviest US tank deployed during World War II. In Korea, it proved to be underpowered and was withdrawn. However, it served as the basis for the Patton series of the 1950s and 1960s.

Chaffee tanks of World War II vintage. These were followed by the M26 Pershing heavy tank, developed late in the war and having seen minimal action, and the main battle tanks of the Patton series, the M47, M48 and M60. Like Great Britain, the United States also developed a heavy tank, the M103, in response to the Soviet IS-2 and IS-3, which would undoubtedly be encountered in the event of war; however, only one battalion of M103s was deployed. In the 1960s, the M113 armoured personnel carrier replaced the older armoured personnel carriers previously in service.

Specifications
Crew: 4
Weight: 52,617kg (116,020lb)
Length: 9.44m (31ft)
Width: 3.63m (11ft 11in)
Height: 3.27m (10ft 8in)
Engine: 559.7kW (750hp) Continental AVDS-
1790-2A V12 turbo-charged diesel
Speed: 48km/h (30mph)
Range: 500km (311 miles)
Armament: 1 x M68 105mm (4.1in) gun; 1 x
12.7mm (0.5in) MG; 1 x 7.62mm (0.3in) MG
Radio: n/k

▲ M60A1 Main Battle Tank
US Army / 3rd Armored Division, Germany, 1963
Based on the M26 Pershing, the Patton main battle tank was developed in the United States during the 1950s. By 1957, the M60A1 emerged in response to a need for upgraded armour protection, better suspension and an improved turret shape. The M60A1 remained in service for more than 30 years.

▲ M103 Heavy Tank
US Army / 4th Armored Group / 899th Tank Battalion, Germany, 1959
With its 120mm (4.7in) M58 main gun, the M103 was the heaviest tank in the US inventory until the 1980s. With the rise of the main battle tank concept, the M103 was produced in only small numbers. A single battalion was deployed to Europe.

Specifications
Crew: 5
Weight: 56,610kg (124,544lb)
Length: 11.3m (37ft 1.5in)
Width: 3.8m (12ft 4in)
Height: 2.9m (9ft 5.3in)
Engine: 604kW (810hp) Continental AV-1790-5B
or 7C V12 petrol
Speed: 34km/h (21mph)
Range: 130km (80 miles)
Armament: 1 x 120mm (4.7in) rifled gun, plus
1 x 12.7mm (0.5in) anti-aircraft HMG and 1 x
7.62mm (0.3in) coaxial MG
Radio: n/k

Specifications

Crew: 3 or 4
Weight: 6930kg (15,280lb)
Length: 4.46m (14ft 7.5in)
Width: 2.33m (7ft 7.6in)
Height: 2.16m (7ft 1in)
Engine: 119kW (160hp) Chevrolet 283-V8 8-
 cylinder petrol
Speed: 58km/h (36mph)
Range: 440km (270 miles)
Armament: 1 x 20mm (0.79in) M139
 or 1 x 12.7mm (0.5in) HMG;
 1 x 7.62mm (0.3in) MG
Radio: n/k

▲ M114A1E1 Reconnaisance Carrier
US Army / 4th Infantry Division, 1963

Also known as the M114A2, a variant of the M114 armoured personnel carrier that entered service with the US military in 1962, the M114A1E1 reconnaissance carrier was heavily armed with a 20mm (0.79in) M139 gun mounted in a hydraulically powered cupola.

Specifications

Crew: 2 + 10
Weight: 18,828kg (41,516lb)
Length: 5.19m (17ft .36in)
Width: 2.84m (9ft 3in)
Height: 2.77m (9ft 1in)
Engine: 220kW (295hp) Continental AO-895-4
 6-cylinder petrol
Speed: 71km/h (44mph)
Range: 185km (115 miles)
Armament: 1 x 12.7mm (0.5in) Browning
 M2 HB HMG

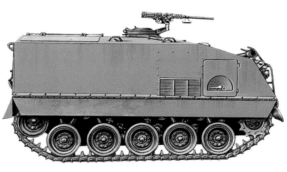

▲ M75 Armoured Personnel Carrier
US Army / 1st Infantry Division, Germany, 1955

Based on the chassis of the T43 cargo carrier, the M75 armoured personnel carrier also shared suspension components with the M41 light tank and was developed in the autumn of 1946. Produced briefly from 1952 to 1954, it was replaced by the M59.

▲ M59 Armoured Personnel Carrier
US Army / 1st Infantry Division, Germany, 1959

Replacing the older M75 armoured personnel carrier, the amphibious and less expensive M59 entered service with the US military in 1953. It carried up to 10 combat infantrymen or one jeep, and more than 6000 were built by 1960.

Specifications

Crew: 2 + 10
Weight: 19,323kg (38,197lb)
Length: 5.61m (18ft 5in)
Width: 3.26m (10ft 8in)
Height: 2.27m (7ft 5in)
Engine: 2 x 95kW (127hp) General Motors Model
 302 6-cylinder petrol
Speed: 51km/h (32mph)
Range: 164km (102 miles)
Armament: 1 x 12.7mm (0.5in) Browning
 M2 HB HMG

▲ **M113 Armoured Personnel Carrier**

US Army / 3rd Infantry Division, 1961

Entering service with the US Army in 1960, the M113 armoured personnel carrier is an iconic vehicle of the Cold War and Vietnam era. Its distinct boxlike silhouette was similar to its predecessors, the M59 and M75; however, its aluminium armour was much lighter and offered greater protection.

Specifications

Crew: 2 + 11

Weight: 12,329kg (27,180lb)

Length: 2.686m (8ft 9in)

Width: 2.54m (8ft 4in)

Height: 2.52m (8ft 3in)

Engine: 205kW (275hp) Detroit Diesel 6V53T

Speed: 66km/h (41mph)

Range: 483km (300 miles)

Armament: 1 x 12.7mm (0.5in) MG

Late Cold War

As the Cold War intensified with armed conflict and proxy wars around the globe, the military establishments of NATO and the Warsaw Pact continued their programmes of armoured vehicle development.

AT THE DAWN of the Cold War's fourth decade, the strategic arms race was centre stage. Tensions between the superpowers had come to the brink of conventional, and then quite probably nuclear, conflict over access to West Berlin and during the Cuban Missile Crisis.

In the event of any armed confrontation between East and West, the role to be played by troops on the ground in Europe was likely to be only a prelude to global thermonuclear war. However, the wary adversaries maintained their armies in a state of readiness, weighing the economic cost and the immediate necessities to fulfil obligations elsewhere around the world. Until 1974, the United States was still directly involved in the Vietnam War, while the Soviet Union was supplying arms to client states in the Middle East and Southeast Asia.

At the same time, advancing technology contributed to the requirement for both NATO and Warsaw Pact nations to continually research and develop better weapons systems. Improved powerplants, armour protection and suspension systems were combined with computerized fire control, defences against nuclear, biological and chemical (NBC) weapons, a new generation of heavy

guns and a variety of special purpose ammunition to encompass a modern main battle tank of extraordinary firepower, protection and mobility. The proving grounds for many of these innovations were the smaller, intense wars of the Middle East, Southeast Asia and Africa which occurred during the last 40 years of the twentieth century.

▲ **Show of force**

Soviet T-64 tanks take part in a parade in Moscow's Red Square.

Warsaw Pact
1970–91

Evolving Soviet nuclear and conventional arms doctrine diminished and then increased the significance of the tank and armoured fighting vehicle during the later years of the Cold War.

SOVIET AND WARSAW PACT military strategists never fully discounted the advantages of a preemptive nuclear strike against the West, but once nuclear parity with the NATO powers was achieved in the early 1970s, the Soviets considered an all-out nuclear war less likely. Weighing various scenarios, they envisioned a possible combined offensive strike, first by nuclear weapons and then followed by conventional forces, or possibly a conventional offensive alone – with the threat of Soviet nuclear capabilities dissuading NATO forces from launching a nuclear attack of their own in response.

Given these scenarios for war in Europe, the Soviets invested heavily in improving their conventional weapons systems. Further, the Brezhnev Doctrine asserted that the Soviet Union reserved the right to intervene militarily in neighbouring countries should the situation be deemed a threat to Soviet security. Tangible evidence of this posture occurred during the suppression of the 1968 revolt in Czechoslovakia and the invasion of Afghanistan in 1979.

Deep Battle theory

Advocated as early as the 1920s, the concept of Deep Battle was resurrected by Soviet military planners during the 1970s. The five major components of Deep Battle theory were the use of tactical formations to prosecute offensive operations; pressure across a large area to prevent an opponent from manoeuvring efficiently in response; deep penetration to shock enemy forces into inaction; coordinated firepower and manoeuvre leveraging technology to effect deep penetration of enemy defences; and a commander's holistic view of the battle – seeing the beginning of hostilities and the end game in total.

Speed was essential to the success of Deep Battle theory, preventing the enemy from regrouping and coordinating an effective defence. Combined infantry and armour would first find and fix the enemy. Then a strong armoured spearhead would attack on a narrow front and achieve the decisive breakthrough. Rapid exploitation of the breach would result in the continuous pursuit of the enemy, steadily degrading

▲ **T-64 Main Battle Tank**
Soviet Army / Kiev Military District / 41st Guards Tank Division, 1967
An innovative Soviet design, the T-64 main battle tank equipped elite units of the Red Army in Eastern Europe and was never exported. Its 115mm (4.5in) gun was later replaced by a 125mm (4.9in) smoothbore. Expensive to produce, the T-64 was augmented by the cheaper T-72.

Specifications

Crew: 3
Weight: 42,000kg (92,610lb)
Length (hull): 7.4m (24ft 3in)
Width: 3.64m (11ft 11in)
Height: 2.2m (7ft 3in)
Engine: 560kW (750bhp) 5DTF 5-cylinder opposed diesel
Speed: 75km/h (47mph)
Range: 400km (248 miles)
Armament: 1 x 125mm (4.9in) smoothbore gun, plus 1 x 12.7mm (0.5in) NSVT AA MG and 1 x coaxial 7.62mm (0.3in) PKT MG
Radio: R-123M

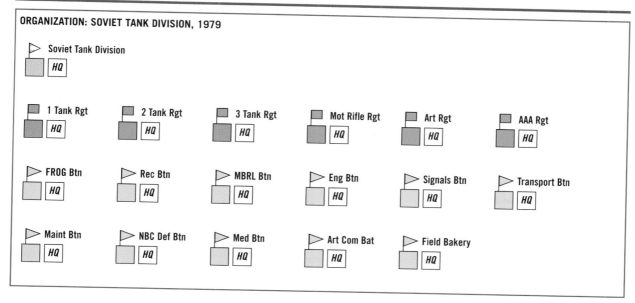

ORGANIZATION: SOVIET TANK DIVISION, 1979

Soviet Tank Division — HQ

1 Tank Rgt — HQ | 2 Tank Rgt — HQ | 3 Tank Rgt — HQ | Mot Rifle Rgt — HQ | Art Rgt — HQ | AAA Rgt — HQ

FROG Btn — HQ | Rec Btn — HQ | MBRL Btn — HQ | Eng Btn — HQ | Signals Btn — HQ | Transport Btn — HQ

Maint Btn — HQ | NBC Def Btn — HQ | Med Btn — HQ | Art Com Bat — HQ | Field Bakery — HQ

his armed forces and diminishing his will to resist. The outcome would be both militarily and psychologically debilitating to the enemy. By the 1980s, Soviet ground forces consisted of more than 200 infantry and armoured divisions, each of them mechanized, and more than 50,000 main battle tanks were in service.

Soviet tank divisions contained three tank regiments and one motorized rifle regiment, while the motorized rifle division consisted of three motorized rifle regiments and a single tank regiment. Such a configuration allowed supporting infantry to keep pace with the advance of armour and in turn allowed armour to mutually support accompanying infantry.

Armoured innovation

The deployment of the T-64 main battle tank in 1966 marked a significant advancement in Soviet tank design with the introduction of an automatic

▲ **T-72G Main Battle Tank**

Polish Army / Silesian Military District, 1979

A licensed version of the T-72 main battle tank, the T-72G was manufactured in Poland and protected by thinner armour plating than T-72s built in the Soviet Union. The T-72G was provided to the armed forces of several Warsaw Pact nations.

Specifications

Crew: 3
Weight: 38,894kg (85,568lb)
Length: 9.24m (30ft 4in)
Width: 4.75m (15ft 7in)
Height: 2.37m (7ft 9in)
Engine: 626kW (840hp) V-46 V12 diesel

Speed: 80km/h (50mph)
Range: 550km (434 miles)
Armament: 1 x 125mm (4.9in) gun, plus
1 x 12.7mm (0.5in) anti-aircraft HMG and
1 x 7.62mm (0.3in) coaxial MG
Radio: R-123M

Specifications

Crew: 2 + 11
Weight: 14,900kg (32,900lb)
Length: 7.47m (24ft 6in)
Width: 2.85m (9ft 4in)
Height: 2.42m (7ft 11in)
Engine: 164kW (220hp) YaMZ-238N 8-cylinder
 diesel
Speed: 62km/h (39mph)
Range: 525km (330 miles)
Armament: 1 x 12.7mm (0.5in) DShK HMG or
 1 x 7.62mm (0.3in) MG
Radio: R-123M

▲ MT-LB Armoured Personnel Carrier

Soviet Army / 35th Guards Motor Rifle Division, 1980

Utilized as a small armoured personnel carrier, ambulance, artillery tractor and in other roles, the amphibious MT-LB was based on the chassis of the PT-76 light tank. The MT-LB was armed with a light machine gun and had entered service with the Red Army by the early 1970s.

Specifications

Crew: 6
Weight: 24,945kg (54,880lb)
Length: 8.4m (27ft 6.7in)
Width: 3.2m (10ft 6in)
Height: 2.8m (9ft 2.25in)
Engine: 388kW (520hp) V12 diesel
Speed: 55km/h (34mph)
Range: 300km (186 miles)
Armament: 1 x 152mm (6in) gun, plus
 1 x 7.62mm (0.3in) anti-aircraft MG
Radio: n/k

▲ 2S3 M-1973 152mm SP Gun-Howitzer

Soviet Army / 6th Guards Separate Motor Rifle Brigade, 1981

Introduced to the Red Army in 1973, the 2S3 M-1973 152mm (6in) self-propelled gun-howitzer replaced the older D-20 system in artillery regiments of the Soviet and Warsaw Pact forces to provide fire support for tank and motorized rifle regiments.

Specifications

Crew: 3
Weight: 14,000kg (30,800lb)
Length: 7.65m (25ft 25in)
Width: 3.14m (10ft 3.7in)
Height: 2.26m (7ft 4.75in)
Engine: 179kW (240hp) V-6 6-cylinder diesel
Speed: 44km/h (27mph)
Range: 260km (160 miles)
Armament: 1 x 76mm (3in) gun, plus
 1 x 12.7mm (0.5in) AA HMG and 1 x coaxial
 7.62mm (0.3in) MG
Radio: R-123

▲ PT-76 Amphibious Light Tank

Soviet Navy / Red Banner Northern Fleet / 63rd Guard Kirkenneskaya Naval Infantry Brigade, Baltic region, 1985

Originally a mainstay of the Soviet Red Army, the PT-76 provides amphibious support for attacking infantry formations. First entering service in 1952, the PT-76 is still operated by Russian naval infantry today, although it is being gradually phased out in favour of the T-80 MBT. More than 12,000 PT-76s have been built, of which 2000 were exported to Soviet client states.

loading system for the tank's 115mm (4.5in) main gun, which effectively reduced the size of the standard tank crew from four to three. Later variants of the T-64 were upgunned to a 125mm (4.9in) cannon and were capable of firing anti-tank missiles. Upgraded fire control systems and improved armour were included, and the T-64 was never exported to foreign countries. It equipped many of the elite guards units stationed opposite NATO forces in Eastern Europe and constituted the basis for the development of the T-80 main battle tank, which emerged in the mid-1970s.

New tanks

While the T-64 was originally intended to fill a perceived void created by the obsolescence of the IS-3 heavy tank of the early Cold War period, the T-72 main battle tank was in development concurrently with the T-64. The initial purpose of the T-72 was to equip the majority of Red Army armoured forces and to be exported to Warsaw Pact countries and arms purchasers around the world. Indeed, along with the T-54/55, the T-72 became an icon of the wars of the Middle East during the 1970s and served as the main battle tank for the armies of North Vietnam and several Arab states and of Soviet satellite countries during the 1970s and 1980s.

The T-72 combined elements of the T-62 and the T-64, entering production about 1970 and service with the Red Army in 1973. The T-72 maintained the characteristic 'frying pan' style turret of prior Soviet tank designs, sacrificing the comfort and operational efficiency of the crew by limiting space within but in turn diminishing the tank's silhouette. The T-72 was relatively inexpensive to produce compared with the T-64 and served as the primary Soviet main battle tank for the last 20 years of the Warsaw Pact.

The T-80, which was deployed to Red Army units in 1976 and was subsequently improved several times, marked the pinnacle of Soviet main battle tank design. Its most advanced variant was the T-80U, which included explosive reactive armour, improved target acquisition equipment and the 9M119M Refleks anti-tank missile system along with its 125mm (4.9in) 2A46-2 smoothbore gun. Its powerplant was similar to the turbine engine of the US Abrams main battle tank.

Improvements to infantry fighting vehicles continued as well, with the BMP-1 of the 1960s

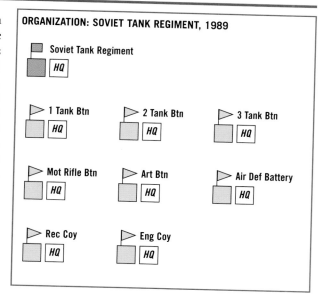

ORGANIZATION: SOVIET TANK REGIMENT, 1989

- Soviet Tank Regiment / HQ
- 1 Tank Btn / HQ
- 2 Tank Btn / HQ
- 3 Tank Btn / HQ
- Mot Rifle Btn / HQ
- Art Btn / HQ
- Air Def Battery / HQ
- Rec Coy / HQ
- Eng Coy / HQ

SOVIET TANK REGIMENT, 1989

Type	Number	Vehicle	Strength
Headquarters	–	MBT	1
		BTR	2
		SA-7/14/16	3
Tank Btn	3	MBT	31
		BMP	2
Motorized Rifle Btn	1	BMP	43
		120mm mortar	8
		SA-7/14/16	9
		AGS-17	6
		BRDM-2	3
Artillery Btn	1	2SI	18–24
Air Defence Battery	1	SA-13	4
		ZSU-23-4	4
		BMP	3
Reconnaissance Coy	1	BRM	1
		BMP	3
		BRDM-2	4
		Motorcycles	3
Engineer Coy	1	MT-55	3
		TMM	4

giving way to the improved BMP-2 and BMP-3 of the 1980s, which were armed with 30mm (1.18in) autocannon, light machine guns and anti-tank guided missile systems. Capable of carrying up to seven combat infantrymen, the BMP-1 and BMP-2 were observed in large numbers during the Soviet invasion of Afghanistan.

Specifications

Crew: 2 + 10
Weight: 14,500kg (31,900lb)
Length: 7.44m (24ft 5in)
Width: 2.55m (8ft 4.4in)
Height: 2.06m (6ft 9in)
Engine: 134KW (180hp) Tatra V8 diesel
Speed: 94.4km/h (59mph)
Range: 710km (441 miles)
Armament: 1 x 14.5mm (0.6in) KPV HMG;
  1 x 7.62mm (0.3in) PKT coaxial MG
Radio: R-112

▲ **SKOT-2A Wheeled Amphibious Armoured Personnel Carrier**

Polish Army / Silesian Military District, 1970

Known in the West as the OT-64C, this amphibious armoured personnel carrier was jointly developed by Czechoslovakia and Poland during the late 1950s and deployed to army units by 1963. The engine, transmission and other components were of Czech manufacture, while the hull and light machine gun armament were made in Poland. The SKOT-2A also included the turret from the BRDM-2.

Specifications

Crew: 4/5
Weight: 23,000kg (50,600lb)
Length: 10.5m (34ft 5in)
Width: 2.8m (9ft 2in)
Height: 2.6m (8ft 6in)
Engine: 257kW (345hp) V12 diesel
Speed: 80km/h (49.71mph)
Range: 600km (375 miles)
Armament: 1 x 152mm (6in) gun, plus
  1 x 12.7mm (0.5in) HMG
Radio: n/k

▲ **DANA SP Howitzer**

Czech Army / 7th Mechanized Brigade, 1988

The world's first wheeled 152mm (6in) self-propelled artillery system to enter active service, the DANA howitzer was developed in Czechoslovakia during the 1970s and is similar to the Soviet 2S3 self-propelled gun-howitzer. The heavy weapon is mounted atop the 8X8 Tatra T815 truck.

Specifications

Crew: 3 + 8
Weight: 11,000kg (24,300lb)
Length: 7.22m (23ft 8in)
Width: 2.83m (9ft 3in)
Height: 2.7m (8ft 9in)
Engine: 2 x 104kW (140hp) 6-cylinder petrol
Speed: 95km/h (60mph)
Range: 500km (310 miles)
Armament: 1 x 14.5mm (0.57in) MG, plus
  1 x 7.62mm (0.3in) PKT MG
Radio: R-113

▲ **TAB-72 Armoured Personnel Carrier**

Romanian Army / 1st Motorized Rifle Division, 1977

The Romanian TAB-72 armoured personnel carrier was a variant of the TAB-71, a licensed version of the Soviet-designed BTR-60. The vehicle design dates to the mid-1950s, and its deployment to the end of that decade. The TAB-72 had an improved turret, upgraded optical equipment and gun sights, and increased elevation angles for its machine guns for use in the anti-aircraft role.

Specifications

Crew: 3

Weight: 46,000kg (101,413lb)

Length: 9.66m (31ft 8in)

Width: 3.59m (11ft 10in)

Height: 2.2m (7ft 2in)

Engine: 932kW (1250hp) GTD-1250 multi-fuel
gas turbine

Speed: 70km/h (44mph)

Range: 440 km (273 miles)

Armament: 1 x 125mm (4.9in) smoothbore gun,
plus 1 x 12.7mm (0.5in) MG, 1 x 7.62mm
(0.3in) MG and 1 x 9K119 Refleks missile
system

Radio: n/k

▲ T-80U Main Battle Tank

Soviet Army / 4th Guards Tank Division, 1990

The most advanced of Soviet main battle tanks, the T-80U was equipped with the latest explosive reactive armour, target acquisition equipment and anti-tank missile firing capability. Based on the original T-80 design of the mid-1970s, it remains in service with forces of the Ukraine and the Russian Federation.

▲ FUG-65 Amphibious Armoured Scout Car

Hungarian Ground Forces, 1985

The Hungarian FUG amphibious armoured scout car, based on the Soviet-designed BRDM-1, entered service in 1964 and was deployed to the armed forces of at least six Warsaw Pact countries. Variants remain in service today.

Specifications

Crew: 2 + 4

Weight: 7000kg (15,400lb)

Length: 5.79m (18ft 11in)

Width: 2.5m (8ft 2in)

Height: 1.91m (6ft 3in)

Engine: 75kW (100hp) Csepel D.414.44
4-cylinder diesel

Speed: 87km/h (54mph)

Range: 600km (370 miles)

Armament: 1 x 7.62mm (0.3in) SGMB MG

Radio: R-113 or R-114

Specifications

Crew: 2 + 6

Weight: 14,500kg (31,900lb)

Length: 7.44m (24ft 5in)

Width: 2.55m (8ft 4.4in)

Height: 2.06m (6ft 9in)

Engine: 134kW (180hp) Tatra V8 diesel

Speed: 94.4km/h (59mph)

Range: 710km (441 miles)

Armament: 1 x 7.62mm (0.3in) MG

Radio: R-114

▲ PSZH-IV Amphibious Armoured Scout Car

Czech Army / 7th Mechanized Brigade, 1980

Developed as an improvement to the FUG amphibious armoured scout car, the PSZH-VI incorporated a small turret mounting a 14.5mm (0.57in) machine gun and a coaxial 7.62mm (0.3in) machine gun. It was capable of transporting six combat-ready soldiers.

NATO – Canada
1970–91

A charter member of NATO, Canada contributed forces to the defence of Western Europe and championed the concept of United Nations peacekeeping during the Cold War.

THROUGHOUT THE COLD WAR PERIOD, the Canadian armed forces maintained two bases in West Germany under the auspices of Canadian Forces Europe. These were CFB Lahr and CFB Baden-Soellingen, and each supported armoured formations of the Canadian Army.

Canadian forces had supported the NATO alliance since 1951, when the 27th Infantry Brigade was deployed to Hanover. By the 1970s, the Canadian troop strength in Europe had diminished significantly. However, for much of the Cold War the 4th Canadian Mechanized Brigade Group was headquartered at Soest with its complement of Centurion and, later, main battle tanks, Ferret armoured cars and armoured personnel carriers, while at least a battalion of mechanized infantry was stationed at Baden-Soellingen along with light infantry formations.

Among the units serving with the 4th Canadian Mechanized Brigade Group were Lord Strathcona's Horse, the Royal Canadian Dragoons, the 8th Canadian Hussars and the Fort Garry Horse, as well as numerous mechanized infantry and horse artillery regiments.

Canadian tanks of the early Cold War era included British- and American-built models such as the Centurion and the M4 Sherman of the World War II period, during which a number of Sherman variants had been built under licence in Canada. In the late 1970s, Canada concluded the purchase of 127 Leopard C1 tanks from Germany. The Leopard C1 was equipped with laser rangefinding equipment similar to that of the German Leopard 1A3. Further improvements made by the Canadians included the addition of thermal night vision equipment, modular appliqué armour and improved fire control systems, and the upgraded Leopard was redesignated the C1A1.

Other Canadian armoured vehicles of the Cold War included the Cougar wheeled fire support vehicle, based on the Swiss-designed Piranha 6X6 fighting vehicle, which entered service in 1976, and the Lynx command and reconnaissance vehicle,

▲ **Cougar Gun Wheeled Fire Support Vehicle**

Canadian Army / Royal Canadian Dragoons, Germany, 1978

Fitted with the turret of the FV 101 Scorpion light tank, the Cougar fire support vehicle mounted a 76mm (3in) main gun. The Cougar entered service with Canadian forces in 1976 and was gradually replaced during the 1990s.

Specifications

Crew: 3	Engine: 160kW (215hp) Detroit Diesel 6V-53T
Weight: 9526kg (21,004lb)	6-cylinder diesel
Length: 5.97m (19ft 7in)	Speed: 102km/h (63mph)
Width: 2.53m (8ft 4in)	Range: 602km (374 miles)
Height: 2.62m (8ft 7in)	Armament: 1 x 76mm (3in) gun, plus
	1 x 7.62mm (0.3in) coaxial MG

similar in profile to the US M113 armoured personnel carrier. The Lynx was, in fact, built by the American FMC Corporation, which manufactured the M113, and the vehicle was supplied to the armed forces of Canada and the Netherlands. While US forces opted to purchase the M114 fighting vehicle in the early 1960s, Canada had deployed the Lynx by the middle of the decade as an amphibious reconnaissance and command platform.

Peacekeeping

Canada is often credited with advancing the concept of United Nations peacekeeping efforts during the half-century of the Cold War, and its troops and armoured assets have been deployed to the Middle East, the Balkans and other hotspots. Canadian troops were first deployed in such a role in 1957, patrolling along with the forces of several other nations in the Sinai Peninsula following the Suez Crisis that had erupted the previous year.

More than 100 Canadian personnel have been killed while fulfilling peacekeeping duties. The Royal Canadian Dragoons, an armoured regiment of the Canadian Army, has participated in peacekeeping efforts in the Korean demilitarized zone, in Kosovo in the Balkans and in Somalia on the Horn of Africa.

Canadian Reconnaissance Squadron

The Canadian reconnaissance squadron of Canadian Forces Europe included 10 Lynx armoured command and reconnaissance vehicles. Each Lynx had a crew of three – commander, driver and observer. The reconnaissance squadron was grouped into three troops, each fielding a complement of the Lynx vehicle. The combat support company of a Canadian infantry battalion included nine Lynxes.

Platoon (10 x Lynx APC)

▲ Lynx Command and Recon (CR) Vehicle

Canadian Army / Royal Canadian Regiment, Germany, 1971

In 1968, the Canadian Army procured the Lynx command and reconnaissance vehicle to replace its inventory of ageing Daimler Ferret armoured cars. The Lynx was armed with both heavy 12.7mm (0.5in) and light 7.62mm (0.3in) machine guns and was withdrawn from frontline units in the 1990s.

Specifications

Crew: 3

Weight: 8775kg (19,300lb)

Length: 4.6m (15ft 1in)

Width: 2.41m (7ft 11in)

Height: 1.65m (5ft 5in)

Engine: 160kW (215hp) Detroit Diesel GMC 6V53 6-cylinder

Speed: 70km/h (43mph)

Range: 525km (325 miles)

Armament: 1 x 12.7mm (0.5in) MG and 1 x 7.62mm (0.3in) MG

France
1970–91

Following its withdrawal from military participation in the NATO alliance in 1966, France continued its programme of armoured vehicle development and became a major exporter.

B Y THE 1970S, THE FRENCH AMX-30 main battle tank had matured as a weapons system. In production from 1966, the AMX-30 underwent several upgrades, including the installation of a stabilization system for its 105mm (4.1in) Modèle F1 main gun and the replacement of its coaxial heavy machine gun with a more powerful 20mm (0.79in) autocannon, an effective weapon against light armoured vehicles. Modernization was continued for the next 20 years and included the introduction of improved fire control systems, drive train elements and eventually laser rangefinding equipment and low light television targeting apparatus. The production of new AMX-30s was ongoing from 1979, while many of those already in service were upgraded. Numerous variants were also produced, including armoured recovery and bridgelaying vehicles.

From 1974 to 1984, the AMX-30 was also built under licence in Spain, while nearly 3000 examples of the main battle tank were produced for the French

military and the export arms market. The Spanish manufactured nearly 300 AMX-30s and deployed them with their army following an initial order of 19 placed in 1970. The primary reasons for Spanish interest in the AMX-30 were the reluctance of other nations to sell arms to the fascist regime of Generalissimo Francisco Franco and the attractive price point of the French system compared with others such the British Chieftain and the US M60. During the 1970s, such diverse nations as Saudi Arabia, the United Arab Emirates, Chile, Venezuela and Cyprus purchased the AMX-30. A delivery of 190 tanks was completed to Greece, the first nation to agree to purchase the French design.

Emerging Leclerc

A large number of AMX-30 variants remain in service around the world today, but by the 1980s it was apparent that the tank was inferior to the main battle tanks of other nations, including the American Abrams,

▲ **AMX-10 PAC 90 Light Tank**

French Army / 1st Armoured Division, France, 1984

Designed to complement the offensive capabilities of main battle tanks and infantry, the AMX-10 PAC 90 entered service with the French Army in 1979. The vehicle is also considered a self-propelled anti-tank weapon and is serviced by a crew of three. It also carries four infantrymen for defence or reconnaissance purposes.

Specifications

Crew: 3 + 4	V8 diesel
Weight: 14,500kg (31,967lb)	Speed: 65km/h (40.4mph)
Length: 5.9m (19ft 4.3in)	Range: 500km (310.7 miles)
Width: 2.83m (9ft 3.4in)	Armament: 1 x 20mm (0.79in) gun, plus
Height: 2.83m (9ft 3.4in)	1 x 7.62mm (0.3in) coaxial MG
Engine: 193.9kW (260hp) Hispano-Suiza HS 115	Radio: n/k

British Challenger, German Leopard and later Israeli Merkava. In light of the situation, French engineers reinvigorated the development of a new generation of main battle tank. Actually, research into a replacement for the AMX-30 had begun as early as the 1960s.

In a repeat performance of the 1950s fiasco, a joint venture with German designers had fallen apart by 1982, while France had also evaluated the main battle tanks offered for sale by other countries and decided

against purchasing a foreign design. Meanwhile, the AMX-40 main battle tank, engineered purely for export sales, failed to gain orders and was cancelled. The high cost of the new Leclerc tank, with its 120mm (4.7in) main gun and a host of state-of-the-art systems, was offset somewhat by a partnership with the United Arab Emirates, who agreed to purchase more than 400 examples of the vehicle, and full production was begun in 1990.

▲ AMX-10RC Armoured Car
French Army / 2nd Regiment of Hussars, France, 1981
Developed in the early 1970s with full production commencing by 1976, the amphibious AMX-10RC served with the French Army in fire support and reconnaissance roles and is no longer in production. Heavily armed, it mounted a 105mm (4.1in) BK MECA L/48 main gun.

Specifications

Crew: 4	Speed: 85km/h (53mph)
Weight: 15,880kg (35,015lb)	Range: 1000km (620 miles)
Length: 6.36m (20ft 10in)	Armament: 1 x 105mm (4.1in) gun; 1 x 7.62mm
Width: 2.95m (9ft 8in)	(0.3in) coaxial MG; 2 x 2 smoke grenade
Height: 2.66m (8ft 8in)	launchers
Engine: 209kW (280hp) Badouin Model 6F 11	Radio: n/k
SRX diesel	

▲ ERC 90 F4 Sagaie
French Army / 31st Heavy Half-Brigade, Ivory Coast, 1982
The wheeled ERC 90 F4 Sagaie was developed by the Panhard Corporation as a light armoured vehicle capable of destroying Soviet main battle tanks such as the T-72. Its 90mm (3.5in) cannon was mounted in a turret manufactured by the government defence contractor GIAT.

Specifications

Crew: 3	Speed: 100km/h (62mph)
Weight: 8300kg (18,300lb)	Range: 700km (430 miles)
Length (gun forwards): 7.69m (25ft 2in)	Armament: 1 x 90mm (3.5in) gun, plus
Width: 2.5m (8ft 2in)	1 x 7.62mm (0.3in) coaxial MG and 2 x 2 smoke
Height: 2.25m (7ft 4in)	grenade launchers
Engine: 116kW (155hp) Peugeot V6 petrol	Radio: n/k

Artillery

The most prominent of the French anti-tank vehicles produced during the latter years of the Cold War was perhaps the AMX-10 PAC 90, a variant of the AMX-10P infantry fighting vehicle. Mounting a 90mm (3.5in) rifled main gun, the AMX-10 PAC 90 entered service in 1979 and is sometimes classified as a light tank in its own right.

Armoured cars such as the AMX-10RC and the ERC 90 F4 came on line, while the heavy GCT 155mm (6.1in) self-propelled gun improved long-range fire support capabilities.

Specifications

Crew: 4	12-cylinder water-cooled multi-fuel
Weight: 41,949kg (92,288lb)	Speed: 60km/h (37mph)
Length: 10.25m (33ft 7.5in)	Range: 450km (280 miles)
Width: 3.15m (10ft 4in)	Armament: 1 x 155mm (6.1in) gun, plus 1 x
Height: 3.25m (10ft 8in)	7.62mm (0.3in) or 12.7mm (0.5in) AA MG
Engine: 537kW (720hp) Hispano-Suiza HS 110	Radio: n/k

▲ **GCT 155mm SP Artillery**

French Army / 7th Armoured Brigade, France, 1980

Replacing the French Mk 3 155mm (6.1in) self-propelled gun, the GCT 155mm (6.1in) was developed in the 1970s and entered service with the armies of France and Saudi Arabia near the end of the decade. The gun was originally mounted on the chassis of the AMX-30 main battle tank.

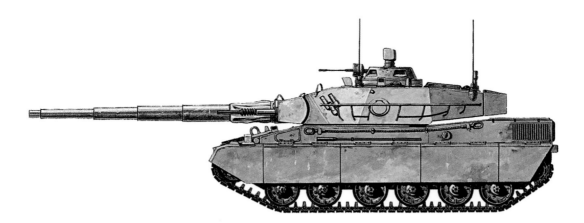

▲ **AMX-40 Main Battle Tank**

French Army, Undeployed, 1985

The AMX-40 main battle tank was designed specifically for the export market, mounting a 120mm (4.7in) smoothbore gun and a 20mm (0.79in) autocannon for use against aircraft and light armoured vehicles. By 1990, the project was scrapped due to lack of orders from foreign countries.

Specifications

Crew: 4	diesel
Weight: 43,000kg (94,600lb)	Speed: 70km/h (44mph)
Length: 10.04m (32ft 11.3in)	Range: 600km (373 miles)
Width: 3.36m (11ft 0.3in)	Armament: 1 x 120mm (4.7in) gun; 1 x 20mm
Height: 3.08m (10ft 1.3in)	(0.79in) gun in cupola; 1 x 7.62mm (0.3in) MG
Engine: 820kW (1100hp) Poyaud 12-cylinder	Radio: n/k

NATO – West Germany
1970–91

During the final decades of the Cold War, German tanks and armoured fighting vehicles gained a reputation as some of the finest of their type in the world.

WITH THE DEPLOYMENT of the Leopard 1 main battle tank in the 1960s, Germany established itself as a leading producer of armoured fighting vehicles. Employing some of the world's latest technology, the Leopard 1 was steadily improved through the mid-1970s; however, by the end of the decade its successor, the Leopard 2, was in production. The Leopard 2 was actually the product of joint research with the United States during the MTB-70 project of the late 1960s. While the German and US designers agreed on a number of points, the venture failed. A few years later, a second attempt was also cancelled following the shipment of a Leopard 2 prototype to the United States for evaluation against the XM-1 Abrams main battle tank prototype. Since the Germans favoured speed over armour protection and the Americans concentrated on tank survivability, each nation chose to pursue its own main battle tank independently.

The first order by the German government for the Leopard 2 was placed in 1977, and 1800 of the new main battle tanks were to be delivered in five batches.

Mounting a 120mm (4.7in) Rheinmetall L55 smoothbore gun, acknowledged as the best weapon of its kind in the world, the Leopard 2 also incorporated modern protection against nuclear, biological and chemical weapons, state-of-the-art fire control and rangefinding systems and an 1109kW (1479hp) turbodiesel engine. A series of upgrades occurred during the 1980s, including the addition of improved radio equipment and automated fire and explosion suppression systems.

Belated export bonanza

During the 1980s, the export market was cool to the latest German main battle tank offering; however, by the 1990s the Leopard 2 was in high demand and being produced under licence in Switzerland, while Canada, Denmark, Greece, Sweden and Turkey were among its buyers. From 1991 to 1996, the Netherlands purchased nearly 450 examples of the German main battle tank.

Leopard 2 tanks have equipped the organic armoured units of the *Deutsches Heer* since the 1980s,

Specifications

Crew: 4	10-cylinder diesel
Weight: 19,500kg (42,900lb)	Speed: 90km/h (56mph)
Length: 7.743m (25ft 4.75in)	Range: 800km (500 miles)
Width: 2.98m (9ft 9.3in)	Armament: 1 x 20mm (0.79in) gun, plus
Height (with AA MG): 2.905m (9ft 6.3in)	1 x 7.62mm (0.3in) MG
Engine: 291kW (390hp) Daimler-Benz OM 403 A	Radio: n/k

▲ Luchs Armoured Reconnaissance Vehicle
German Army / 5th Armoured Division, Germany, 1977

An 8X8 wheeled amphibious reconnaissance armoured fighting vehicle, the *Spähpanzer Luchs* mounted a 20mm (0.79in) Rheinmetall MK 20 autocannon and a light 7.62mm (0.3in) machine gun. The amphibious vehicle replaced the SPz 11-2 *kurz* and entered service in 1975.

facing the armour of the Warsaw Pact across the frontier between East and West. More than 400 Leopard 2 main battle tanks are estimated to be deployed with the German armed forces currently, and their service life has been extended by means of numerous upgrades.

In addition to the Leopard main battle tank, Germany's Marder armoured fighting vehicle also traces its development to the 1960s, and by 1971 it had entered production. It is capable of carrying up to seven combat infantrymen and mounts a 20mm (0.79in) autocannon and MILAN anti-tank guided missile launch system. More than 2100 Marders were produced. The vehicle was originally designed to work in cooperation with the Leopard 1, but several improvements have made it capable of keeping up with the latest Leopard 2 on the battlefield.

Since the end of the Cold War, the armed forces of the former East German People's Army have been integrated into the unified German armed forces.

▲ **Marder Schützenpanzer**

German Army / 10th Armoured Division, Germany, 1979

The Marder infantry fighting vehicle was the primary transport of the mechanized infantry formations of the West German Army. Numerous variants have been developed, and the vehicle mounts a 20mm (0.79in) autocannon as well as the MILAN anti-tank guided missile system. The Marder carries up to seven combat infantrymen.

Specifications

Crew: 3 + 6 or 7 troops	Ea-500 6-cylinder diesel
Weight: 33,500kg (73,855lb)	Speed: 65km/h (40.4mph)
Length: 6.88m (22ft 6.8in)	Range: 500km (310 miles)
Width: 3.38m (11ft 1in)	Armament: 1 x 20mm (0.79in) gun, plus MILAN
Height: 3.02m (9ft 10.7in)	ATGM launcher and 1 x 7.62mm (0.3in) MG
Engine: 447kW (600hp) MTU MB 833	Radio: n/k

Specifications

Crew: 4	8-cylinder diesel
Weight: 23,000kg (50,700lb)	Speed: 70km/h (43mph)
Length: 6.43m (21ft 1in)	Range: 400km (250 miles)
Width: 2.98m (9ft 9in)	Armament: 14 x SS-11 ATGWs, plus 2 x 7.62mm
Height: 2.15m (7ft 0.6in)	(0.3in) MG3 MGs
Engine: 373kW (500hp) Daimler-Benz MB 837A	

▲ **Raketenjagdpanzer (RJPZ) 2 Anti-tank Vehicle**

German Army / 5th Armoured Division, Germany, 1979

The tracked *Raketenjagdpanzer* (RJPZ) 2 anti-tank vehicle was designed to defeat Warsaw Pact armour with the Nord SS.11 anti-tank missile launcher system. Its development was begun in the 1960s, and it was deployed with armoured infantry brigades of the German Army, remaining in service until 1982.

▲ **Leopard 2A2 Main Battle Tank**

German Army / 10th Panzer Division, Germany, 1986

The latest generation of German main battle tanks, the Leopard 2 began its development during the 1970s. Replacing the Leopard 1 in frontline units of the German Army during the following decade, the tank mounts the 120mm (4.7in) Rheinmetall L55 smoothbore gun.

Specifications

Crew: 4	12-cylinder diesel
Weight (approx): 59,700kg (131,616lb)	Speed: 72km/h (45mph)
Length: 9.97m (32ft 8.4in)	Range: 500km (310 miles)
Width: 3.74m (12ft 3.25in)	Armament: 1 x 120mm (4.7in) smoothbore gun,
Height: 2.64m (8ft 7.9in)	plus 2 x 7.62mm (0.3in) MGs
Engine: 1119kW (1500hp) MTU MB 873 Ka501	Radio: SEM 80/90 digital

German Army, 23rd Panzer Battalion, 1989

As the Cold War came to a close, the German 23rd Panzer Battalion fielded 40 Leopard 2 main battle tanks, considered one of the finest weapons of its kind in the world, along with a complement of four M577 command vehicle variants of the M113 armoured personnel carrier and 12 M113s, transporting the battalion's mechanized infantry personnel.

(40 x Leopard 2 MBT)

(4 x M577 command vehicles)

(12 x M113 APC)

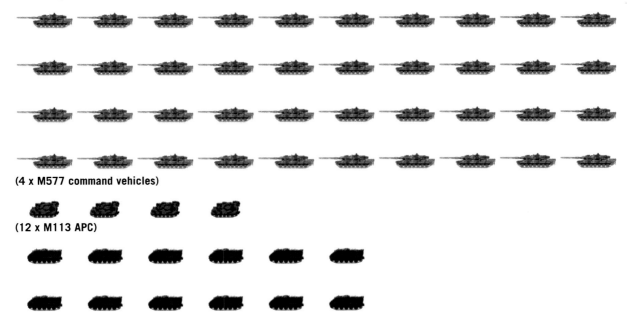

▶ **M113 Green Archer**

German Army / 13th Mechanized
Infantry Division, 1990

The platform for mobile Green Archer
mortar and artillery locating radar utilized
by the German Army during the latter
years of the Cold War, the M113 Green
Archer variant demonstrates the
versatility of the US-manufactured
armoured personnel carrier.

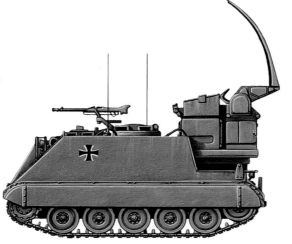

Specifications
Crew: 4
Weight: 11,900kg (26,200lb)
Length: 4.86m (15ft 11in)
Width: 2.7m (8ft 10in)
Height: 4.32m (14ft 2in)
Engine: 160kW (215hp) Detroit Diesel 6V-53N
        6-cylinder diesel
Speed: 68km/h (42mph)
Range: 480km (300 miles)
Armament: 1 x 7.62mm (0.3in) MG
Radio: SEM-80/90 digital

Specifications
Crew: 4
Weight: 25.5 tonnes (56,200lb)
Length: 6.61m (21ft 8in)
Width: 3.12m (10ft 3in)
Height: 2.55m (8ft 4in)
Engine: 1 x 373kW (500hp) Daimler-Benz
        MB837A 8-cylinder diesel
Speed: 68km/h (42mph)
Range: 400km (250 miles)
Armament: 1 x HOT ATGW system; 1 x 7.62mm
        (.3in) MG3 MG
Radio: SEM-80/90 digital

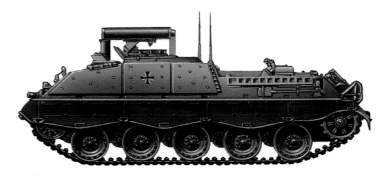

▲ **Jagdpanzer Jaguar**

German Army, 1990

The Jadgpanzer Jaguar 1 self-propelled anti-tank vehicle upgraded the Raketenjagdpanzer 2. It mounted the
Euromissile K3S HOT ATGW, a command-to-line-of-sight system with a range of 4000m (4374 yards), able to
penetrate modern explosive-reactive armour.

▲ **TPz 1A3 Fuchs NBC reconnaissance vehicle**

German Army, 1988

The Transportpanzer 1 Fuchs is an amphibious 6x6 vehicle, carrying 10 soldiers in a rear compartment. In water, it
reaches 10.5km/h (6.5mph) using twin propellers beneath the rear of the hull. Variants include an EOD vehicle and a
RASIT radar carrier.

Specifications
Crew: 2 + 10
Weight: 18.3 tonnes (40,350lb)
Length: 6.76m (22ft 2in)
Width: 2.98m (9ft 9in)
Height: 2.3m (7ft 6.6in)
Engine: 1 x 239kW (320hp) Mercedes-Benz
        OM402A 8-cylinder diesel
Speed: 105km/h (65mph)
Range: 800km (500 miles)
Armament: 1 x 7.62mm (0.3in) MG
Radio: SEM-80/90 digital

NATO – Italy
1970–91

Organic Italian armoured development during the latter years of the Cold War began with the influence of the German Leopard 1 main battle tank.

WHEN THE ITALIAN GOVERNMENT obtained licensing to produce a variant of the German Leopard 1 main battle tank in the early 1970s, Italian engineers were allowed to gain valuable insight into the design of the modern armoured fighting vehicle. In time, the Italians produced more than 700 of the licensed Leopard, which served as the impetus for a world-class main battle tank of Italian manufacture.

While the OF 40, designed by Otobreda and Fiat, may have incorporated numerous features of the Leopard 1, its performance proved unremarkable. Entering service in 1980, its original 105mm (4.1in) main cannon was not stabilized. Within a year, the OG 14 LR fire control system had been installed, improving its accuracy tremendously. Designated the OF 40 Mk 2, this improved version of the tank was subsequently purchased by the United Arab Emirates in the only recorded export sale of the tank. Still, the OF 40 offered no system of defence against nuclear,

biological and chemical weapons, and ammunition storage capacity was minimal.

During the 1980s, research continued on a new Italian main battle tank, and the Ariete was slated to enter production during the mid-1990s. The principal armoured personnel carrier of the Italian Army during the period was the VCC-1, a highly modified version of the US-designed M113 which was built under licence.

Artillery

Another Italian foray into the arms export market was the Palmaria 155mm (6.1in) self-propelled howitzer. Developed during the era of the superb US, German and British weapons of similar configuration, the Palmaria main weapon was mounted atop the chassis of the OF 40 main battle tank. Its development was undertaken in 1977, and the first prototype was tested in 1981. The former Italian colony of Libya was the first foreign country to purchase the

▲ **VCC-1 Armoured Personnel Carrier**
Italian Army / Folgore Mechanized Infantry Division, Italy, 1974
A licence-built and highly modified version of the American M113 armoured personnel carrier, the Italian VCC-1 featured sloped rear and side armour, firing ports for infantrymen, shields for its Browning 12.7mm (0.5in) machine guns and smoke grenade launchers.

Specifications

Crew: 2 + 7	Speed: 65km/h (40mph)
Weight: 11,600kg (25,578lb)	Range: 550km (340 miles)
Length: 5.04m (16ft 6in)	Armament: 2 x Browning 12.7mm (0.5in) MGs
Width: 2.69m (8ft 10in)	Radio: n/k
Height: 2.03m (6ft 8in)	
Engine: 156kW (210bhp) GMC V6 diesel	

Palmaria, followed by Nigeria and Argentina later in the 1980s. The system featured an automatic loader with a rate of fire of a single round every 15 seconds.

During the Cold War, the Italian Army was tasked with protecting its own borders against Warsaw Pact aggression. The *Ariete* Armoured Division and *Mantova* and *Folgore* Mechanized Infantry Divisions were deployed along the Italian northern frontier. The army also contributed to NATO operations around the world and to the efforts of United Nations peacekeeping forces.

Typical of the Italian Army's mobility was the *Aosta* Mechanized Brigade, its infantry regiments equipped

with numerous M113 armoured personnel carriers and variants of the Centauro infantry fighting vehicle. Cavalry formations fielded the wheeled Centauro tank destroyer, and artillery units the M109 self-propelled howitzer.

The *Ariete* Armoured Division, which traces its lineage to the fascist regime of Benito Mussolini during the 1930s, was redesignated a brigade in 1986 and included three tank regiments, an elite *Bersaglieri* regiment, and supporting artillery and engineers. The elite *Garibaldi Bersaglieri* Brigade was a mechanized infantry formation which included three infantry and one armoured battalions along with supporting artillery.

Specifications

Crew: 2 + 11
Weight (approx): 12,000kg (26,500lb)
Length: 6.87m (22ft 6.4in)
Width: 2.95m (9ft 8in)
Height: 2.05m (6ft 8.7in)
Engine: 160kW (215hp) Detroit 6V-53N 6-cylinder diesel
Speed: 68km/h (42mph)
Range: 550km (340 miles)
Armament: 1 x 12.7mm (0.5in) Browning M2 HB HMG

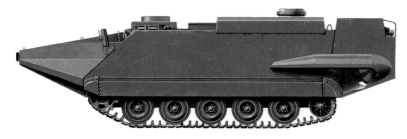

▲ **Arisgator Amphibious APC**

Italian Army / Mantova Mechanized Infantry Division, Italy, 1975

A fully amphibious version of the American M113 armoured personnel carrier, the Arisgator was heavily modified by the Italian firm Aris. Readily identifiable due to its boat-shaped forward section, the Arisgator could carry a complement of up to 11 combat infantrymen.

▲ **Type 6616 Armoured Car**

Italian Army / Carabinieri, Italy, 1977

The wheeled Otobreda Fiat Type 6616 armoured car entered service with the Italian Army during the early 1970s and was made available on the export market as well. Capable of traversing water hazards, it featured a turret-mounted 20mm (0.79in) cannon and a light 7.62mm (0.3in) machine gun.

Specifications

Crew: 3
Weight: 8000kg (17,600lb)
Length: 5.37m (17ft 7in)
Width: 2.5m (8ft 2in)
Height: 2.03m (6ft 8in)
Engine: 119kW (160hp) Fiat Model 8062.24 supercharged diesel
Speed: 100km/h (75mph)
Range: 700km (450 miles)
Armament: 1 x Rheinmetall 20mm (0.79in) Mk 20 Rh 202 gun, plus 1 x 7.62mm (0.3in) coaxial MG
Radio: n/k

NATO – Spain
1982–PRESENT

In May 1982, seven years after the death of fascist leader Generalissimo Francisco Franco, Spain joined the NATO alliance and initiated an effort to modernize its armoured force.

DURING THE EARLY YEARS OF THE COLD WAR, many Western nations refused to export arms to the fascist regime of Generalissimo Francisco Franco. One notable exception was France. Unable to purchase main battle tanks from other countries, the Spanish settled on the AMX-30, purchasing and producing under licence more than 300 examples of the French tank from 1973 to 1984.

By the mid-1980s, approximately 700 US tanks were also in the Spanish arsenal, including the venerable M41 Walker Bulldog light tank and the M47, M48 and M60 tanks of the Patton series. A number of the M41s, dating to the Korean War era, were reportedly updated as tank destroyers during the period. The Spanish Army fielded one armoured division, which included a pair of active armoured brigades and a reserve brigade. In addition to the array of tanks, it included armoured personnel carriers such as the American-built M113 and armoured cars such as the French AML-60 and AML-90. The Pegaso 3560 BMR armoured personnel carrier was a wheeled 6X6 vehicle that was produced in Spain from 1979

onwards. Several variants have been developed, and armament ranges from a 40mm (1.57in) grenade launcher to light machine guns and anti-tank guided missile systems. Nearly 700 of these vehicles have seen service with the Spanish military.

Armoured upgrade
The Spanish military establishment briefly considered the purchase of a new main battle tank during the early 1990s; however, that option was declined and the existing inventory of ageing AMX-30s was upgraded with explosive reactive armour, laser rangefinding equipment and high-performance diesel engines manufactured in Germany. Later, the Spanish Army acquired more than 300 of Germany's outstanding Leopard 2 main battle tanks. More than 100 of these were Leopard 2A4s previously in service with the downsizing German Army, while 219 were the brand new Leopard 2E, a variant of the 2A6 jointly manufactured by Germany and Spain and featuring greater armour protection than the domestic German tank.

▲ AMX-30 Main Battle Tank
Spanish Army / 1st Armoured Division, Spain, 1978
The AMX-30 main battle tank, purchased directly from France and also built in Spain under licence, served as the backbone of the Spanish Army's armoured forces for decades. Upgraded during the 1990s, a large number of the AMX-30s continue on active duty today.

Specifications
Crew: 4
Weight: 35,941kg (79,072lb)
Length: 9.48m (31ft 1in)
Width: 3.1m (10ft 2in)
Height: 2.86m (9ft 4in)
Engine: 537kW (720hp) Hispano-Suiza

12-cylinder diesel
Speed: 65km/h (40mph)
Range: 600km (373 miles)
Armament: 1 x 105mm (4.1in) gun, plus 1 x 20mm (0.79in) gun and 1 x 7.62mm (0.3in) MG
Radio: n/k

The NATO-era Spanish armoured force includes four heavy armoured brigades and one cavalry brigade. Among the light armoured vehicles of the Spanish Army are at least 30 examples of the ASCOD Pizarro infantry fighting vehicle, which entered service in 2002 and is a product of the Austrian–Spanish Cooperative Development (ASCOD). The Pizarro carries a crew of three and up to eight combat-ready infantrymen. Its armament includes a turret-mounted 30mm (1.18in) cannon and a 7.62mm (0.3in) light machine gun. Functioning in battlefield cooperation with the Leopard 2 tank, the Pizarro has proven a capable replacement for the ageing M113 armoured personnel carrier in the Spanish inventory.

As the Cold War neared its end, the 1st *Brunete* Armoured Division of the Spanish Army was grouped within the IIF (Immediate Intervention Force), a corps-sized unit of the NATO armed forces. Among its components were the 11th Mechanized Brigade and the 12th Armoured Brigade which

Specifications

Crew: 5	Speed: 21km/h (13.5mph)
Weight: 46,500kg (102,533lb)	Range: 144km (90 miles)
Length: 12.3m (40ft 6.5in)	Armament: 1 x 76mm (3in) gun, plus 1 x
Width: 3.2m (10ft 8in)	12.7mm (0.5in) MG and 1 x 7.62mm (0.3in) MG
Height: 2.4m (8ft 2in)	Radio: n/k
Engine: 261.1kW (350hp) Bedford petrol	

▲ **M41 Walker Light Tank**

Spanish Army / 1st Armoured Division, Spain, 1982

The M41 light tank was a US design of the Korean War era, which replaced the M24 Chaffee during the early 1950s. The M41 initially mounted a 76mm (3in) M32 main gun. In addition to the M41, the Spanish Army had previously received a quantity of M24s.

▲ **Pegaso VAP 3550/1 Amphibious Vehicle**

Spanish Army / 1st Armoured Division, Spain, 1980

The Pegaso VAP 3550/1 amphibious wheeled vehicle was produced in Spain during the 1970s. It mounted a light machine gun for defence, and its crew rode in an enclosed cab, while combat troops or cargo were carried in its spacious rear compartment.

Specifications

Crew: 3 + 18	Engine: 142kW (190hp) Pegaso 9135/5
Weight: 12,500kg (27,550lb)	6-cylinder turbo diesel
Length: 8.85m (29ft 0.4in)	Speed: 87km/h (54mph)
Width: 2.5m (8ft 2in)	Range: 800km (500 miles)
Height: 2.5m (8ft 2in)	Armament: 1 x 7.62mm (0.3in) MG (export
	versions only)

included, as representative of its strength, the 11th Armoured Battalion with 27 AMX-30 main battle tanks, 14 French BMR 600 armoured personnel carriers licence-built in Spain, an 81mm (3.2in) mortar section, nine rifle squads and a pair of MILAN anti-tank guided missile launchers. The 11th Artillery Battalion fielded 18 M109 155mm

(6.1in) self-propelled howitzers. The 2nd Motorized and 3rd Mechanized Divisions were also capable of rapid deployment.

Since the end of the Cold War, Spanish forces have participated with NATO in operations in Afghanistan, Lebanon, the Balkans, Iraq and other hotspots around the globe.

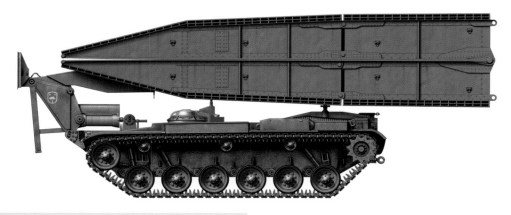

Specifications

Crew: 4	Speed: 48km/h (30mph)
Weight: 51.33 tonnes (50.5 tons)	Range: 500km (311 miles)
Length: 9.44m (31ft)	Bridge: length: (extended) 191.9m (63ft),
Width: 3.63m (11ft 11in)	(folded) 8.75m (32ft); span: 18.28m (60ft);
Height: 3.27m (10ft 8in)	width: (overall) 3.99m (13.1ft), (roadway)
Engine: 559.7kW (750hp) Continental AVDS-	3.81m (12.5ft); height: 0.94m (3.1ft); weight:
1790-2A V12 turbo-charged diesel	13.28 tonnes (13.07 tons)

▲ M60A1 AVLB

Spanish Army / 1st Armoured Division, Spain, 1993

Based on the M60 Patton chassis, the M60A1 AVLB is used for launching and retrieving an 18m (60ft) scissors-type bridge. The AVLB consists of three major sections: the launcher, the hull and the bridge. The launcher is mounted as an integral part of the chassis. The bridge, when emplaced, is capable of supporting most tracked and wheeled vehicles.

▲ M60A3E Patton Main Battle Tank

Spanish Army / 1st Armoured Division, Spain, 1993

The M60A3E Patton main battle tank featured an unusual turret configuration, with a small machine gun mount atop the main 105mm (4.1in) M68 gun turret. The Spanish Army acquired at least 50 of the M60A3E variant.

Specifications

Crew: 4	2 V12 diesel
Weight: 49 tonnes (48.2 tons)	Speed: 48km/h (30mph)
Length: 6.9m (22ft 9.5in)	Range: 500km (300 miles)
Width: 3.6m (11ft 11in)	Armament: 1 x 105mm (4.1in) M68 gun;
Height: 3.2m (10ft 6.5in)	1 x 12.7mm (0.5in) M85 MG; 1 x 7.62mm
Engine: 560kW (750hp) Continental AVDS-1790-	(0.3in) MG

Sweden
1970–91

An innovative Swedish armoured force has adopted the German Leopard 2 main battle tank while maintaining a willingness to experiment with radical designs of its own.

EARLY IN THE POST-WORLD WAR II PERIOD, the Swedish armed forces relied on the British Centurion as their primary tank. However, as Soviet tank designs progressed, a Swedish engineer proposed a departure from the expected: a turretless tank. The idea was not new, however. German armoured assault guns of World War II had been successful, their heavy weapons mounted within the hull.

The elimination of a turret would accomplish several things. The hull would provide a stable gun platform, potentially improving accuracy; the profile of the tank would be significantly lower, improving its ability to hide in revetments or fight from ambush; and the tank would be less expensive to manufacture. On the other hand, the tank would be at a distinct disadvantage in the hull-down position, and reorienting the main weapon would essentially mean moving the entire vehicle.

Nevertheless, the experiment went forward and the Stridsvagn 103 was developed. Beginning in the late

1950s, the prototype was tested, and by 1967 production was under way. The first unit was soon delivered to the Swedish Army, and production ceased at 290 units in 1971. During the late 1960s, the Stridsvagn 103, or S Tank as it came to be known, was tested against the Chieftain main battle tank of the British Army of the Rhine; and in 1975 trials were conducted in the US comparing the tank with the M60A1E3 Patton. In both cases, the S Tank came out favourably despite its inability to fire on the move.

Modern arms

Sweden sought a new main battle tank during the 1990s and has recently operated 280 German Leopard 2 tanks, 160 of which are the Leopard 2A4, designated the Stridsvagn 121; the remainder are the Leopard 2(S), or Stridsvagn 122. Since the early 1990s, Sweden has deployed the CV 90, or Stridsfordon 90, infantry fighting vehicle, designed by Hagglünds Bofors and built by BAE Land

Specifications	
Crew: 3	(490hp) Boeing 553 gas turbine
Weight: 38,894kg (85,568lb)	Speed: 50km/h (31mph)
Length (hull): 7.04m (23ft 1in)	Range: 390km (242 miles)
Width: 3.26m (10ft 8.3in)	Armament: 1 x 105mm (4.1in) gun, plus
Height: 2.5m (8ft 2.5in)	3 x 7.62mm (0.3in) MGs
Engine: 1 x 119kW (240hp) diesel; 1 x 366kW	Radio: n/k

▲ **Stridsvagn 103 Light Tank**

Swedish Army / Skaraborgs Regiment, Sweden, 1974

The turretless Stridsvagn 103 was an innovative main battle tank design and the only one of its kind deployed in large numbers. It mounted the 105mm (4.1in) L/62 rifled gun in the hull along with two light machine guns.

Systems. The development of the CV 90 was begun in 1984, and testing of the prototype began four years later, successfully concluding in 1991. The first deliveries to the Swedish Army were made in 1993. The CV 90 carries a crew of three and a complement of seven combat infantrymen. More than 1000 CV 90s have been produced to date, and a variant was exported to Finland. The Swedish Army currently possesses three regiments of armoured and mechanized troops (*Pansartrupperna*).

Specifications

Crew: 5

Weight: 53,000kg (116,600lb)

Length: 11m (36ft 1in)

Width: 3.37m (11ft 0.7in)

Height: 3.85m (12ft 7.5in)

Engine: 1 x 179kW (240hp) Rolls-Royce diesel; 1 x 224kW (300hp) Boeing gas turbine

Speed: 28km/h (17.4mph)

Range: 230km (143 miles)

Armament: 1 x 155mm (6.1in) gun, plus 1 x 7.62mm (0.3in) anti-aircraft MG

▲ **Bandkanon**

Swedish Army / Södra Skånska Regiment, Sweden, 1981

The 155mm (6.1in) Bandkanon self-propelled artillery vehicle was developed by Bofors in the early 1960s and combined the chassis of the Stridsvagn 103 with the heavy cannon. The system entered service with the Swedish Army in 1967.

Specifications

Crew: 2 + 8

Weight: 2900kg (6400lb)

Length: 6.17m (20ft 2in)

Width: 1.76m (5ft 9in)

Height: 2.21m (7ft 3in)

Engine: 68kW (91hp) Volvo B18 4-cylinder diesel

Speed: 39km/h (24mph)

Range: 400km (250 miles)

Armament: None

Radio: n/k

▲ **BV 202**

Swedish Army / Skaraborgs Regiment, Sweden, 1982

Developed by Volvo, the BV 202 troop carrier vehicle includes two Kegresse track units, with the crew and powerplant in the first and up to eight soldiers in the trailer. It was produced from 1964 to 1981 and last used by Swedish cavalry units, which perform training functions in the Swedish Army.

Switzerland
1970–91

The Swiss Army has rarely mobilized during the modern era. Nevertheless it maintains two armoured brigades in readiness for self-defence and to complement four brigades of infantry and three brigades of mountain troops.

THE SWISS ARMY maintains approximately 380 German Leopard 2A4 main battle tanks, designated the Panzer 87. In addition, more than 500 examples of the US-manufactured M113 armoured personnel carrier remained in service into the 1990s, while the APC 2000 variant of the Swedish CV 9030 infantry fighting vehicle was purchased early in the decade.

The Swiss MOWAG corporation has produced a series of armoured fighting vehicles, including the Roland and MR8 armoured personnel carriers of the 1970s and the Grenadier, an updated version of the Roland. Earlier, the Entpannungspanzer armoured recovery vehicle was designed by RUAG Land Company of Switzerland and entered service in 1970.

Specifications
Crew: 1 + 8
Weight: 6100kg (13,450lb)
Length: 4.84m (15ft 10in)
Width: 2.3m (7ft 6in)
Height: 2.12m (6ft 11in)
Engine: 150kW (202hp) MOWAG 8-cylinder
    petrol
Speed: 100km/h (62mph)
Range: 550km (340 miles)
Armament: 1 x 20mm (0.79in) cannon

▲ **MOWAG Grenadier**
Swiss Army / 11th Armoured Brigade, Switzerland, 1984
Mounting a 7.62mm (0.3in) light machine gun or the heavy 20mm (0.79in) M-2HB cannon in a small turret, the MOWAG corporation Grenadier infantry fighting vehicle was a modernization of the Roland fighting vehicle and entered service with the Swiss Army during the late 1970s.

Specifications
Crew: 5
Weight: 38,000kg (83,800lb)
Length: 7.6m (24ft 11in)
Width: 3.06m (10ft 4in)
Height: 3.25m (10ft 8in)
Engine: 525kW (704hp) MTU MB 837
    8-cylinder diesel
Speed: 55km/h (34mph)
Range: 300km (190 miles)
Armament: 1 x 7.5mm (0.295in) MG, plus
    8 x smoke dischargers
Radio: n/k

▲ **Entpannungspanzer**
Swiss Army / 1st Armoured Brigade, Switzerland, 1971
Fitted with a large winch, the RUAG Land Systems Entpannungspanzer armoured recovery vehicle was developed during the 1960s, with the first prototypes evaluated late in the decade and the initial deliveries to the Swiss Army in 1970.

NATO – United Kingdom
1970–91

As the Cold War dragged on, the British forces committed to NATO on the European continent continued to deploy more powerful and versatile armoured fighting vehicles.

DURING THE 1970s, the British Army of the Rhine maintained three divisions, increased to four by the end of the decade, each with considerable armoured strength. By the middle of the decade the Chieftain main battle tank had arrived in large numbers. Developed during the 1960s as a successor to the long-serving Centurion, the Chieftain was the most heavily armoured tank of its time and mounted the most powerful main weapon, the 120mm (4.7in) rifled L11A5 gun. The Chieftain crew was well protected, the tank provided firepower that was second to none and laser rangefinding gear was installed to replace a ranging machine gun.

The last Chieftain production model, the Mk 5, was also fully protected against nuclear, biological and chemical weapons. There was, however, a price to pay in speed and mobility. The question nagged as to whether the Chieftain was mobile enough to react swiftly to the onslaught of the latest Soviet-built tanks of the Warsaw Pact, namely the T-64 and T-72. A number of Chieftain variants were purpose built,

including armoured recovery and bridging vehicles, and these served with NATO forces.

Flexible Response
Should the Warsaw Pact attack, the role of the British Army of the Rhine would be to halt the advance under the doctrine of Flexible Response, which basically dictated one of three courses of action. In the event of a Soviet attack other than a nuclear first strike, NATO forces would respond in kind.

The first response was called Direct Defence and involved stopping a Warsaw Pact conventional offensive with conventional forces. The second stage was Deliberate Escalation. It was fully expected that Warsaw Pact conventional forces would overwhelm NATO forces due to superior numbers. Therefore a response with tactical nuclear weapons would occur. Third, a General Nuclear Response would correspond to the 'mutually assured destruction' theory set out by Robert S. McNamara, US Secretary of Defense under President John F. Kennedy.

▲ **Alvis Saracen Armoured Personnel Carrier**
British Army of the Rhine / 3rd Armoured Division, Germany, 1978
The FV603 Alvis Saracen armoured personnel carrier was one of numerous armoured fighting vehicles produced by the Alvis Corporation during the 1960s and 1970s. It was armed with light machine guns for protection against enemy infantry and transported up to nine soldiers.

Specifications

Crew: 2 + 9	Engine: 119kW (160hp) Rolls-Royce B80 Mk 6A
Weight: 8640kg (19,008lb)	8-cylinder petrol
Length: 5.233m (17ft 2in)	Speed: 72km/h (44.7mph)
Width: 2.539m (8ft 4in)	Range: 400km (248 miles)
Height: 2.463m (8ft 1in)	Armament: 2 x 7.62mm (0.3in) MGs
	Radio: n/k

Specifications

Crew: 4

Weight: 54,880kg (120,736lb)

Length: 10.795m (35ft 5in)

Width: 3.657m (11ft 8.5in)

Height: 2.895m (9ft 6in)

Engine: 560kW (750hp) Leyland 6-cylinder
  multi-fuel

Speed: 48km/h (30mph)

Range: 500km (310 miles)

Armament: 1 x 120mm (4.7in) rifled gun, plus
  1 x 7.62mm (0.3in) coaxial machine gun and
  12 x smoke dischargers

Radio: Twin Clansman VRC 353 VHF radio sets,
  plus 1 x C42 1 B47 Larkspur VHF radio

▲ Chieftain Mk 5 Main Battle Tank

British Army of the Rhine / 7th Armoured Brigade, Germany, 1976

The Chieftain main battle tank combined the powerful 120mm (4.7in) L11A5 gun with the heaviest armour protection in the world. Its final production variant, the Mk 5, was equipped with defences against nuclear, biological and chemical weapons and had laser rangefinding equipment.

Specifications

Crew: 2 + 10

Weight: 15,280kg (33,616lb)

Length: 5.251m (17ft 7in)

Width: 2.8m (9ft 2in)

Height (with machine gun): 2.286m (7ft 6in)

Engine: 170kW (240hp) Rolls-Royce K60
  6-cylinder multi-fuel

Speed: 52.2km/h (32mph)

Range: 483km (300 miles)

Armament: 1 x 7.62mm (0.3in) MG

Radio: n/k

▲ FV432 Armoured Personnel Carrier

British Army of the Rhine / 2nd Division, Germany, 1975

The FV432 was developed in the 1960s and served as the primary armoured personnel carrier of the British Army for more than two decades. The vehicle was capable of transporting up to 10 combat infantrymen, and by the 1980s more than 2500 examples of the FV432 had been deployed.

While speed was essential to the success of a deep penetration offensive according to Warsaw Pact doctrine, rapid response was equally significant in NATO plans to stem a Soviet-led tide of armour and infantry. In 1983, the British Army of the Rhine received yet another improved main battle tank, the Challenger 1. Integral in helping the British forces fulfil their charge in stopping a Warsaw Pact offensive, the Challenger 1 maintained the proven 120mm (4.7in) L11A5 rifled gun. However, it was considerably faster than the Chieftain with a top road speed of 56 km/h (37mph).

Although only 420 examples of the Challenger were actually built, the tank represented a great improvement in armour protection as well. Lighter Chobham armour, a ceramic and metal composite, was installed for the first time on the Challenger 1 and provided protection many times greater than that of rolled steel. Aside from serving with British forces in Europe, the Challenger 1 was the latest British main battle tank to see combat during Operations Desert Shield and Desert Storm in 1991, compiling an impressive record against Iraqi tanks. Even as the Challenger 1 was deployed during the mid-1980s, its

British Army, 2nd Royal Tank Regiment, 1989

As the Cold War waned, the strength of the 2nd Royal Tank Regiment was typical of comparable armoured formations of the British Army of the Rhine. Its 56 Challenger tanks mounted heavy 120mm (4.7in) L11A5 main guns, while supporting infantry was transported aboard the ageing FV432 armoured personnel carrier. The Alvis Sultan and Scorpion vehicles, along with the venerable Daimler Ferret armoured car, provided command, reconnaissance and fire support structure.

Regiment (56 x Challenger, 4 x Sultan, 8 x Scorpion, 10 x FV432, 8 x Ferret)

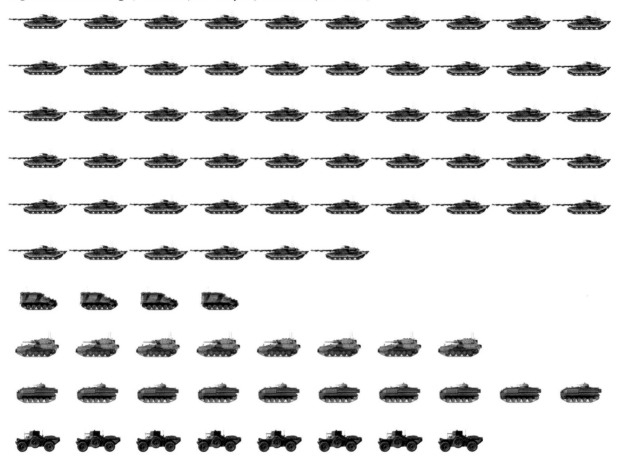

successor, the Challenger 2, was on the drawing board. A radical departure from its predecessor, the Challenger 2 was scheduled to come on line by the end of the twentieth century.

Armoured fighting vehicles

During the 1970s, British armoured fighting vehicles such as the Alvis Saracen and the later FV101 Scorpion combat reconnaissance vehicle were utilized extensively in fire support and scouting roles. The FV432 armoured personnel carrier was capable of transporting up to 10 combat infantrymen and entered service during the 1960s.

Evaluating the capabilities of the Soviet-built BMP infantry fighting vehicles, British designers undertook the development of a comparable vehicle in 1972. Intended to replace the ageing FV432, the Warrior was designed for maximum cross-country speed and later to keep pace with the Challenger 1 and 2 tanks in Europe. An agonizingly slow development period led to the delay of the prototype until 1979. Further, the new vehicle did not enter service until 1987. Nevertheless, armed with a 30mm (1.18in) RARDEN cannon and 7.62mm (0.3in) machine guns, the Warrior has been proven effective, and long-range upgrade and sustainment programmes continued into the 1990s.

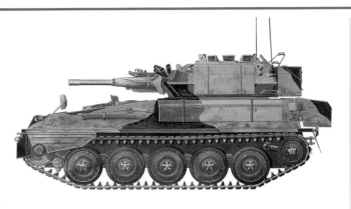

Specifications

Crew: 3
Weight: 8073kg (17,760lb)
Length: 4.794m (15ft 8.75in)
Width: 2.235m (7ft 4in)
Height: 2.102m (6ft 10.75in)
Engine: 142kW (190hp) Jaguar 4.2-litre petrol
Speed: 80km/h (50mph)
Range: 644km (400 miles)
Armament: 1 x 76mm (3in) gun, plus
  1 x 7.62mm (0.3in) coaxial MG
Radio: Clansman VRC 353

▲ FV101 Scorpion CVR(T)

British Army of the Rhine / 7th Armoured Brigade, Germany, 1984

One of seven Alvis-produced armoured vehicles, the FV101 Scorpion entered service with the British Army in 1973 and was deployed for more than 20 years. Serving in a reconnaissance role, it was originally armed with a 76mm (3in) cannon and upgunned to a 90mm (3.5in) weapon.

Specifications

Crew: 3 + 4
Weight: 8172kg (17,978lb)
Length: 5.125m (16ft 9in)
Width: 2.24m (7ft 4in)
Height: 2.26m (7ft 5in)
Engine: 142kW (190hp) Jaguar 6-cylinder petrol
Speed: 80km/h (50mph)
Range: 483km (301 miles)
Armament: 1 x MILAN ATGM launcher, plus
  1 x 7.62mm (0.3in) MG
Radio: Clansman VRC 353

▲ FV120 Spartan with MILAN Compact Turret (MCT)

British Army of the Rhine / 1st Armoured Division, Germany, 1977

The anti-tank version of the Alvis FV103 Spartan armoured personnel carrier, the FV120 mounted a two-man turret with the MILAN anti-tank guided missile launching system. Two missiles were loaded to fire, while an additional 11 were transported.

▲ FV106 Samson CVR(T) Armoured Recovery Vehicle

British Army of the Rhine / 3rd Armoured Division, Germany, 1978

An armoured recovery adaptation of the FV120 Spartan, the FV106 Samson was equipped with a winch to remove vehicles that had bogged down or were damaged in combat. It carried a light machine gun for defensive purposes.

Specifications

Crew: 3
Weight: 8740kg (19,300lb)
Length: 4.78m (15ft 8in)
Width: 2.4m (7ft 10.4in)
Height: 2.55m (8ft 4.4in)
Engine: 145kW (195hp) Jaguar J60 N01 Mk100B
  6-cylinder petrol
Speed: 55km/h (34mph)
Range: 483km (300 miles)
Armament: 1 x 7.62mm (0.3in) MG
Radio: n/k

Specifications

Crew: 1

Weight: 2120kg (4664lb)

Length: 3.65m (12ft)

Width: 1.68m (5ft 6in)

Height: 1.97m (6ft 5in)

Engine: 30kW (51hp) 4-cylinder OHV diesel

Speed: 105km/h (65.6mph)

Range: 560km (350 miles)

Armament: None

Radio: n/k

▲ **Land Rover 4x4 Light Utility Vehicle**

British Army of the Rhine / 2nd Infantry Division, Germany, 1980

The modified military version of the Land Rover Defender series, the 4x4 light utility vehicle was a workhorse of the British military deployed in Europe. Excellent cross-country capability facilitated the rapid deployment of combat units.

NATO – United States
1970–90

US armour in service with NATO included the latest generation of main battle tank along with sophisticated weapons systems designed to defeat a Warsaw Pact ground offensive.

WHILE THE NATO TACTIC of Follow On Forces Attack had been standard procedure since the 1960s, the role of the alliance's ground defence component evolved from one of early warning or 'tripwire' involvement to one of defeat of the Warsaw Pact armour and infantry arrayed against it. In tandem with Flexible Response (outlined on page 131), the Follow On Forces Attack doctrine involved coordinated action against an enemy. The three elements of Follow On Forces Attack were Long-Range Attack, Immediate-Range Attack and Cross-Corps Support.

In Long-Range Attack, strikes would be conducted against Warsaw Pact marshalling areas, where troop and tank assets moving forward would be most vulnerable, concentrated for transport or choked in column along roads. Immediate-Range Attack involved identifying the most critical area requiring defence, concentrating forces and denying Warsaw Pact commanders an effective next move. Cross-Corps Support involved attacking long-range follow-on forces of the Warsaw Pact to diminish the strength of an attack against a specific sector.

Armour component

Into the 1980s, the Patton series remained a significant main battle tank for US forces, particularly the most advanced variant, the M60A3, which had resulted from an improvement programme undertaken in 1978 and included a 105mm (4.1in) main weapon, ballistic computer and turret stabilization system for improved accuracy.

However, it had become apparent to the American military establishment that a replacement for the Patton was needed. Following the failed MBT-70 project of the 1960s and an abortive joint tank development venture with West Germany, the research and development of the XM815, later known as the M1 Abrams main battle tank, was begun in about 1972. Eight years later, the first M1 Abrams tank entered service with the US Army. Mounting the M68 105mm (4.1in) rifled cannon, a licence-built version of the British Royal Ordnance L7 gun, the Abrams was later rearmed in the M1A1 upgrade with the M256 120mm (4.7in) smoothbore cannon developed by the Rheinmetall AG corporation of Germany for the Leopard 2 main battle tank. By 1986, the M1A1 had become the primary production model, and it was this version which was deployed during Operation Desert Storm.

The M1A1 Abrams was protected by a composite armour similar to the British Chobham and was powered by a 1120kW (1500hp) gas turbine engine, which later earned it the nickname 'Whispering Death'. Its pressurized nuclear, biological and chemical defence system increased survivability, and the advanced fire control system resulted in tremendous accuracy.

After a long delay in development, the M2/M3 Bradley Fighting Vehicle entered service in 1981 in both infantry and cavalry configurations. Mounting a 25mm (1in) M242 chain gun and the TOW anti-tank missile system, the Bradley was capable of carrying up to seven combat infantrymen. A significant requirement for the Bradley vehicle was that it keep pace with the M1 Abrams main battle tank under combat conditions while also providing protected transportation and direct fire support for infantry.

▲ **M1A1 Abrams Main Battle Tank**

US Army / 1st Armored Division, Germany, 1987

The M1A1 Abrams was the primary variant of the US main battle tank deployed during the mid-1980s. Its 120mm (4.7in) smoothbore gun, developed by Rheinmetall of Germany, was accurate up to a range of more than 2469m (2700 yards).

Specifications

Crew: 4	Speed: 67km/h (42mph)
Weight: 57,154kg (126,024lb)	Range: 465km (289 miles)
Length (over gun): 9.77m (32ft 3in)	Armament: 1 x 120mm (4.7in) M256 gun, plus
Width: 3.66m (12ft)	1 x 12.7mm (0.5in) MG and 2 x 7.62mm
Height: 2.44m (8ft)	(0.3in) MGs
Engine: 1119.4kW (1500hp) Textron Lycoming	Radio: n/k
AGT 1500 gas turbine	

▲ **M901 TOW APC**

US Army / 1st Infantry Division, Germany, 1987

Based on the M113A1 APC, the M901 entered production in 1978 and mounts 2 x M27 TOW anti-tank missiles. The M901 must come to a stop before it can fire, though it takes only 20 seconds for the TOW system to target and launch. Reloading takes around 40 seconds.

Specifications

Crew: 4 or 5
Weight: 11,794kg (26,005lb)
Length: 4.88m (16ft 1in)
Width: 2.68m (8ft 9in)
Height: 3.35m (10ft 11.8in)
Engine: 160kW (215hp) Detroit Diesel 6V-53N
6-cylinder diesel
Speed: 68km/h (42mph)
Range: 483km (300 miles)
Armament: 1 x TOW 2 ATGW system (2 missles);
1 x 7.62mm (0.3in) MG
Radio: n/k

Specifications

Crew: 3 + 25
Weight: 22,837kg (50,241lb)
Length: 7.943m (26ft 0.7in)
Width: 3.27m (10ft 8.7in)
Height: 3.263m (10ft 8.5in)
Engine: 298kW (400hp) Detroit-Diesel Model
  8V-53T engine
Speed: 64km/h (40mph)
Range: 482km (300 miles)
Armament: 1 x 12.7mm (0.5in) M2HB HMG, plus
  optional 40mm (1.57in) Mk19 grenade
  launcher
Radio: AN/VIC-2 intercom system

▲ LVTP7 amphibious vehicle

US Marine Corps / 31st Marine Expeditionary Unit, 1990

Currently the primary amphibious armoured personnel carrier of the US Marine Corps, the LVTP7 entered service
in the early 1980s. With a troop-carrying capacity of 25, it was armed with grenade launchers or a 25mm (1in) chain gun.

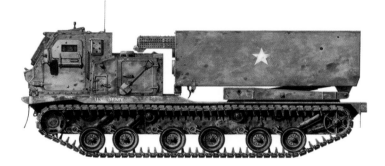

Specifications

Crew: 3
Weight: 25,191kg (55,420lb)
Length: 6.8m (22ft 4in)
Width: 2.92m (9ft 7in)
Height: 2.6m (8ft 6in)
Engine: 373kW (500hp) Cummings VTA-903
  turbo-charged 8-cylinder diesel
Speed: 64km/h (40mph)
Range: 483km (302 miles)
Armament: 2 x rocket pod containers, each
  holding 6 rockets
Radio: n/k

▲ M270 Multiple Launch Rocket System (MLRS)

US Army / 1st Infantry Division, Germany, 1989

The M270 Multiple Launch Rocket System entered service with the US Army in 1983. Mounting the M269 launcher module,
the system was capable of firing a variety of munitions at a rate of up to 12 per minute.

Specifications

Crew: 4
Weight: 50,803kg (112,020lb)
Length: 8.27m (27ft 1.5in)
Width: 3.43m (11ft 3in)
Height: 2.92m (9ft 7in)
Engine: 730kW (980hp) Continental
  AVDS-1790-2DR 12-cylinder diesel
Speed: 42km/h (26mph)
Range: 450km (280 miles)
Armament: 1 x 12.7mm (0.5in) Browning
  M2HB HMG
Radio: n/k

▲ M88A1 Armoured Recovery Vehicle

US Army / 1st Armored Division, Germany, 1985

Based on the M88, one of the heaviest armoured recovery vehicles in the world, the M88A1 medium armoured recovery
vehicle entered service with the US Army in 1977. Powered by a diesel engine, it also transported ammunition and supplies.

Chapter 2

The Korean War, 1950–53

When elements of the North Korean People's Army crossed the 38th Parallel on 25 June 1950, communist forces rapidly overwhelmed those of the South attempting to stand against them. In the vanguard of the communist offensive were Soviet-designed T-34 tanks, battle-tested during World War II and considered among the finest armoured fighting vehicles in the world. As United Nations forces, primarily those of the United States and the British Commonwealth, bolstered the South Koreans, a new generation of Western tanks and armoured vehicles reached the combat zones. The Korean War, therefore, became a proving ground for tactical and technological innovation – particularly in the role of the armoured fighting vehicle on the modern battlefield.

◀ **US Marine armour**

US Marine M26 Pershing tanks roll through a village in Korea as a line of prisoners of war are marched into captivity, September 1950.

Organization and armour

At the dawn of the Nuclear Age, senior military planners around the world grappled with redefining the nature of conventional warfare.

THE MOBILITY AND FIREPOWER of the modern tank were to take on added significance during the ebb and flow of the Korean War. The armoured fighting vehicle had come of age during World War II. The rapid advancement of technology and the unparalleled proving ground of the battlefield – particularly in the desert of North Africa, across the Western Front in Europe, and on the vast steppes of the Soviet Union in the East – had fostered a quantum leap in the development, deployment and doctrine of the armoured fighting vehicle. The tank was, without doubt, the mobile sledgehammer of a land army's combat arsenal. However, while the strength of an armoured formation was readily apparent, its shortcomings had been laid bare as well.

In the United States, the report of the War Department Equipment Board, popularly known as the Stilwell Board and presided over by General Joseph Stilwell of World War II fame, was published

in January 1946. Its findings concluded that ground and air forces must cooperate fully in combat situations, while tanks could not operate without the support of infantry. The role of armour was defined as one of exploiting a breakthrough against the enemy on the ground.

Although the tank provided mobile firepower, it could not sustain the advantage indefinitely on its own. Therefore, the combined arms approach was deemed appropriate. The highest and best future use of the tank would be in concert with infantry and air assets. US infantry divisions were to be assigned their own organic tank battalions to facilitate the combined arms approach.

Furthermore, the United States Army would no longer field tank destroyer formations. The advent of the modern tank, with heavy firepower, rendered the tank destroyer obsolescent. The M26 Pershing heavy tank, for example, fielded a 90mm (3.5in) main gun

▲ **Tank destroyer**
First serving towards the end of World War II, the US-made M36 tank destroyer saw action in Korea. The M36 was later used in Indochina and the Indo-Pakistan War.

and afforded crewmen better protection with a closed turret than the most recent tank destroyers of the World War II period had provided. Three types of tanks were recommended: the light tank for scouting, reconnaissance and the security of a defensive perimeter; the medium tank for combat assault and advance; and the heavy tank for further exploitation of a tactical advantage.

Development of the role of the modern tank in battle aside, the reality of a war-fatigued nation and the post-war budget constraints placed upon the military establishment resulted in the reduction of many battalion-sized tank formations within army divisions to mere company strength. Additionally, the manufacture of the M24 Chaffee light and M26 Pershing heavy tanks, and later the M46 Patton, was seriously curtailed and even suspended by the eve of the Korean War. Indeed, during the early days of the Korean War, the World War II vintage M4 Sherman was a mainstay.

Girding for war

While a financially strapped Great Britain wrestled with the lessons of the armoured experience during World War II as well, its Cromwell, Centurion and Churchill tanks were modified and field operations reassessed. However, as the chill of the Cold War settled in, Western defensive posture remained decidedly focused on the security of Western Europe. Although the security of its borders and the consolidation of its grip on the client states of Eastern Europe were paramount, the Soviet Union supported the build-up of arms in North Korea. The T-34 had been produced in staggering numbers during World War II, and its upgunned variant, the T-34/85, was made available in some numbers.

As North Korea prepared for war, its army consisted of eight full-strength infantry divisions, two more infantry divisions at partial strength, other independent units and an armoured brigade, the 105th. With an overall strength of 6000 men, the 105th was well trained and included 120 T-34s evenly distributed among three tank regiments and supported by a 2500-man mechanized infantry regiment. In contrast, there were no tanks organic to the eight infantry divisions of the South Korean Army in 1950.

Less than two weeks after the North Koreans crossed the 38th Parallel, a small, lightly armed

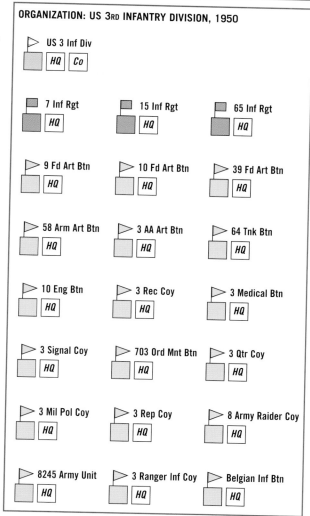

contingent of the US 21st Infantry Regiment, 24th Division, had been airlifted to Pusan and hurried north to confront the invaders. Spearheaded by T-34s, the North Koreans decimated Task Force Smith, named for its commander, Lieutenant-Colonel Charles B. Smith, and inflicted more than 150 casualties. By August, the 1st Provisional Marine Brigade and its M26s had reached Pusan, while army armoured units had also deployed, providing some measure of tenuous stability.

Armoured advantage

For several reasons, including the nature of the terrain, the real tactical value of the tank during the Korean War has been questioned. It may be reasoned that the presence of tanks directly affected the outcomes of numerous engagements; however, taken as a whole, their collective influence is open to conjecture. It has been estimated that total UN tank strength in Korea never exceeded 600 at any one time. Among these were many of the World War II-era Shermans, Cromwells and Challengers. The T-34/85 of the same vintage was by far the most prevalent tank employed by the North Korean forces. One Chinese armoured formation may actually have been fielded during the war but never engaged in any hostile action.

Korean proving ground
Still, the North Koreans had used the tank in its exploitative role, taking advantage of a breakthrough to rapidly advance southwards, while the arrival of UN armour had helped to avert total collapse, and armoured formations were again shown to be vulnerable to air attack. Even though large-scale armoured operations were few and tanks rarely engaged one another in significant numbers, the evolution of the main battle tank continued with the Korean War experience.

The Korean battlefield served as something of a narrow proving ground for the early tanks of the US Patton series, which was continually upgraded and

became the backbone of US armoured forces during the next 30 years. For Britain, the Centurion had already incorporated many of the lessons learned during World War II and included in the earlier Cromwell design.

The improvements to later British tanks such as the Challenger and Chieftain were undoubtedly influenced. Furthermore, the Soviet Union was far from idle, continuing to develop its T-54/55 series of main battle tanks, which would eventually equip the armed forces of nations across the globe.

Firepower, mobility and armour protection became the watchwords of the future. Bigger, stronger and faster tanks were on the horizon, and the perceived division of labour among light, medium and heavy tanks was beginning to noticeably wane. The Cold War demanded technology and treasure, while maintaining the balance of power and economic viability contributed to the development of the modern main battle tank.

Perhaps the influence of the Korean War on the development of the main battle tank has been underestimated. Regardless of opinion or perspective, the main battle tank of the twenty-first century has been, to some extent, shaped by the experience of both older designs and more innovative post-World War II features that were battle-tested in Korea.

▲ Light Tank M24
Republic of Korea Army Training Center, Kwang-Ju 1953
The M24 Chaffee was lightly armed and armoured. Although quantities of both the Chaffee and the M4E8 Sherman had been promised by the US, the South Korean Army had no tanks when war broke out.

Specifications

Crew: 5	Speed: 55km/h (34mph)
Weight: 18.28 tonnes (18 tons)	Range: 282km (175 miles)
Length: 5.49m (18ft)	Armament: 1 x 75mm (2.9in) M6 gun, plus
Width: 2.95m (9ft 8in)	1 x 12.7mm (0.5in) HMG on AA mount and
Height: 2.46m (8ft 1in)	2 x 7.62mm (0.3in) MGs (1 coaxial,
Engine: 2 x 82kW (110hp) Cadillac 44T24	1 ball-mounted in hull front)
V8 8-cylinder petrol	Radio: SCR 508

Pusan

AUGUST–SEPTEMBER 1950

The hard-pressed forces of the United Nations and the South Korean Army relied on armoured support to stem the North Korean tide and to defend the Pusan Perimeter.

B Y THE LATE SUMMER OF 1950, reinforcements had slowed the North Korean advance, which had followed a string of victories from Seoul to Osan and beyond. The defence of the Pusan Perimeter in the extreme southeast corner of South Korea was facilitated largely by the deployment of US armoured forces. As the Korean War intensified, many of the American M26 Pershing tanks had been slated for upgrade to the M46A1 Patton, primarily to address mechanical problems and improve engine performance and to implement a better suspension system. The 90mm (3.5in) main gun of the Pershing, however, remained in the M46A1 Patton and proved to be a potent weapon during the bleak early months in Korea. The sheer availability of the M4 Sherman variants, including the 'Firefly' with its 76mm (3in) high-velocity cannon, made these tanks instrumental in defensive operations.

More than half the North Korean complement of tanks were reported to be the improved T-34/85, while the earlier T-34, with its 76mm (3in) main gun, nevertheless constituted a major threat. The numbers of Shermans, Pershings, Pattons, Centurions, Cromwells and Churchills increased over time. In tank-versus-tank combat, the United Nations armour proved at least equal to the prowess of the legendary T-34. On 3 September 1950, a platoon of US Marine M26 Pershings engaged three T-34s near Hill 117 during the Second Naktong Offensive, destroying all three.

More than 500 US medium tanks, mostly M26s and M4s, had reached the Pusan Perimeter by the end of August 1950, while a single battalion of M46s had been deployed. In contrast to the rapid offensive movement of North Korean infantry and armour during the opening weeks of the war, the defensive infantry support of these tanks proved a key element in the eventual breakout from the Pusan Perimeter and the concurrent amphibious landing at Inchon, far to the north, on 15 September.

▲ **M26 Pershing Heavy Tank**

Eighth United States Army / 1st US Marine Division / 1st Tank Battalion

The M26 Pershing tank was developed late in World War II and saw limited action. In Korea, its reputation for mechanical unreliability diminished its performance and hastened its withdrawal in favour of the improved M46 Patton.

Specifications

Crew: 5	Range: 161km (100 miles)
Weight: 41.86 tonnes (41.2 tons)	Armament: 1 x 90mm (3.5in) M3 gun,
Length: 8.61m (28ft 3in)	plus 1 x 12.7mm (0.5in) AA HMG and
Width: 3.51m (11ft 6in)	2 x 7.62mm (0.3in) MGs (1 coaxial and
Height: 2.77m (9ft 1in)	1 ball-mounted in hull front)
Engine: 373kW (500hp) Ford GAF V8 petrol	Radio: SCR508/528
Speed: 48km/h (30mph)	

The initial armoured engagements of the war had been fought between the North Korean T-34s and the light US-made M24 Chaffees, which mounted 76mm (3in) cannon of their own but proved inadequate against the communist tanks. The anticipated service life of the M24 with the US Army was drawing to a close, at least on paper. The new M41 was being developed; the 'Walker Bulldog' was named for General Walton Walker, killed in a jeep accident in Korea in December 1950.

As war wore on, armoured engagements became fewer and the role of the tank did gravitate towards infantry support; however, statistical analysis yielded some valuable information. An evaluation of 256 T-34s destroyed in US-controlled territory concluded that 97 had been knocked out by United Nations armour, including 45 by the M4 Sherman, 32 by the M26 Pershing, 19 by the M46 Patton and one by the M24 Chaffee. The T-34 was estimated to have claimed 16 per cent of the American armour lost.

Specifications

Crew: 5

Weight: 41.86 tonnes (41.2 tons)

Length: 8.61m (28ft 3in)

Width: 3.51m (11ft 6in)

Height: 2.77m (9ft 1in)

Engine: 373kW (500hp) Ford GAF V8 petrol

Speed: 48km/h (30mph)

Range: 161km (100 miles)

Armament: 1 x 105mm (4.1in) M4 howitzer,
    plus 1 x 12.7mm (0.5in) AA HMG and
    2 x 7.62mm (0.3in) MGs (1 coaxial and
    1 ball-mounted in hull front)

Radio: SCR508/528

▲ **M45 Medium Tank**

Eighth United States Army / 6th Tank Battalion

The close infantry support version of the US M26 Pershing heavy tank, the M45 mounted a powerful 105mm (4.1in) howitzer. Production was begun in the summer of 1945, and the M45 designation standardized after World War II. The 6th Tank Battalion fought in defence of the Pusan Perimeter in 1950.

▲ **M46A1 Patton Medium Tank**

Eighth United States Army / 7th Infantry Division / 73rd Heavy Tank Battalion

During the winter of 1950/51, the M46 Patton tanks of the 73rd Heavy Tank Battalion operated with elements of the 7th Infantry Division. The unit was commended for its eventual participation in six campaigns of the Korean War.

Specifications

Crew: 5	Speed: 48km/h (30mph)
Weight: 44 tonnes (43.3 tons)	Range: 130km (81 miles)
Length: 8.48m (27ft 10in)	Armament: 90mm (3.5in) M3A1 gun;
Width: 3.51m (11ft 6in)	1 x 12.7mm (0.5in) AA HMG;
Height: 3.18m (10ft 5in)	2 x 7.62mm (0.3in) M1919A4 MGs
Engine: 604kW (810hp) Continental AVDS-1790-	Radio: SCR508/528
5A V12 air-cooled twin-turbo petrol	

◀ M29C Weasel

Eighth United States Army

Designed by the Studebaker company for use in snow, the M29 Weasel was utilized in Korea as a supply and personnel transport vehicle. The M29C was equipped with flotation tanks.

Specifications

Crew: 4

Weight: 3.9 tonnes (3.8 tons)

Length: 3.2m (10ft 6in)

Width: 1.5m (5ft)

Height: 1.8m (5ft 11in)

Engine: 48kW (70hp) Studebaker Model 6-170 Champion

Speed: 58km/h (36mph)

Range: 426km (265 miles)

Specifications

Crew: 7

Weight: 26.01 tonnes (25.6 tons)

Length: 6.02m (19ft 9in)

Width: 2.88m (9ft 5in)

Height: 2.54m (8ft 4in)

Engine: 298kW (400hp) Continental R975 C1

Speed: 42km/h (26mph)

Range: 201km (125 miles)

Armament: 1 x 105mm (4.1in) M1A2 howitzer, plus 1 x 12.7mm (0.5in) HMG on 'pulpit' AA mount

Radio: SCR608

▲ 105mm Howitzer Motor Carriage (HMC) M7

Eighth United States Army

Nicknamed the 'Priest' by British troops due to the prominent machine-gun ring atop the chassis, which resembled a pulpit, the M7 105mm (4.1in) howitzer provided mobile artillery support for infantry.

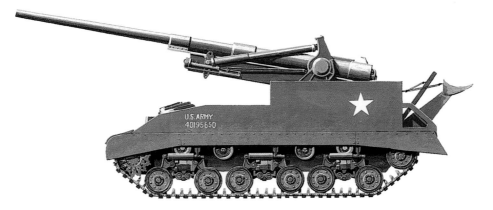

▲ 155mm Gun Motor Carriage (GMC) M40

Eighth United States Army / 25th Infantry Division / 937th Field Artillery Battalion

Introduced late in World War II, the US M40 Gun Motor Carriage was built atop the modified chassis of the M4A3 Sherman tank. Its 155mm (6.1in) cannon provided mobile heavy artillery support for infantry.

Specifications

Crew: 8

Weight: 40.64 tonnes (40 tons)

Length: 9.04m (29ft 9in)

Width: 3.15m (10ft 4in)

Height: 2.69m (8ft 10in)

Engine: 295kW (395hp) Continental 9-cylinder radial petrol

Speed: 39km/h (24mph)

Range: 161km (100 miles)

Armament: 1 x 155mm (6.1in) M1A1 gun

Radio: SCR608

◄ GAZ 67B Command Vehicle
North Korean People's Army

The GAZ 67B was one of a series of multi-purpose Soviet-built vehicles of World War II which were provided to the North Korean armed forces. Inspired by the famous American jeep, the GAZ 67 was first produced in 1943.

Specifications

Crew: 1 driver	Engine: 37.25kW (50hp) 4-cylinder petrol
Weight: 1.32 tonnes (1.3 tons)	Speed: 90km/h (56mph)
Length: 3.35m (11ft)	Range: 450km (280miles)
Width: 1.685m (5ft 6in)	Radio: n/k
Height: 1.7m (5ft 7in)	

Specifications

Crew:
Weight: 5.1 tonnes (5 tons)
Length: 4.65m (15ft 3in)
Width: 2.1m (6ft 11in)
Height: 2.2m (7ft 3in)
Engine: 30kW (40hp) GAZ-A
Speed: 55km/h (34mph)
Range: 200km (124 miles)
Armament: 45mm (1.8in) 20-K gun;
    2 x 7.62mm (0.3in) DT MGs

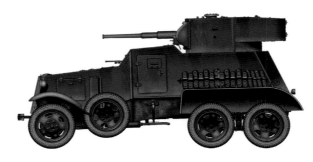

▲ BA-6 Armoured Car
North Korean People's Army

The BA-6 armoured car was developed in the Soviet Union during the early 1930s and usually mounted a 45mm (1.8in) cannon atop a primitive turret. By the time of the Korean War, the vehicle was obsolescent.

▲ SU-76M SP Assault Gun
North Korean People's Army

Second only to the T-34 in production during World War II, the SU-76M was the main production variant of the widely used self-propelled 76mm (3in) assault gun. The assault gun was based on the obsolete T-70 chassis. Large numbers of these were used by communist forces in Korea.

Specifications

Crew: 4	Engine: 2 x 52kW (70hp) GAZ 6-cylinder petrol
Weight: 10.8 tonnes (10.6 tons)	Speed (road): 45km/h (28mph)
Length: 4.88m (16ft)	Range: 450km (280miles)
Width: 2.73m (8ft 11.5in)	Armament: 1 x 76mm (3in) gun, plus
Height: 2.17m (7ft 1.4in)	1 x 7.62mm (0.3in) MG

Seoul
July 1950 – September 1951

The war-torn city of Seoul endured four separate battles for control of the South Korean seat of government in a 10-month period during the Korean War.

CONTROL OF THE SOUTH KOREAN capital city changed hands several times during the first year of war in Korea. Within a week of the opening of hostilities, North Korean forces had captured Seoul; however, their hold was to be short-lived. By September 1950, United Nations forces under the command of General Douglas MacArthur had initiated the breakout from the Pusan Perimeter and brilliantly executed the amphibious end run at the port city of Inchon, and a bloody fight for the city ensued. In December 1950, the intervention of communist China sent the UN forces reeling, and Seoul was again under the control of invaders. The following spring, UN forces recaptured Seoul for the final time prior to stalemate, negotiation and armistice.

The arrival of American armoured units on the Korean peninsula in the autumn of 1950 had been critical in the stabilization of the front at Pusan, blunting the advance of the North Korean People's Army. The latter was spearheaded by columns of the battle-tested T-34 tank supplied by the Soviet Union and client states of the Eastern bloc and supported by self-propelled artillery such as the widely produced SU-76. Control of the air by UN forces was another essential element in the defence against communist armoured formations.

Although tanks were involved in most major battles of the Korean War, the mountainous and forested terrain that covered much of the country was not conducive to large-scale armoured operations. As the war continued, therefore, the number of tank battles declined. One of the larger concentrations of armoured units during the Korean War occurred during the second battle for Seoul in September 1950.

Inchon and beyond

Following the landing at Inchon on 15 September, the advance towards Seoul was slow and painful. UN air power took its toll on exposed North Korean

▲ **Light Tank M24**

Eighth United States Army / 25th Infantry Division / 79th Tank Battalion

Mounting 75mm (2.9in) main guns, the M24 Chaffee light tanks of the US Army's 79th Tank Battalion engaged the North Koreans in the summer of 1950 at the Han River during Operation Ripper, and in other offensive actions during the spring of 1951.

Specifications

Crew: 5	Speed: 55km/h (34mph)
Weight: 18.28 tonnes (18 tons)	Range: 282km (175 miles)
Length: 5.49m (18ft)	Armament: 1 x 75mm (2.9in) M6 gun, plus
Width: 2.95m (9ft 8in)	1 x 12.7mm (0.5in) HMG on AA mount and
Height: 2.46m (8ft 1in)	2 x 7.62mm (0.3in) MGs (1 coaxial,
Engine: 2 x 82kW (110hp) Cadillac 44T24	1 ball-mounted in hull front)
V8 petrol	Radio: SCR 508

T-34s operating in daylight. Successive North Korean counterattacks were beaten back, and the M26 gained a slight upper hand in tank-versus-tank actions. On the morning of the landings, American aircraft destroyed three North Korean T-34s with 227kg (500lb) bombs, while three more were destroyed by M26 Pershings of the US Marines. The following day, Pershing tanks of D Company, 5th Marines destroyed five more T-34s, while a sixth was dispatched with bazooka fire. Only one Marine was wounded, while over 200 North Korean soldiers were killed in the engagement.

During the advance towards Seoul on 17 September, M26s of the 1st Marines destroyed four T-34s, and two

Specifications

Crew: 5	Speed: 48km/h (30mph)
Weight: 28.14 tonnes (27.7 tons)	Range: 241km (150 miles)
Length: 6.15m (20ft 2in)	Armament: 1 x 90mm (3.5in) M3 gun,
Width: 3.05m (10ft)	plus 1 x 12.7mm (0.5in) AA HMG
Height: 2.72m (8ft 11in)	Radio: SCR610
Engine: 373kW (500hp) Ford GAA V8 petrol	

▲ 90mm Gun Motor Carriage, M36 Tank Destroyer
Eighth United States Army

Deployed late in World War II, the M36 tank destroyer, with its 90mm (3.5in) main weapon, was effective against enemy armour in Korea. Many of those deployed in Korea added a ball-mounted machine gun in the hull.

▲ Sherman M4A3 (76)W Dozer
Eighth United States Army / 3rd Engineer Combat Battalion (Hyzer's Tigers II)

This Sherman M4A3 (76)W Dozer operated with Hyzer's Tigers II, the US Army's 3rd Engineer Combat Battalion, during Operations Ripper and Killer in the spring of 1951. Note the tank's 76mm (3in) main cannon.

Specifications

Crew: 5	Speed: 48km/h (30mph)
Weight: 33.65 tonnes (33.1 tons)	Range: 193km (120 miles)
Length: 6.27m (20ft 7in) (with sandshields)	Armament: 76mm (3in) M1A1 gun; 1 x 12.7mm
Width: 3m (9ft 10in)	(0.5in) M2HB MG; 1 x 7.62mm (0.3in) M1919A4
Height: 2.97m (9ft 9in)	coaxial MG
Engine: 298 kW (400hp) Continental R975 C1	Radio: SCR508/528/538
petrol	

days later elements of the 1st Marines struck again, wiping out a battalion of North Korean troops and five T-34s. In a small-scale tank battle, typical of those which occurred during the Korean War, tanks of B Company, 73rd Tank Battalion engaged a pair of North Korean T-34s, with each side losing a tank.

On 22 September, the US Marine vanguard of the UN forces entered the capital city, and Seoul was officially declared liberated three days later. Meanwhile, North Korean forces still engaged to the south near Pusan were rapidly in danger of being cut off. However, the UN objective of liberating Seoul took precedence and more than 30,000 North Korean soldiers were allowed to withdraw.

The UN advance continued to the Chinese frontier, and MacArthur appeared poised to cross the Yalu River, significantly widening the war. In December, the People's Republic of China launched a massive attack that drastically altered the military situation in Korea.

OT-34/76 Medium Tank
North Korean People's Army

Supplied by the Soviet Union, the T-34/76 equipped the early armoured formations of the North Korean People's Army. First produced in 1940, the tank was revolutionary in its day, combining sloped armour for added protection with a powerful 76mm (3in) gun. The OT-34 was a flamethrower model, developed during World War II and first deployed in 1944. The OT-34 carried 200 litres (44 gallons) of fuel and could be effective up to a range of 90m (98 yards).

Specifications
Crew: 4
Weight: 26.5 tonnes (26.2 tons)
Length: 5.92m (19ft 5in)
Width: 3m (9ft 10in)
Height: 2.44m (8ft)
Engine: 373kW (500hp) V-2-34 V12
 diesel
Speed (road): 53km/h (33mph)
Range: 400km (250 miles)
Armament: 1 x 76mm (3in) F-34 gun;
 1 x ATO-41 flamethrower (hull-mounted);
 1 x 7.62mm (0.3in) DT MG (coaxial)
Radio: 10R

Specifications
Crew: 5
Weight: 32 tonnes (31.5 tons)
Length: 6m (19ft 7in)
Width: 3m (9ft 10in)
Height: 2.6m (8ft 6in)
Engine: 372 kW (493hp) V-2 V12 diesel
Speed (road): 55km/h (33mph)
Range: 360km (223 miles)
Armament: 1 x 85mm (3.4in) ZiS-S-53 cannon;
 2 x 7.62mm (0.3in) DT MGs (1 in the bow and
 1 coaxial)
Radio: 10R

Type 58 (T34/85) Medium Tank
Chinese People's Volunteer Army

The Type 58 was a Chinese copy of the Soviet T-34/85 Model 1944. The upgunned successor to the T-34/76, the T-34/85 medium tank mounted an 85mm (3.4in) cannon. In Korea the 85mm (3.4in) cannon was capable of knocking out the latest in United Nations tanks.

Imjin River
APRIL–MAY 1951

The Centurion tank stood tall while the British 29th Infantry Brigade achieved legendary status during an epic battle against overwhelming odds. A major Chinese offensive against Seoul was stalled in the process.

WHEN THE BRITISH ARMY'S 8th King's Royal Irish Hussars arrived at Pusan on 14 November 1950, they brought with them three squadrons of the heavy Centurion Mk 3 tank, equipped with 84mm (3.3in/20-pounder) main cannon. Although the Centurion had been developed during World War II as a counter-measure to the superb German PzKpfw V Panther medium and PzKpfw VI Tiger tanks, it gained lasting fame on the battlefield in Korea.

The 51.8-tonne (51-ton) Centurion had been developed too late to take on the German armour in Western Europe, instead emerging in late 1945 as the primary British battle tank of the early Cold War era. Intended to eventually supplant earlier designs such as the Churchill and the Cromwell, the Centurion was originally armed with a 76mm (3in/17-pounder) main weapon. By the time of its deployment to Korea, the Mk 3 variant included not only the heavier gun but also additional storage positions for track links on the glacis and a stabilizer for the main weapon. Powerful though it was, the Centurion in the Korean War is best remembered for crucial infantry support rather than direct encounters with communist armour.

The earliest of 12 eventual Centurion marks, or variants, was powered by a 485kW (650hp) Rolls-Royce Meteor Mk IVB engine, and while the tank's limited range and relatively low speed were significant shortcomings, its overall performance was strong enough that some observers believed it capable of multiple roles as the 'universal tank' of the British Army.

Stand on the Imjin

On 22 April 1951, communist Chinese forces launched a spring offensive against the United Nations lines north of Seoul, the South Korean capital. The Chinese plan involved the quick exploitation of a breakthrough along the lower Imjin River, and powerful communist forces attacked positions held by the British 29th Infantry Brigade. A rapid breakthrough might have outflanked

▲ **Centurion Mk 3 Main Battle Tank**

British Commonwealth Occupation Force (BCOF) / 29th Infantry Brigade /
8th King's Royal Irish Hussars

During nearly two decades of production, more than 4400 Centurion tanks were produced in a dozen or so variants. The Mk 3 shown incorporated additional machine-gun mounts and was later upgunned to a 105mm (4.1in) main weapon.

Specifications

Crew: 4	Engine: 485 kW (650hp) Rolls-Royce Meteor
Weight: 51.8 tonnes (51 tons)	Speed: 34km/h (21mph)
Length: 7.6m (25ft)	Range: 450km (280 miles)
Width: 3.38m (11ft 1in)	Armament: 84mm (20pdr) gun, plus
Height: 3.01m (9ft 10in)	1 x 7.62mm (0.3in) Browning MG
	Radio: n/k

supporting United Nations units to the east and west, unhinged the enemy line and opened the way to Seoul. Through the course of the coming battle, British, Belgian, US, Filipino and South Korean troops engaged the Chinese.

Battling overwhelming odds, the British and Belgians suffered tremendous losses but slowed the Chinese advance. A combined force of Filipino M24 Chaffee light tanks and Centurions of the 8th Hussars attempted to relieve a nearly surrounded position held by the 1st Battalion, The Gloucestershire Regiment on Hill 235. However, the lead tank was destroyed by Chinese fire and the effort was halted 1830m (2000 yards) from the Glosters' position. As the remnants of the 29th Infantry Brigade retreated from a series of hills it had heroically defended for several days, the Centurions of the 8th Hussars covered the withdrawal and lost five tanks in the process, three of these to enemy fire.

Centurions in the thick of it

The sheer weight of Chinese numbers at times overwhelmed the British positions near the Imjin River, and repeatedly the tanks of the 8th Hussars braved enemy artillery fire to rescue pockets of trapped infantrymen. Although supported by their own infantry, the tanks were assailed by Chinese soldiers attempting to pry turrets and hatches open to drop grenades inside. Turning their machine guns on one another, the buttoned-up tanks mowed down the

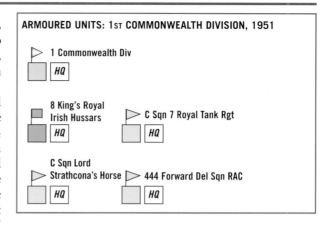

ARMOURED UNITS: 1st COMMONWEALTH DIVISION, 1951

- 1 Commonwealth Div — HQ
- 8 King's Royal Irish Hussars — HQ
- C Sqn 7 Royal Tank Rgt — HQ
- C Sqn Lord Strathcona's Horse — HQ
- 444 Forward Del Sqn RAC — HQ

Chinese infantrymen clinging to their hulls. One eyewitness remembered three platoons of Chinese soldiers emerging from a riverbed and being devastated by the guns of the Centurions. Major Henry Huth, commander of C Squadron, 8th Hussars, received the Distinguished Service Order (DSO) for his heroism at the Imjin River, and described the withdrawal of the 29th Infantry Brigade as 'one long, bloody ambush'.

The tanks of the 8th Hussars evacuated a large number of troops while under fire. One soldier remembered, 'We were told there was a chance that we wouldn't get through and that we'd be safer going up the hills, but anyway two or three of us took the chance and climbed up on the back of the tank. The Chinese were still running alongside the tanks,

▲ **Cruiser Mk VIII Cromwell IV**

British Commonwealth Occupation Force (BCOF) / 29th Infantry Brigade / 8th King's Royal Irish Hussars

Developed in the early 1940s, the British Cromwell tank marked a comprehensive design effort to combine speed, firepower and armour protection in a single package. The Cromwell was largely outmoded by 1950.

Specifications

Crew: 5	V12 petrol
Weight: 27.94 tonnes (27.5 tons)	Speed: 64km/h (40mph)
Length: 6.35m (20ft 10in)	Range: 280km (174 miles)
Width: 2.9m (9ft 6in)	Armament: 1 x 75mm (2.9in) OQF gun,
Height: 2.49m (8ft 2in)	plus 2 x 7.92mm (0.31in) Besa MGs
Engine: 447kW (600hp) Rolls-Royce Meteor	Radio: Wireless Set No. 19

throwing grenades on to the tanks, trying to disable them. I mean we couldn't do a lot about it because we had nothing left, we just laid there quiet and still, watching them, listening to them actually being crushed by the tank tracks.'

Although the terrain near the Imjin was far from ideal tank country, the 8th Hussars had played a key role in facilitating the withdrawal of the 29th Infantry Brigade and sapping the strength of the Chinese offensive. One American officer noted, 'In their Centurions, the 8th Hussars have evolved a new type of tank warfare. They taught us that anywhere a tank can go is tank country, even the tops of mountains.'

The Chinese 63rd Army reportedly sustained more than 10,000 casualties during the Battle of the Imjin River and was withdrawn from combat. The 29th Infantry Brigade lost nearly 1100 killed, wounded and captured.

▲ Sherman M4 Firefly
British Commonwealth Occupation Force (BCOF)

A World War II British improvement to the original 75mm (2.9in) main armament version of the Sherman tank was known as the Firefly. Upgraded with the 76mm (3in/17-pounder) high-velocity gun for increased firepower, the Firefly was deployed to Korea as well.

Specifications
Crew: 4
Weight: 32.7 tonnes (32.18 tons)
Length: 7.85m (25ft 9in)
Width: 2.67m (8ft 9in)
Height: 2.74m (8ft 11in)
Engine: 316.6kW (425hp) Chrysler Multibank A57 petrol
Speed: 40km/h (24.8mph)
Range: 161km (100 miles)
Armament: 1 x 76mm (3in) 17pdr OQF, plus 1 x coaxial 7.62mm (0.3in) MG
Radio: Wireless Set No. 19

▲ M4A3 Sherman Flail
British Commonwealth Occupation Force (BCOF) / 7th Royal Tank Regiment / C Squadron

The M4A3 Sherman Flail was one of many variants of the World War II workhorse tank which continued in service throughout the Korean War. The flail apparatus mounted on the chassis was intended to detonate landmines.

Specifications
Crew: 5
Weight: 31.8 tonnes (31.3 tonnes)
Length: 8.23m (27ft)
Width: 3.5m (11ft 6in)
Height: 2.7m (9ft)
Engine: 373kW (500hp) Ford GAA V8 petrol
Speed: 46km/h (29mph)
Range: 100km (62 miles)
Armament: 1 x 75mm (2.9in) M3 gun, plus 1 x 12.7mm (0.5in) AA HMG and 1 x 7.62mm (0.3in) MG
Radio: Wireless Set No. 19

▶ **Daimler Scout Car**

British Commonwealth Occupation Force (BCOF)
Produced throughout World War II by the British, the
lightly armed and armoured Daimler Scout Car
proved so successful that its service life was
extended through the Korean conflict.

Specifications

Crew: 2

Weight: 3.22 tonnes (3.2 tons)

Length: 3.23m (10ft 5in)

Width: 1.72m (5ft 8in)

Height: 1.5m (4ft 11in)

Engine: 41kW (55hp) Daimler 6-cylinder petrol

Speed: 89km/h (55mph)

Range: 322km (200 miles)

Armament: 1 x 7.62mm (0.3in) MG

Radio: Wireless Set No. 19

HQ (1 x M10 tank destroyer)

Tank Squadron, Lord Strathcona's Horse (Canada)

During and after the Korean War, from 1951 to 1954, A, B and C Squadrons of Lord Strathcona's Horse served in
rotation with the 1st Commonwealth Division. A tank squadron was divided into five troops of three tanks each plus
one tank as HQ vehicle. Initially equipped with the American M10 tank destroyer, the regiment later received the M4A3
Sherman tank. The 1st Commonwealth Division encompassed all British Commonwealth land units in Korea after July
1951, including troops from Britain, Canada, Australia, New Zealand and India.

Troop 1 (3 x M10 tank destroyer)

Troop 2 (3 x M10 tank destroyer)

Troop 3 (3 x M10 tank destroyer)

Troop 4 (3 x M10 tank destroyer)

Troop 5 (3 x M10 tank destroyer)

Chapter 3

The Vietnam War, 1965–75

For many observers, the employment of armoured forces during the Vietnam War might well deserve only a footnote to the overall prosecution of a conflict which raged, hot and cold, for more than 30 years. The attitudes of commanders were shaped largely by the combat experiences of World War II, Korea and the limited use of armour during France's ill-fated attempt to sustain its colonial empire in the Far East. In fact, the continued prosecution of the war in Vietnam led to improvisation and the eventual realization that armour could, in certain circumstances, prove to be decisive in combat.

◀ **Aussie armour**

Crew from the Royal Australian Armoured Corps (RAAC) service their Centurion tank. Between 1967 and 1970 the Australians employed 58 Centurions in Vietnam, mostly providing a fire base for infantry operations.

Introduction

The notion of mechanized combat in Vietnam was for many military strategists as remote as Asia itself as NATO and the Soviet Bloc were fully engaged in the throes of the Cold War.

DURING THE VIETNAM ERA, armoured doctrine for both the United States and the Soviet Union was decidedly centred on 'Battlefield Europe'. Surely, if armour were to be utilized on a grand scale, such events would occur in the West. Large tank formations had not participated in the liberation of islands across the Pacific during World War II, and the China–Burma–India theatre had not seen major clashes of armour.

As the US military presence in Vietnam gradually increased, the role of the tank was considered limited at best. During the Korean War, tanks had served a purpose; however, the perspective of time had not refined the contribution made to the United Nations effort there. Furthermore, the French experience in Vietnam had apparently offered a lesson in the use of armour in Southeast Asia. By the spring of 1954, the French armed forces in what was then Indochina included more than 450 tanks and tank destroyers along with nearly 2000 half-tracks, armoured cars and amphibious tracked vehicles. Much of this materiel had been acquired through American aid and consisted of the M24 Chaffee light tank, M4 Sherman and other vehicles of World War II vintage.

The French deployed a few tanks in the defence of the doomed airhead at Dien Bien Phu, and these had been unable to stem the communist Viet Minh assault. Aside from that disastrous defeat in the far north of Indochina, the debacle which befell a French task force known as *Groupement Mobile* 100 weighed heavily on Western armoured doctrine, or lack thereof, in Southeast Asia. *Groupement Mobile* 100, wrongly assessed as an armoured formation by many, actually included infantry, armoured and support units. Hastily evacuated from an exposed position, the French force was set upon and nearly annihilated by Viet Minh forces in the spring of 1954.

Terrain timidity

US military planners were wary of Vietnam's dense jungle, rice paddies and interior mountains of the Central Highlands, and General William Westmoreland, who would later command American troops in Vietnam, remarked matter-of-factly, 'Except for a few coastal areas …Vietnam is no place for either tanks or mechanized infantry units.'

Indicative of the US preoccupation with massive armoured assaults on the plains of northern Europe was the fact that in the early 1960s the US Army field manual for the operations of an armoured brigade included a single section of only 14 pages dealing with tactics in difficult terrain. Armoured formations, it said, should bypass such areas and allow infantry to clear them. The fatal flaw in such doctrine, which mirrored the failed French attitude, was that by definition armour would be vulnerable while confined to the few suitable roads. While the US military establishment asserted officially that the tank was 'not appropriate for counter-insurgency operations', combat conditions in Vietnam would eventually prove otherwise.

In addition to the hazards of jungle and mountain, the rainy season in Southeast Asia presented another obstacle to armoured operations. Certain geographic areas of Vietnam were actually designated off limits to tanks, armoured personnel carriers and other tracked vehicles during the months of the monsoon. However, a 1967 survey of the country by a group of US officers familiar with the capabilities of the frontline tanks in the American arsenal – particularly the M24 Chaffee, M41 Walker Bulldog and M48 Patton – indicated that nearly half of Vietnam was suitable for the use of armour during much of the year.

Increasing influence

By the time the communist Tet Offensive had been blunted in the winter of 1968, the concentrated firepower of the tank had proven itself a valuable weapon in Vietnam. Actually, the scope of the armoured vehicle had widened considerably as first South Vietnamese and then American and Australian troops adapted the M113 armoured personnel carrier into a true fighting vehicle with the addition of machine guns, a gun shield and even a small turret. Meanwhile, communist forces gained in armoured proficiency as the war dragged on. The growing number of North Vietnamese Army formations in the South included armoured units consisting of Soviet-built PT-76 amphibious tanks, T-34 variants and the later T-54/55 main battle tanks fielded by this well-trained communist army and to a lesser extent the insurgent Viet Cong.

In Vietnam, the anti-tank weapon came of age as well. The communists deployed their lethal shoulder-fired rocket-propelled grenade (RPG) in great numbers, and the US fielded the LAW and wire-guided TOW missiles. Powerful anti-tank mines took their toll and slowed the progress of armour considerably. Capable of destroying some tanks and lightly armoured vehicles or blowing the tread off a heavier tank, many of these were planted on roadways or rigged as booby traps.

Find and fix

Perhaps the greatest contrast to more than half a century of US armoured doctrine was the altered role of the tank in battle in Vietnam. Certainly, the tank's firepower in direct support of infantry operations was undeniable. Its mobility, albeit limited at times, was significant. Its psychological impact was notable.

However, in previous wars the tank had been envisioned and employed as the mailed fist which exploited the breakthrough of the enemy lines. Defined battle lines were seldom seen in Vietnam. The enemy often hit hard and then melted into the jungle or countryside. Therefore, to a great extent the tank became the 'fixer' of the enemy, joining battle, taking hold and pounding away with heavy weaponry. In conjunction with tanks and supporting infantry, the concept of airmobile warfare was implemented. Rather than the tank slashing through the enemy rear, combat infantrymen transported by helicopter could often serve as the enveloping force.

Although it must be acknowledged that Southeast Asia was far from an ideal proving ground for large tank formations to operate in, it was nevertheless indicative of the fighting which was to take place in other parts of the world as the superpowers fought proxy wars and avoided the direct confrontation for which they had so long prepared.

▲ **Light support**
French forces employed the versatile M24 Chaffee light tank in Indochina from the early 1950s. The tank proved ideal in the infantry support role, especially in mountainous and jungle terrain.

US/ARVN forces
1965–75

US and South Vietnamese forces came to rely on the armoured fighting vehicle in routine operations against an elusive enemy, although direct armoured confrontations were rare.

BY THE SUMMER OF 1969, the United States had deployed more than 600 tanks and 2000 other armoured vehicles to combat areas in Vietnam. This was in sharp contrast to the initial belief among ranking military strategists that armour would be of little or no value in fighting a lightly armed insurgency. Possibly the American perspective changed as better trained and more heavily armed North Vietnamese Army units appeared in the South.

Regardless, the markedly changed point of view may be best illustrated by the directive of General William Westmoreland, a one-time opponent of armour in Vietnam, which followed the Tet Offensive of 1968. Westmoreland asserted that future reinforcements sent to Southeast Asia should be armoured, rather than infantry. Doubtless, he recalled that the first American tanks had arrived in Vietnam somewhat by accident when the organic armour of 3rd Platoon, Company B, 3rd Marine Tank Battalion arrived at Da Nang on 9 March 1965

with the Marine Battalion Landing Team. Apparently, some commanders already 'in country' had not realized that M48A3 Patton tanks were included in the force.

Another US Marine Battalion Landing Team came ashore in South Vietnam in August, and this was followed by the first US Army armoured units in Vietnam with elements of the 1st Infantry Division. In one of their first recorded actions during the Vietnam War, Marine tanks took part in Operation Starlite in the summer of 1965. During two days of heavy fighting, the tanks were instrumental in destroying numerous Viet Cong strongpoints, capturing a large number of weapons and killing 68 insurgents. Seven tanks were damaged in the fighting, and one was considered beyond repair.

Early in the war, US infantry brigades were often supported by a cavalry troop, which primarily consisted of the M114, and later the M113, armoured personnel carrier. Most of the heavy

▲ **M41A3 Light Gun Tank 'Bulldog'**

Army of the Republic of South Vietnam (ARVN)

In 1964 the M41 light tank was selected to replace the M24 Chaffee light tank, which the ARVN had inherited from the French. The first M41A3s arrived in January 1965, equipping five ARVN squadrons. The tanks entered combat in October 1965, when 15 M41s joined the relief force for the besieged Plei Mei Special Forces camp.

Specifications

Crew: 5	12-cylinder petrol
Weight: 46,500kg (102,533lb)	Speed: 21km/h (13.5mph)
Length: 12.3m (40ft 6.5in)	Range: 144km (90 miles)
Width: 3.2m (10ft 8in)	Armament: 1 x 76mm (3in) gun, plus 1 x
Height: 2.4m (8ft 2in)	12.7mm (0.5in) MG and 1 x 7.62mm (0.3in) MG
Engine: 261.1kW (350hp) Bedford	Radio: n/k

M48A3 tanks which had been deployed with the infantry were held out of the 'jungle fighting'.

Although some convincing was required, tanks were eventually allowed to join in combat operations. Chief among the proponents of armour in Vietnam was Major-General Frederick Weyand, commander of the US 25th Infantry Division, who demanded the deployment of his armoured units, which included the 3rd Squadron, 4th Cavalry; the 1st Battalion, 5th Infantry (Mechanized); and the 1st Battalion, 69th Armor.

In a classic example of the evolving armoured doctrine employed in Vietnam, Task Force Dragoon, consisting of Troops B and C, 1st Squadron, 4th

US Armoured Cavalry Squadron, 1969

The standard US armoured cavalry squadron of the Vietnam era packed substantial firepower, including the ACAV (Armored Cavalry Assault Vehicle) and infantry versions of the M113 armoured personnel carrier, which transported up to 11 combat-ready soldiers. The light M551 Sheridan tank was capable of being transported by air but proved a disappointment in combat. A company of four M48A3 Patton tanks mounted 90mm (3.5in) cannon, and a self-propelled M109 155mm (6.1in) howitzer provided heavy artillery support.

HQ (1 x M577 APC)

Armoured Cavalry Troop (3 x M113 ACAV, 2 x M551 Sheridans, 1 x M113 infantry combat team)

Armoured Cavalry Troop (3 x M113 ACAV, 2 x M551 Sheridans, 1 x M113 infantry combat team)

Howitzer Battery: 1 x M109 155mm SP howitzer

Armoured Cavalry Troop (3 x M113 ACAV, 2 x M551 Sheridans, 1 x M113 infantry combat team)

Tank Company (4 x M48A3 medium tanks)

Cavalry and Company B, 1st Battalion, 2nd Infantry, lured strong Viet Cong forces into a trap near An Loc in July 1966. M48A3 tanks and machine-gun-equipped M113s held onto the enemy while infantry converged from the flanks. At least two M113s were destroyed; however, more than 240 Viet Cong were killed.

Throughout the Vietnam War, the South Vietnamese Army (ARVN) was dependent upon the United States for arms. In the 1950s, ARVN armoured cavalry units were equipped with light tanks and armoured personnel carriers. By 1966, six armoured cavalry squadrons and units equipped solely with tanks were being added to ARVN infantry divisions. In 1969, two armoured brigades were constituted, equipped with tanks and other vehicles. In the spring of 1971, the 20th Tank Regiment was formed and equipped with the M48, and following the communist Easter Offensive the following year two more M48 tank regiments were added.

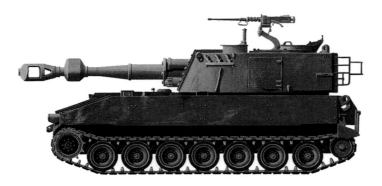

▲ M109 155mm SP Howitzer

1st Infantry Division / 4th Cavalry Regiment / 1st Squadron

The M109 self-propelled howitzer, mounting a 155mm (6.1in) main weapon, was first delivered to the US Army in 1962 and served in numerous armoured formations throughout the Vietnam War, adding heavy artillery capability to combined arms operations.

Specifications

Crew: 6	71T diesel
Weight: 23,723kg (52,192lb)	Speed: 56km/h (35mph)
Length: 6.612m (21ft 8.25in)	Range: 390km (240 miles)
Width: 3.295m (10ft 9.75in)	Armament: 1 x 155mm (6.1in) howitzer, plus
Height: 3.289m (10ft 9.5in)	1 x 12.7mm (0.5in) AA HMG
Engine: 302kW (405hp) Detroit Diesel Model 8V-	Radio: N/a

▲ M110A2 SP Howitzer

15th Field Artillery Regiment / 7th Battalion / Battery A

The M110 self-propelled howitzer was the largest weapon of its kind in the US arsenal during the Vietnam era. The 203mm (8in) main weapon of the M110A2 was distinguished from the M110A1 model by its double baffle muzzle brake.

Specifications

Crew: 5	Engine: 335.5kW (405hp) Detroit Diesel V-8
Weight: 28,350kg (62,512lb)	Speed: 56km/h (35mph)
Length: 5.72m (18ft 9in)	Range: 520km (325 miles)
Width: 3.14m (10ft 4in)	Armament: 1 x 203mm (8in) howitzer
Height: 2.93m (9ft 8in)	Radio: N/a

THE VIETNAM WAR, 1965-75

▲ M578 Light Recovery Vehicle

4th US Artillery / 8th Battalion

The M578 light recovery vehicle utilized the same chassis as the M110 203mm (8in) and M107 175mm (6.9in) self-propelled weapons. It was developed to facilitate the changing of the gun barrels, which experienced rapid wear during combat conditions.

Specifications

Crew: 3	Engine: 302kW (405hp) General Motors 8V-71T
Weight: 24,300kg (53,600lb)	8-cylinder diesel
Length: 6.42m (21ft .75in)	Speed: 55km/h (33mph)
Width: 3.15m (10ft 4in)	Range: 725km (450 miles)
Height: 2.92m (9ft 7in)	Armament: 1 x 12.7mm (0.5in) Browning
	M2 HB MG

North Vietnamese forces
1959–75

The armoured forces of the North Vietnamese Army began to take shape in the mid-1950s with the acquisition of armoured cars and half-tracks and the development of anti-tank tactics.

ALTHOUGH THE NORTH VIETNAMESE ARMY had established armoured vehicle units as early as 1956, it emphasized defence and acquired a number of towed anti-tank guns, including the Soviet 57mm (2.24in) and German Pak 40 75mm (2.9in) weapons. In 1959, the 202nd Armoured Regiment, the first tank unit in the North Vietnamese Army, was established. The unit received 35 T-34/85 tanks and 16 SU-76 self-propelled guns, and its designation referred to the 202 members of its command cadre who had been trained in the Soviet Union and China.

By 1965, a formal Armed Forces Directorate had been established to refine armoured doctrine and foster cooperative efforts among infantry, armour and artillery units. The 202nd Armoured Regiment had been expanded to include three battalions and fielded the modern T-54/55 main battle tank, the SU-76 and the PT-76 amphibious tank.

Acknowledging that its armoured assets were limited, reportedly fewer than 100 serviceable tanks, the North Vietnamese Army adopted a philosophy of limited use. Tanks were to be primarily deployed during offensive operations in order to reduce casualties, and only the minimum number of tanks necessary would be engaged at any one time. The close coordination of armour and infantry was deemed essential. It was not until late 1967 that North Vietnamese armour went into harm's way in appreciable strength.

Organization

Although the standard organization of armoured units was generally followed, it was not unusual for detached units to operate independently or for tank battalions to mix vehicle types liberally. A single tank battalion might, for example, include one or more companies of light PT-76 or heavier T-34/85 tanks, and one or more companies of BTR-50 armoured personnel carriers. A complete armoured battalion might include as many as 40 tanks or 35 armoured personnel carriers.

North Vietnamese armoured regiments were reorganized in 1971, and those formed subsequent to the 202nd Armoured Regiment were raised to three battalions, each including three companies of up to 12 tanks or 11 of the Soviet-built BTR-50PK or Chinese-manufactured K-63 armoured personnel carriers. By the 1970s, the People's Republic of China had begun to supply the North Vietnamese with its own Type 59 tank, a copy of the Soviet T-34, and the Type 63, which was quite similar to the amphibious PT-76. China also became the principal supplier of armoured personnel carriers with the K-63.

On those occasions when North Vietnamese armour ventured forward in force, the results were often predictable. US control of the air contributed to heavy losses during the Easter Offensive of 1972, and by mid-June more than 80 tanks had been destroyed. When the offensive ended, over 400 tanks and armoured personnel carriers had been lost. Anti-tank missiles and chance encounters with US and South Vietnamese M48s often left the lightly armoured PT-76 a smoking ruin.

Following the heavy losses of the Easter Offensive, the North Vietnamese replenished their armoured formations with more T-54/55s, T-34/85s and

NVA ARMOURED REGIMENT, 1971			
Type	Number	Vehicle	Strength
Headquarters	–	T34/85	1
Armoured Btn	3		
Headquarters	1	T34/85	1
Armoured Coy	3	T34/85	10
Reconnaissance Ptn	1	T34/85	3–5
Reconnaissance Btn	1		
Headquarters	1	BTR-40	1
Light Tank Coy	1	T34/85	7–10
Recce Coy	2	BTR-60PA	5
AA Battery	1	BTR-40A or ZSU-57-2	2

PT-76s supplied by the Soviets. Tactics were revised to include two offensive options, the sudden assault, which would shock the enemy and open the way for the deep thrust, which would then wreak havoc in the enemy rear.

On the eve of the decisive 1975 offensive against the ARVN, now fighting alone, the North Vietnamese Army could boast nine armoured regiments organized into 29 battalions with more than 600 tanks and 400 other armoured vehicles. The outcome of the final assault was a foregone conclusion, and the image of a T-54 crashing through the gate of the presidential palace in Saigon is an icon of the communist victory.

▲ **T-34/85M Medium Tank**

North Vietnamese Army / 202nd Armoured Regiment

The Soviet-built T-34/85 medium tank was a mainstay of the early armoured formations of the North Vietnamese Army. The T-34/85M, also known as the Model 1969, was developed in the late 1960s, with a V-54 engine, wide, T-55-style road wheels and several other modifications, including an improved radio set and an external fuel pump to ease refuelling.

Specifications

Crew: 5

Weight: 32 tonnes (31.5 tons)

Length: 6m (19ft 7in)

Width: 3m (9ft 10in)

Height: 2.60m (8ft 6in)

Engine: 433 kW (581 hp) Model V-55 12-cyl.

38.88-l diesel

Speed (road): 55km/h (33mph)

Range: 360km (223 miles)

Armament: 1 x 85mm (3.4in) ZiS-S-53 cannon; 2 x 7.62mm (0.3in) DT MGs (bow and coaxial)

Radio: R-123

NVA Armoured Regiment, 1971

At the height of the Vietnam War, the North Vietnamese armoured regiment fielded a complement of more than 90 tanks in three battalions, each comprising three companies, along with reconnaissance platoons and headquarters vehicles. Mechanized infantry was transported by up to 35 BTR-50 or K-63 armoured personnel carriers. By 1975, the North Vietnamese armoured strength had grown to nine regiments and was estimated at 600 tanks and over 400 armoured personnel carriers.

HQ

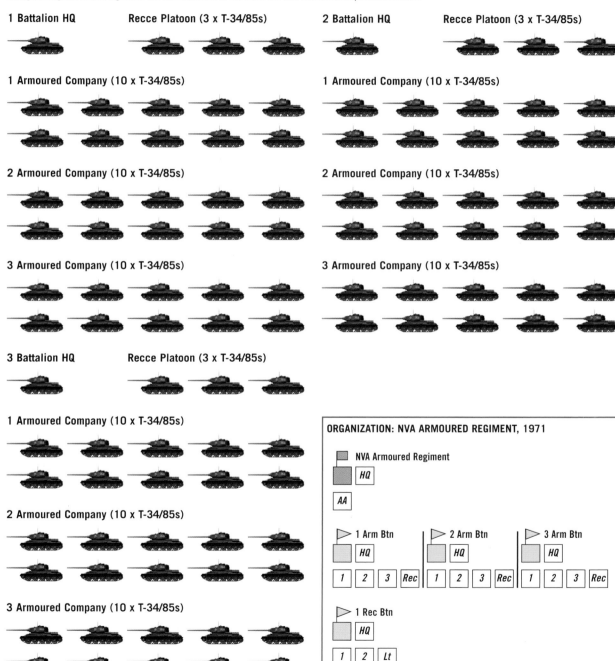

▲ Norinco Type 63 Amphibious Light Tank

NVA / 574th Armoured Regiment

The Chinese Type 63 amphibious light tank resembled the Soviet PT-76 and was first produced in 1963. In 1969, North Vietnam placed an order for 150 of the Type 63, and these tanks were delivered during the following three years.

Specifications

Crew: 4

Weight: 18,400kg (40,572lb)

Length: 8.44m (27ft 8in)

Width: 3.2m (10ft 6in)

Height: 2.52m (8ft 4in)

Engine: 298kW (400bhp) Model 12150-L V12

diesel

Speed: 64km/h (40mph)

Range: 370km (230 miles)

Armament: 1 x 85mm (3.4in) gun, plus 1 x
12.7mm (0.5in) HMG and 1 x 7.62mm (0.3in) MG

Radio: n/k

▲ BTR-40 Amphibious Armoured Scout Car

NVA / 198th Armoured Battalion

Indicative of the Soviet preference for wheeled armoured personnel carriers in the years following World War II, the BTR-40 was exported in large numbers to North Vietnam and also served as a command, reconnaissance and scout vehicle during the Vietnam War.

Specifications

Crew: 2 + 8

Weight: 5300kg (11,660lb)

Length: 5m (16ft 5in)

Width: 1.9m (6ft 3in)

Height: 1.75m (5ft 9in)

Engine: 60kW (80hp) GAZ-40 6-cylinder

Speed: 80km/h (50mph)

Range: 285km (178 miles)

Armament: 1 x 7.62mm (0.3in) MG

Specifications

Crew: 6

Weight: 28,100kg (61,820lb)

Length: 8.48m (27ft 10in)

Width: 3.27m (10ft 9in)

Height: 2.75m (9ft)

Engine: 388kW (520hp) Model V-54 V12 diesel

Speed: 50km/h (31mph)

Range: 420km (260 miles)

Armament: 2 x 57mm (2.24in) anti-aircraft guns

Radio: n/k

▲ ZSU-57-2 SP Anti-Aircraft Gun (SPAAG)

NVA / 201st Armoured Regiment

Its twin 57mm (2.24in) anti-aircraft cannon mounted atop the chassis of the T-34 medium tank, the ZSU-57-2 entered service in the mid-1950s and provided the North Vietnamese Army with mobile defence against enemy aircraft during the Vietnam War.

Tet Offensive/Battle for Hue
1968

Direct armoured combat was a rarity during the Vietnam War; however, the employment of the tank and the armoured personnel carrier was pivotal during numerous actions, particularly the defeat of the communist Tet Offensive.

O N 26 JANUARY 1968, less than a week before their commencement of the Tet Offensive, communist forces sent tanks into battle in the South for the first time. Assaulting South Vietnamese positions at Ta May, amphibious PT-76 tanks of the 3rd Company, 198th Armoured Battalion supported troops of the 24th Infantry Regiment, forcing the ARVN soldiers to abandon their position. Moving forward, the North Vietnamese attacked the US Special Forces position at Lang Vei, losing six PT-76s but overwhelming the garrison, which retreated to the US Marine base at Khe Sanh, which was under siege for months to come.

The majority of US and South Vietnamese armour losses in Vietnam were caused by anti-tank weapons such as the B-40 rocket launcher (RPG) and powerful landmines. As the war progressed, additional armour packages were installed on the undersides of many vehicles to minimize casualties and damage from mines. Tanks began to employ screens to detonate RPG rounds before they could directly impact hull or turret armour. North Vietnamese armoured vehicles often fell prey to both tactical and strategic bombers, as well as tank-killing Bell Huey Cobra gunships – heavily armed attack helicopters.

Tanks at Tet

When communist forces launched coordinated attacks throughout the South on 31 January 1968, to coincide with the new year celebration of Tet, regular army and guerrilla forces hit military and civilian targets, creating confusion and spawning a media event in the United States. Militarily, the Tet Offensive proved disastrous for the communists; however, images of fighting in the streets of Saigon, the South Vietnamese capital, and in the grounds of the US embassy provided a propaganda coup for the communists and hastened the US withdrawal from Vietnam.

▲ M48A1 Medium Tank

11th Armored Cavalry Regiment / 3rd Squadron / Company M

The M48A1 Patton medium tank featured the commander's cupola of the original M48, which allowed the M2HB 12.7mm (0.5in) anti-aircraft machine gun to function, including reloading, from inside the tank. Many early M48s were converted to the M48A3 and deployed to Vietnam.

Specifications	
Crew: 4	cooled petrol
Weight: 47,273kg (104,219lb)	Speed: 42km/h (26mph)
Length: 7.3m (23ft 11in)	Range: 216km (134 miles)
Width: 3.6m (11ft 11in)	Armament: 1 x 105mm (4.1in) gun, plus
Height: 3.1m (10ft 2in)	3 x 7.62mm (0.3in) MGs
Engine: 604kW (810hp) AV1790-7C V12 air-	Radio: n/k

When US and South Vietnamese forces brought armour to bear, the result was often successful. At Quang Ngai City the concentrated firepower of South Vietnamese tanks and M113 armoured personnel carriers cleared the city of communist forces in about eight hours. During the two-day battle at the Pineapple Forest near Tam Ky, armoured cavalry units killed 180 Viet Cong and North Vietnamese soldiers.

Battle for Hue

The longest and most bitter battle during the Tet Offensive was the contest for the provincial capital of Hue, which lasted 26 days. Armoured cavalry and US Marine tanks, some of which mounted flame-throwers, rooted out communist soldiers who had occupied houses and administrative buildings within the walled 'Citadel'. The fighting was heavy, and US tank crews were rotated on a daily basis due to heavy contact, including multiple RPG hits on a single tank.

Although the Marines' M48s had not been intended for close, urban combat and were shown to be vulnerable to anti-tank weapons, their firepower was instrumental in the eventual recapture of Hue. Primitive urban combat tactics were developed, such as the tandem use of the M48 and the six-barrelled self-

▲ **Rifle, Multiple 106mm, Self-propelled, M50 Ontos**
1st Marine Division / 1st Anti-Tank Battalion
An airmobile tank destroyer, the M50 Ontos was lightly armoured but offered heavy firepower with six 106mm (4.17in) recoilless rifles and was utilized primarily as an infantry support weapon in Vietnam. The M50 was withdrawn from service by the mid-1970s.

Specifications
Crew: 3
Weight: 8640kg (19,051lb)
Length: 3.82m (12ft 6in)
Width: 2.6m (8ft 6in)
Height: 2.13m (6ft 11in)
Engine: 108kW (145hp) General Motors
 302 petrol
Speed: 48km/h (30mph)
Range: 240km (150 miles)
Armament: 6 x 106mm (4.17in) recoilless rifles;
 4 x 12.7mm (0.5in) M8C spotting rifles
Radio: n/k

▲ **M42 SP Anti-Aircraft Gun**
3rd Marine Division / 44th Artillery Regiment / 1st Battalion
The self-propelled M42 Duster anti-aircraft gun was developed during the 1950s and deployed to Vietnam in response to disappointing results from early anti-aircraft missile systems. The 40mm (1.57in) guns of the M42 also proved outstanding in an infantry support role.

Specifications
Crew: 6
Weight: 22,452kg (49,394lb)
Length: 6.35m (20ft 10in)
Width: 3.225m (10ft 7in)
Height: 2.847m (9ft 4in)
Engine: 373kW (500hp) Continental AOS-895-3

6-cylinder air-cooled petrol
Speed: 72.4km/h (45mph)
Range: 161km (100 miles)
Armament: 2 x 40mm (1.57in) anti-aircraft guns,
 plus 1 x 7.62mm (0.3in) MG
Radio: n/k

propelled 106mm (4.17in) Ontos recoilless rifle. Several tanks were lost; however, the communists suffered more than 5000 killed and wounded.

Armour against armour

One of the few instances when opposing armour met in combat in Vietnam occurred when PT-76 tanks of the North Vietnamese 4th Armoured Battalion, 202nd Armoured Regiment met M48A3s of the US Army's 1st Battalion, 69th Armor at Ben Het on 3 March 1969. One M48 sustained a direct hit from a 76mm (3in) shell fired by a PT-76; however, the damage was slight. One PT-76 struck a mine and exploded, while two others were destroyed by 90mm (3.5in) fire from the M48s. The North Vietnamese had been surprised by the presence of heavier US armour and retreated. During the Vietnam War, the US lost approximately 150 M48 and 200 M551 Sheridan tanks, while North Vietnamese armoured losses were known to be considerably higher.

▲ M551 Sheridan Light Tank

4th Armored Cavalry Regiment / 3rd Squadron / Troop A

Designed as a light, airmobile infantry support tank, the M551 Sheridan equipped many armoured cavalry units in Vietnam. The vehicle was susceptible to mines. Although its Shillelagh missile system was disappointing, the 152mm (6in) gun offered welcome firepower.

Specifications

Crew: 4

Weight: 15,830kg (34,826lb)

Length: 6.299m (20ft 8in)

Width: 2.819m (9ft 3in)

Height: 2.946m (9ft 8in)

Engine: 224kW (300hp) 6-cylinder Detroit 6V-53T diesel

Speed: 70km/h (43mph)

Range: 600km (310 miles)

Armament: 1 x 152mm (6in) gun/missile launcher, plus 1 x 12.7mm (0.5in) anti-aircraft HMG and 1 x coaxial 7.62mm (0.3in) MG

Radio: n/k

▲ M113A1 Armoured Personnel Carrier

11th Armored Cavalry Regiment

The M113A1 armoured personnel carrier was introduced in 1964 and had the original petrol engine replaced with a reliable 158kW (212hp) diesel. Gun shields and additional machine guns were added, and the M113A1 was later designated ACAV (Armored Cavalry Assault Vehicle).

Specifications

Crew: 2 + 11

Weight: 11,343kg (25,007lb)

Length: 2.52m (8ft 3in)

Width: 2.69m (8ft 10in)

Height (to top of hull): 1.85m (6ft 1in)

Engine: 158kW (212hp) General Motors 6V53 6-cylinder diesel

Speed: 61km/h (38mph)

Range: 480km (298 miles)

Armament: 1 x 12.7mm (0.5in) HMG

Radio: n/k

Chapter 4

Cold War
in Asia

The Cold War and its influence were pervasive
around the globe, and geopolitical wrangling, territorial
disputes and religious fervour fuelled conflict throughout the
twentieth century. With the end of World War II, the newly
independent or reconstituted nations of the Far East and
Central Asia grappled with national identity. Borders were
drawn, and governments raised armies, alternately for
defence and for conquest, often eagerly supplied by the
superpowers. Spheres of influence emerged. Like no other
symbol of military might, tanks and armoured fighting
vehicles became the core elements of these armies
and engaged in some of the largest clashes of
armour since World War II.

◀ **Captured M47**
Indian civilians examine a knocked-out US-built M47 tank during the Indo-Pakistan War of 1965. Although
the M47 was outdated by the early 1960s, it was still capable of taking on lighter opposition armour, such
as the M4A3 Shermans employed by the Indian Army, as well as playing an infantry support role.

Introduction

The armoured formations of numerous Asian countries constituted the backbone of large armies and provided a proving ground for advancing technology, both in the modern design of the tank and in defence against it.

THE VAST CONTINENT OF ASIA, its oil-rich central region, the natural resources and raw materials in the southeast, its immense population and the preeminent colossi of its two communist powers – the Soviet Union and the People's Republic of China – often took centre stage in military conflict during the Cold War.

Exerting their influence throughout the region, the Soviet Union, China and the United States vied for preeminence in Asia, intent on protecting their supplies of oil, maintaining the security of national borders and blunting the perceived aggression of adversarial states. Simultaneously, there were scores to settle. Religious, ethnic, economic and political animosity simmered just below the surface and, on occasion, erupted in open war.

In December 1980, a report by the US Central Intelligence Agency (CIA) claimed that the Soviet Union had delivered nearly $7 billion in arms and military assistance to Third World countries during the previous year and that more than 50,000 Soviet military advisors were scattered across the globe. While the report may indeed have been accurate, the United States was also fully engaged in the worldwide arms trade. Other nations had joined in as well, including Great Britain, France and the nations of both the Warsaw Pact and NATO. The sale of weaponry provided hard currency to benefit teetering economies, extended spheres of influence and could potentially curb the territorial ambitions of aggressors. A by-product of the burgeoning arms sales bonanza was an illegal weapons trade, particularly in small arms, which resulted in billions of dollars in profits for black marketeers.

Since the 1950s, the United States had believed Pakistan to be a valuable buffer against potential

▲ **Soviet invasion**
Soviet BTR-60 APCs stop by the roadside during operations in Afghanistan, 1980. The BTR-60 proved vulnerable to shoulder-fired rocket-propelled grenades.

expansion into Central Asia. On the other hand, India and the Soviet Union maintained cordial relations. One of the world's poorest and most populous nations, India needed Soviet technology for its economic infrastructure and Soviet tanks to protect against its neighbouring enemy. Thus the inevitable clashes of arms that ensued pitted US tanks of the Patton series, particularly the M47 and M48, and the light M24 Chaffee against the Soviet-built T-54/55, T-62 and light amphibious PT-76.

Far East tensions

During the uneasy peace that followed the Korean War, the communist regime of North Korea continued a costly military build-up to the detriment of its overall economy, while the armed forces of South Korea were supported by US troops stationed in the country. North Korea modernized its armoured forces with tanks of both Soviet and Chinese manufacture and later embarked on its own programme of main battle tank development.

In Vietnam, tanks were employed on a somewhat

limited basis, and the tactical deployment of armoured vehicles, their role in combat and their armour protection against a new generation of anti-tank weapons were tested in battle.

The People's Republic of China had long depended on the Soviet Union to equip its armoured units and produced its own version of the venerable T-34 medium tank, the Type 59. Subsequently, China began the development of its own armoured vehicles, including a modern main battle tank.

▶ **War trophy**
Indian troops sit atop a captured Pakistani T-55 after the cessation of hostilities during the Indo-Pakistan War of 1971.

India and Pakistan
1965–80

Heavy casualties and the largest tank battle since World War II failed to resolve a territorial conflict that has persisted into the twenty-first century.

SINCE THE PARTITION OF INDIA in August 1947, the primarily Hindu Republic of India and an Islamic Pakistan have clashed over the disputed border region of Kashmir and the emergence of the independent nation of Bangladesh (formerly East Pakistan). Each nation developed its own substantial armoured force with the assistance of the superpowers, India primarily through the acquisition of arms from the United States, Great Britain, France and later the Soviet Union, and Pakistan, as a counterweight to Soviet influence on the subcontinent, from the United States and the People's Republic of China.

In the mid-1950s, Pakistan and the United States had agreed that the armed forces of Pakistan would include capabilities substantial enough to maintain an uneasy balance with those of India. This included an armoured division and an independent armoured brigade, which would be equipped primarily with American arms. However, when war erupted in 1965, the Pakistani Army had already expanded beyond the limits of its agreement with the United States. This was reportedly in response to a major increase in Indian military strength during the early part of the decade.

The Pakistani 6th Armoured Division was formed less than a year prior to the opening of hostilities with

India in 1965 and included the 100th Independent Armoured Brigade. Subsequently, the United States declined to arm the new division, and existing assets were deployed. At the height of its strength, the 6th Armoured Division consisted of several armoured battalions, including the 10th Guides Cavalry, the 11th PAVO Cavalry, the 13th Lancers and the 22nd Cavalry which had been temporarily attached. The division's armour consisted of more than 160 M48 Patton tanks armed with 90mm (3.5in) main guns and a contingent of M36B tank destroyers, also with 90mm (3.5in) main weapons.

The Pakistani 1st Armoured Division included three armoured brigades, the 3rd, 4th and 5th, which were heavily engaged in the upcoming battle of Assal Uttar and included Patton tanks and motorized infantry. The M24 Chaffee light tank, with a 75mm (2.9in) main weapon, and the battle-tested M4 Sherman, some of which had been modernized, were also part of the Pakistani arsenal.

The Indian Army had at its disposal an array of ageing Sherman tanks, including several that had been upgunned with the high-velocity 75mm (2.9in) French CN 75 50 cannon; the British Centurion Mk 7 mounting the powerful 105mm (4.1in) Royal Ordnance L7 weapon; the French light AMX-13 tank with 75mm (2.9in) or 90mm (3.5in) cannon; and the World War II-vintage US-made M3 Stuart light tank.

When war broke out in 1965, the two Pakistani Army divisions fielded an estimated 15 armoured cavalry regiments, although some of these did operate independently. Each of the cavalry regiments included nearly 50 tanks divided into three squadrons. Along with their large number of M47 and M48 tanks, the Pakistanis were equipped with about 150 M24 Chaffees and 200 M4 Shermans.

By August 1965, Indian relations with the Soviet Union had warmed substantially, and the Indian 7th Light Cavalry received the first shipment to the Indian Army of the Soviet amphibious PT-76 tank, equipped with a 75mm (2.9in) cannon. Three Indian officers had travelled to the Soviet Union to train with Red Army tank crews.

The 1st Armoured Division was the pride of the Indian Army and its only organic armoured division. Some of its components traced their lineage to the early 1800s and the days of British colonial rule. These included the 18th Cavalry, 62nd Cavalry, 2nd Royal Lancers, 7th Light Cavalry, 16th Cavalry, 4th Hodson's Horse, 17th Cavalry and the Poona Horse. Both the 17th Cavalry and the Poona Horse were equipped with the upgunned M4 Shermans and heavy British Centurion tanks. In 1965, the Indian Army consisted of 17 cavalry regiments which included more than 160 AMX-13s, 188 Centurions and a large number of Shermans and Stuarts. The PT-76s were reported to have arrived only hours

Specifications

Crew: 5

Weight: 18.28 tonnes (18 tons)

Length: 5.49m (18ft)

Width: 2.95m (9ft 8in)

Height: 2.46m (8ft 1in)

Engine: 2 x 82kW (110hp) Cadillac 44T24
V8 8-cylinder petrol

Speed: 55km/h (34mph)

Range: 282km (175 miles)

Armament: 1 x 75mm (2.9in) M6 gun, plus
1 x 12.7mm (0.5in) HMG on AA mount and
2 x 7.62mm (0.3in) MGs (1 coaxial,
1 ball-mounted in hull front)

Radio: SCR 508

▲ **Light Tank M24**

Pakistani Army / 1st Armoured Division / 12th Cavalry

Deployed in the reconnaissance regiments of the Pakistani 1st Armoured Division, the M24 Chaffee light tank was of US World War II-era manufacture. Its 75mm (2.9in) weapon remained potent, and its firepower was equal to that of Indian light armour.

11th Prince Albert Victor's Own (PAVO) Cavalry (Pakistan)

A component of the Pakistani 6th Armoured Division, which was constituted early in 1965, the 11th PAVO Cavalry included two squadrons of modern US-manufactured M48A3 Patton tanks with 90mm (3.5in) cannon along with a squadron of M36B2 Jackson tank destroyers, also armed with 90mm (3.5in) weapons. The 6th Armoured Division was heavily engaged in the defeat of the Indian 1st Armoured Division at Chawinda.

HQ plus 2 x Squadrons (30 x M48A3 MBT)

1 x Tank Destroyer Squadron (13 x M36B2)

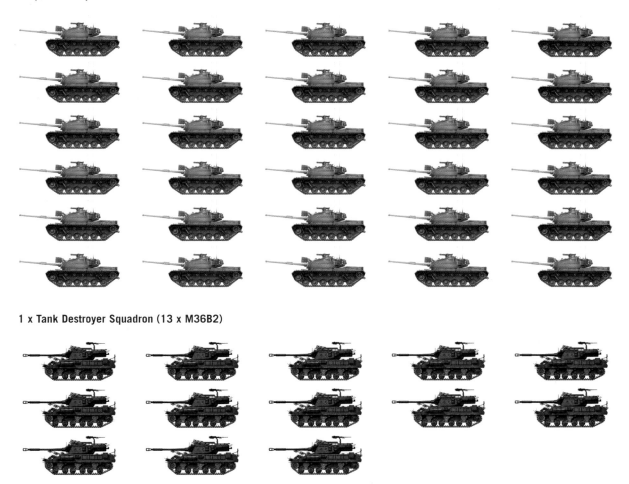

before the opening of hostilities with Pakistan and were committed to battle without even having their guns properly bore-sighted.

Assal Uttar

During three days of intense combat, 8–10 September 1965, the largest tank battle since World War II occurred at Assal Uttar in the Indian state of Punjab. Estimates of the armoured strength involved vary widely; however, it is known that at least several hundred armoured vehicles took part.

Elements of the Pakistani 1st Armoured Division, including the 19th Lancers, 12th Cavalry, 24th Cavalry, 4th Cavalry, 5th Horse and 6th Lancers, blundered into a trap on 10 September, as three Indian armoured regiments, the 3rd Cavalry, Deccan Horse and 8th Cavalry, lay waiting in concealed positions that formed a defensive 'U' shape. The Indian force consisted of Shermans, AMX-13s and Centurions, a total of about 140 tanks, while approximately 300 Pakistani M47s and M24s advanced. Although the Pakistani tanks were more recent designs and possessed heavier armament than most of their Indian opponents, the ensuing action revealed glaring deficiencies in Pakistani tactics.

The Pakistanis advanced into an Indian artillery barrage, while the Indian tanks, concealed in a thick growth of tall sugar cane stalks, held their fire until the enemy was at near point-blank range. Failure to properly reconnoitre the prepared Indian defences was compounded by the inferior training of many of the Pakistani tank crews. Although the Pakistanis' weaponry may well have been superior to that of the Indians, it was rendered ineffective due to the operators' lack of proficiency.

The concentrated 75mm (2.9in) and 90mm (3.5in) fire from the Indian tanks destroyed nearly 100 Pakistani tanks, while dozens were abandoned. The Indians lost 32 tanks and blunted a Pakistani offensive in the process. Rows of destroyed and captured Pakistani tanks were displayed for months afterwards in Indian-held territory.

Chawinda

While the premier armoured force of the Pakistani Army was bloodied at Assal Uttar, the 1st Indian Armoured Division was also pounded during two weeks of fighting, 6–22 September, collectively known as the Battle of Chawinda. During the extended fighting, the 1st Division was severely

mauled, and the Indian Army lost more than 120 tanks, three times the losses of the Pakistanis. The Pakistani Air Force also accounted for some of the Indian tank losses. The fighting at Assal Uttar and Chawinda proved that the tank would be the primary future weapon of war on land, and the inconclusive strategic outcomes led to stalemate and negotiation between the warring nations.

Bangladesh at war

During only 13 days of war in December 1971, the Indian Army forced the surrender of Pakistani forces in East Pakistan. While a concentration of Indian armoured strength remained in the light AMX-13 or PT-76 tanks, which were relatively ineffective in tank-versus-tank fighting against Pakistani M47s and M48s, the tendency of the Pakistanis to deploy their tanks in troops of only two or three negated their superior firepower to an extent when confronted by an entire squadron of Indian light tanks that advanced to within 1000m (1094 yards) before opening fire. On those few occasions when Indian light tanks were caught in the open, the results were predictable, with even the heavily worn 75mm (2.9in) cannon of some Chaffee and obsolete Sherman tanks taking a toll on thinly armoured PT-76s.

The Indian-manufactured Vijayanta main battle tank, introduced in 1965 with a 105mm (4.1in)

Specifications

Crew: 5	1790-5B V12 petrol
Weight: 46 tonnes (45.3 tons)	Speed: 48km/h (30mph)
Length: 8.56m (28ft 1in)	Range: 129km (80 miles)
Width: 3.2m (10ft 6in)	Armament: 1 x M36 90mm (3.5in) gun; 2 x
Height: 3.35m (11ft)	12.7mm (0.5in) MGs; 1 x 7.62mm (0.3in) MG
Engine: 604.5kW (810hp) Continental AVDS-	Radio: n/k

▲ M47 Patton Medium Tank

Pakistani Army / 1st Armoured Division, 1965

Developed in the early 1950s, the M47 Patton was the US Army and Marine Corps primary tank, replacing the M46 and M4 Sherman tanks. After the tank was declared obsolete in 1957 by the US Army, hundreds of M47s were sold to Pakistan. Dozens were destroyed at the battle of Assal Uttar in September 1965.

L7A2 cannon, was based on the design of the Vickers Mk 1 and saw action in the 1971 war, while the number of Soviet- and Warsaw Pact-built T-54/55 tanks supplied to India grew steadily during the latter part of the decade. The Pakistanis were building their own version of the Chinese Type 59MII tank by 1979, while a limited number of T-54/55 tanks, along with upgraded M47 and M48 Pattons, remain in service. The Pakistani Army also fields a large number of BMP and M113 armoured personnel carriers.

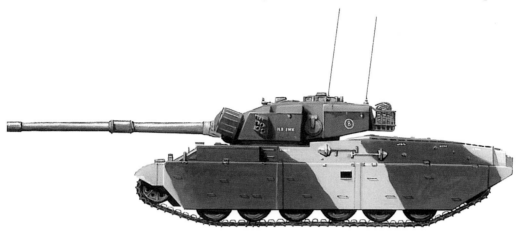

▲ Vijayanta Main Battle Tank

Indian Army / 66th Armoured Regiment, 1971

A licence-built version of the British Vickers Mk 1 main battle tank, the Vijayanta (Victorious) was developed in the early 1960s and participated in the 1971 war with Pakistan. It mounted a 105mm (4.1in) L7A2 gun. The last Vijayanta was withdrawn from active service in 2008.

Specifications

Crew: 4
Weight: 39 tonnes (38.4 tons)
Length: 7.92m (26ft)
Width: 3.168m (10ft 6in)
Height: 2.44m (8ft)
Engine: 484.7kW (650bhp) Leyland L60 6-

cylinder multi-fuel
Speed: 48km/h (30mph)
Range: 480km (300 miles)
Armament: 1 x 105mm (4.1in) gun; 1 x 12.7mm
(0.5in) MG; 2 x 7.62mm (0.3in) MGs
Radio: Twin Clansman VRC 353 VHF

▲ T-55 Main Battle Tank

Indian Army / 72nd Armoured Regiment, 1971

During the 1971 Indo-Pakistani War, India operated T-55s around Chaamb, in the Western Theatre, against Pakistan's US-built M48 Patton and Chinese-built Type 59 tanks. The upgraded T-55 proved qualitatively superior to the T-54-based Type 59 when they met in battle.

Specifications

Crew: 4
Weight: 39.7 tonnes (39 tons)
Length (hull): 6.45m (21ft 2in)
Width: 3.27m (10ft 9in)
Height: 2.4m (7ft 10in)
Engine: 433kW (581bhp) V-55 12-cylinder

Speed: 48km/h (30mph)
Range: 400km (250 miles)
Armament: 1 x 100mm (3.9in) D-10T gun;
1 x 12.7mm (0.5in) DShK AA MG mounted on
turret; 2 x 7.62mm (0.3in) DT MGs
Radio: R-113

Soviet invasion of Afghanistan
1979

Committed to battle in order to support a pro-Soviet regime, the Red Army found that conventional tactics and heavy equipment were often ineffective against guerrilla fighters.

IN DECEMBER 1979, Soviet infantry and mechanized units crossed the border with Afghanistan in force. The nine-year military intervention that followed proved costly as the lives of more than 15,000 Red Army soldiers were taken and large quantities of materiel were destroyed, including nearly 150 tanks and more than 1300 armoured fighting vehicles and personnel carriers. The Soviet military commitment in Afghanistan increased rapidly, and by 1981 numbered more than 100,000 troops from an airborne division, four motorized rifle divisions and other units. More than 1800 tanks and 2000 armoured fighting vehicles had arrived.

Opposing the might of the Red Army were thousands of Islamic guerrillas, known as the Mujahideen. Ill-equipped and poorly trained, the guerrillas nevertheless waged an effective low-intensity war against the Soviets and their Afghan Army proxies. During the course of the conflict, the Mujahideen received substantial aid from the United States and other nations, as the Central Intelligence Agency viewed the conflict as the front line of the Cold War. Anti-tank weapons were supplied, and the arrival of the US-made shoulder-fired FIM-92 Stinger surface-to-air missile was instrumental in making the air a dangerous place for Soviet aircraft.

Soviet commitment

The mountainous terrain of Afghanistan proved challenging for Soviet armoured operations. Hit-and-run tactics employed by the guerrillas and frequent attacks on population, communications and government centres, such as the Afghan capital city of Kabul, obliged the Soviets to commit armoured personnel carriers and tanks to urban environments. Furthermore, control of roads, power facilities and supply depots and the protection of convoys required the deployment of armoured assets most of the time.

By 1984, the United States was spending $200 million per year to supply the Mujahideen. Aside from financial assistance, the guerrillas received Type 69 RPGs (rocket-propelled grenades) and other small arms from the People's Republic of China, along with a limited number of the Chinese-made Type 59 tank.

▲ **BMD-1 Airborne Amphibious Tracked Infantry Fighting Vehicle**

Soviet Fortieth Army / 103rd Guards Airborne Division

Smaller and lighter than other infantry fighting vehicles, the BMD-1 was designed for deployment by air and entered service with Red Army airborne units in 1969. Armed with a 73mm (2.8in) semi-automatic main weapon, it also mounted machine guns and an anti-tank guided-missile launcher.

Specifications

Crew: 3 + 4	Range: 320km (200 miles)
Weight: 6.7 tonnes (14,740lb)	Armament: 1 x 73mm (2.8in) 2A28 'Grom' low-
Length: 5.4m (17ft 9in)	pressure smoothbore short-recoil gun, plus
Width: 2.63m (9ft 8in)	1 x coaxial 7.62mm (0.3in) MG, 2 x front-
Height: 1.97m (6ft 6in)	mounted 7.62mm (0.3in) MGs and 1 x AT-3
Engine: 179kW (240hp) 5D-20 V6 liquid-cooled	'Sagger' ATGW
Speed: 70km/h (43mph)	Radio: R-123

Landmines, concealed explosives and even captured Soviet equipment were used against Red Army troops in Afghanistan.

Although the Soviets did have state-of-the-art technology at their disposal, it has been asserted that the Red Army did not deploy its T-72 and T-80 main battle tanks in large numbers. The majority of Soviet tanks deployed in Afghanistan were modified older T-54/55s and T-62s, which first rolled off assembly lines in 1959. In the spring of 1979, the Soviets had also delivered nearly 250 of these tanks to the Afghan Army. However, it must be understood that heavy armour is less effective than mobile, light armour in combat against guerrillas. Therefore, it is not surprising that an entire tank regiment was eventually

considered of no use in Afghanistan and returned to the Soviet Union by mid-1980. When the Soviets withdrew from Afghanistan, scores of armoured vehicles were abandoned. The rusting hulks of T-55 and T-62 tanks litter the landscape today.

The Soviets employed the ageing BTR-60, BMP-1 and BMD-1 armoured personnel carriers in Afghanistan, and the thin armour protection of these proved vulnerable to shoulder-fired projectiles, mines and shells of any calibre larger than small arms. Petrol engines were also a continual hazard, and a number of these vehicles were destroyed by igniting fuel tanks. Later, the diesel-powered BTR-70 and BTR-80 constituted a significant improvement in survivability.

▲ BTR-60PB Amphibious Armoured Personnel Carrier
Soviet Fortieth Army / 108th Guards Motorized Rifle Division

Two decades old at the time of the Afghan invasion, the BTR-60 armoured personnel carrier was the first of several Soviet eight-wheeled fighting vehicles. Armed with a 14.5mm (0.6in) KPVT heavy machine gun, it entered service in 1959 and could carry up to 14 soldiers.

Specifications

Crew: 2 + 14	petrol
Weight: 10.3 tonnes (22,660lb)	Speed: 80km/h (50mph)
Length: 7.56m (24ft 9.6in)	Range: 500km (311 miles)
Width: 2.825m (9ft 3.2in)	Armament: 1 x 14.5mm (0.6in) KPVT HMG, plus
Height: 2.31m (7ft 6.9in)	2 x 7.62mm (0.3in) MGs
Engine: 2 x 67kW (90hp) GAZ-49B 6-cylinder	Radio: R-113

▲ BTR-70 Armoured Personnel Carrier
Soviet Fortieth Army / 5th Guards Motorized Rifle Division

With heavier armour plating and stronger tyres, the BTR-70 was originally intended as a replacement for the BTR-60 and entered service with the Red Army in 1972. Its troop capacity was scaled down to seven soldiers, and it was armed with 14.5mm (0.6in) and 7.62mm (0.3in) machine guns.

Specifications

Crew: 2 + 7	8-cylinder petrol
Weight: 11.5 tonnes (25,400lb)	Speed: 80km/h (50mph)
Length: 7.53m (24ft 8in)	Range: 600km (370 miles)
Width: 2.8m (9.ft 2in)	Armament: 1 x 14.5mm (0.6in) KPVT MG, plus
Height: 2.23m (7ft 4in)	1 x coaxial PKT 7.62mm (0.3in) MG
Engine: 179kW (240hp) ZMZ-4905	Radio: R-123

Soviet Tank Battalion, 1979

The standard Red Army tank battalion of the 1970s included three companies of three platoons each, a headquarters formation of a single tank and light transport, and a section of supply trucks. Its full complement of armour numbered at least 36 T-72 main battle tanks. Those Soviet heavy tanks which saw service in Afghanistan were often limited to main roads or the protection of facilities.

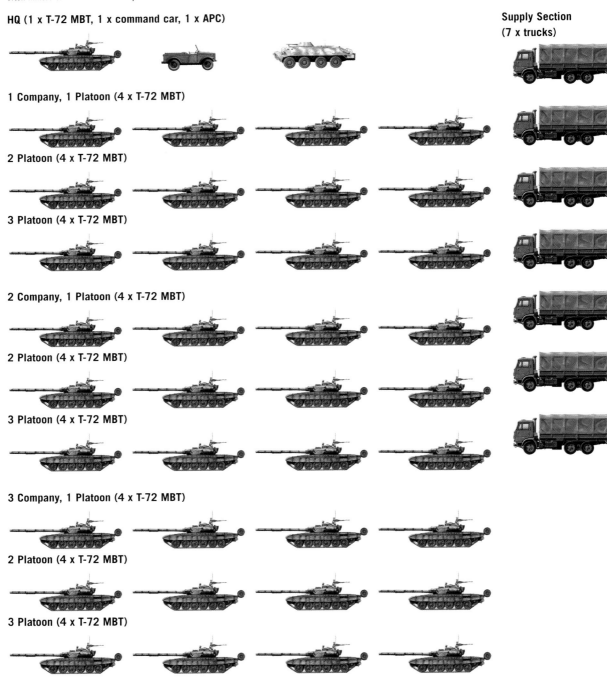

HQ (1 x T-72 MBT, 1 x command car, 1 x APC)

**Supply Section
(7 x trucks)**

1 Company, 1 Platoon (4 x T-72 MBT)

2 Platoon (4 x T-72 MBT)

3 Platoon (4 x T-72 MBT)

2 Company, 1 Platoon (4 x T-72 MBT)

2 Platoon (4 x T-72 MBT)

3 Platoon (4 x T-72 MBT)

3 Company, 1 Platoon (4 x T-72 MBT)

2 Platoon (4 x T-72 MBT)

3 Platoon (4 x T-72 MBT)

Disparate doctrine

Perhaps as challenging as the mountainous terrain and the determined enemy was Soviet armoured doctrine, which had been conceived to battle NATO forces in Europe. Further complicating the military situation was the simple fact that Soviet forces might take and hold territory, but destroying the Mujahideen in the field would require a vast military and financial commitment whose end was indefinite

and could not be sustained. In the end, Soviet firepower was ineffective against a shadowy enemy.

Lieutenant-General Boris Gromov, 45, was the last high-ranking Soviet officer to leave Afghanistan. When he reached a bridge across from the Soviet frontier post at Termez, he climbed down from an armoured personnel carrier and walked the last few steps with his son. He was heard to say, 'I did not look back.'

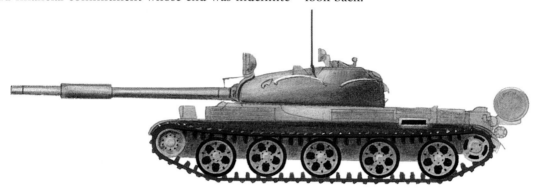

Specifications

Crew: 4	Speed: 60km/h (37.5mph)
Weight: 39.9 tonnes (87,808lb)	Range: 650km (404 miles)
Length: 9.34m (28ft 6in)	Armament: 1 x 115mm (4.5in) U-5TS gun, plus
Width: 3.3m (10ft 1in)	1 x coaxial 7.62mm (0.3in) MG
Height: 2.4m (7ft 5in)	Radio: R-130
Engine: 432kW (580hp) V-55-5 V12 liquid-cooled	
diesel	

▲ **T-62 Main Battle Tank**

Soviet Fortieth Army / 201st Motorized Rifle Division

Produced from 1961 to 1975, the T-62 main battle tank was originally intended to replace the older T-55; however, that tank also remained in production. The T-62 mounted a 115mm (4.5in) U-5TS smoothbore gun, and a number of them were reinforced with additional armour while in Afghanistan.

▲ **T-72A Main Battle Tank**

Soviet Fortieth Army / 5th Guards Motor Rifle Division

The T-72 main battle tank entered production in the Soviet Union in 1971 and has been in service since 1973. Although variants have been exported in large numbers, those deployed to Afghanistan were primarily of the original version, the Ural, with a 125mm (4.9in) 2A46M smoothbore gun.

Specifications

Crew: 3	Speed: 80km/h (50mph)
Weight: 41.5 tonnes (40.8 tons)	Range: 550km (434 miles)
Length: 9.53m (31 ft 3in)	Armament: 1 x 125mm (4.9in) 2A46M gun, plus
Width: 3.59m (11 ft 9in)	1 x 12.7mm (0.5in) NSVT anti-aircraft HMG and
Height: 2.37m (7ft 9in)	1 x coaxial 7.62mm (0.3in) PKT MG
Engine: 626kW (840hp) V-46 V12 diesel	Radio: R-123M

Far East

As the two Koreas faced one another on their troubled peninsula, the People's Republic of China maintained one of the largest land armies in the world.

ALTHOUGH THE CRADLE of the Cold War may indeed have been in Europe, the Korean peninsula was the scene of its first major armed conflict. Since the uneasy armistice that ended the shooting in 1953, the two sides have officially remained at war, staring warily at one another across the 38th Parallel. During the decades that followed, both Koreas increased their military preparedness – the communist North with paranoid intensity and the democratic South with stoic resolve to fend off aggression.

Meanwhile, the People's Republic of China embarked on its own programme of modernization and began transforming itself from being primarily a producer of clones of armoured vehicles designed in the Soviet Union to a sophisticated producer able to manufacture, deploy and export its own modern armoured vehicles.

North and South

The North Korean Army, known officially as the Korean People's Army, totalled approximately 400,000 troops in 1960. By 1990, its number was estimated at close to one million. Capable of both offensive and defensive operations on a large scale, the North Korean Army was originally organized in similar fashion to its early benefactors, the Soviet Union and the People's Republic of China.

During the 1960s, the army contained a single tank division of five armoured regiments, four with the Soviet T-54 and one with the older heavy IS-3. Self-propelled guns, primarily the Soviet SU-76, complemented the firepower of the armoured force. This was followed by the indigenous manufacture of a modified Soviet T-62 beginning in the 1970s.

Although the North Korean armed forces are shrouded in secrecy and much of the Western estimates of strength and equipment are based on sketchy intelligence, glimpses of military machinery are sometimes available during parades or special observances. Therefore it is known that the North Koreans added considerable modifications to the Soviet and Chinese tanks they had acquired during the 1950s and 1960s.

The 820th Armoured Corps and its 105th Armoured Division have long formed the backbone of the North Korean armoured forces. The officers of the 105th Division apparently formed the nuclei of several smaller armoured formations within the 820th Armoured Corps. By 1990, the North Korean armoured arsenal included more than 3000 tanks. The bulk of these were early Soviet T-54/55s, Chinese Type 59s and approximately 800 examples of the T-62, the primary Soviet tank of the 1960s. A number of mechanized units existed within the North Korean Army and operated about 2500 armoured personnel carriers and fighting vehicles.

During the early 1980s, the North Koreans embarked on a programme to improve their Soviet T62A main battle tanks. The result was the Chonma-ho, or Pegasus, which mounts either the 115mm (4.5in) 2A20 or 125mm (4.9in) 2A46 smoothbore gun. Since 1980, it is estimated that more than 1200 Chonma-ho tanks have been built, complementing a force that includes a diverse array of tanks such as the T-72, T-62, T-54/55 and the amphibious light PT-76.

◄ **Tanks on parade**
Chinese Type 59 tanks line up during a parade beneath portraits of Soviet communist leaders Lenin (left) and Stalin (right). China's first home-built main battle tank, the Type 59 was a simple copy of the Soviet T-54.

The army of the Republic of Korea (that is, the South Korean Army) had virtually no armour when the communists attacked in 1950. With the cessation of hostilities, the South Koreans began to organize a defensive armoured force with a core of US-built tanks of the Patton series, and for more than 20 years the M47 and M48 served as the frontline tanks. During the late 1980s, the core of Western tanks, including the improved M48A3K and M48A5K, was augmented with the purchase of a few T-80U main battle tanks from Ukraine. By 1987, each South Korean infantry division was supported by an attached armoured battalion or company. Mechanized infantry divisions included a cavalry battalion or one of nine armoured infantry battalions. In that year, the South Korean Army also began to deploy the K1 main battle tank. Designed by General Dynamics and produced in South Korea by Hyundai Rotem, the K1 mounts a 105mm (4.1in) KM68A1 cannon.

Myanmar militarism

In 1988, the government of Myanmar was overthrown in a coup d'etat carried out by the country's military. Since the 1960s, a total of 337 infantry and light infantry battalions had been supported by armoured reconnaissance and tank battalions which included the Chinese Type 63 light tank, the British Comet of World War II vintage and the Chinese Type 59. Later, Myanmar purchased T-72s from Ukraine and T-55s from India, which were being phased out of service, and began the licensed manufacture of Soviet-designed armoured personnel carriers. The army of Myanmar includes 10 armoured battalions in two divisions. Five of these are equipped with tanks, and five serve with armoured personnel carriers and infantry fighting vehicles, including the Soviet-designed BMP-1, the British Dingo, the Chinese Type 85 and the Brazilian EE-9.

Royal Thai Army

The Royal Thai Army has battled an insurgency for years while also remaining prepared to defend itself from attack by its neighbours. Its seven infantry divisions were initially supported by five organic armoured battalions, while an independent armoured division and an armour-equipped cavalry division completed its armoured forces. More than 300 M48A3 and M48A5 Patton tanks are included in its formations, along with about 100 of the Chinese Type 69II, an upgraded version of the older Type 59. Light tanks include the venerable M41 Walker Bulldog, the British Scorpion and the Stingray, an American design that mounts the 105mm (4.1in) L7A3 rifled gun and is only in use with the Royal Thai Army.

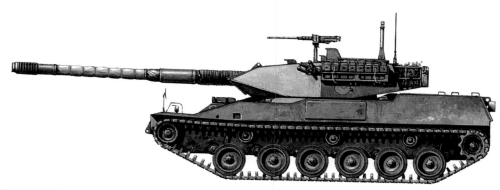

Specifications

Crew: 4
Weight: 19.05 tonnes (41,912lb)
Length: 9.35m (30ft 8in)
Width: 2.71m (8ft 11in)
Height: 2.54m (8ft 4in)
Engine: 399kW (535hp) Detroit Diesel Model 8V-92 TA diesel
Speed: 69km/h (43mph)
Range: 483km (300 miles)
Armament: 1 x 105mm (4.1in) gun, plus 1 x coaxial 7.62mm (0.3in) MG and 1 x 7.62mm (0.3in) anti-aircraft MG
Radio: Long-range, directional

▲ **Stingray Light Tank**
Royal Thai Army / 1st Armoured Division, Thailand, 1990
Developed by Textron Marine and Land Systems during the mid-1980s, the Stingray light tank was originally intended for the US Army. However, it is currently deployed only by the Royal Thai Army. The Stingray mounts a 105mm (4.1in) L7A3 rifled gun.

China
1960–91

The modern People's Liberation Army of China, the largest land fighting force in the world, boasts mechanization of 40 per cent of its combat troops.

DURING ITS INFANCY, the People's Liberation Army fought a guerrilla war for control of the vast Chinese interior. Out of necessity, the communist military fought with small arms and propaganda, and later with tanks, armoured vehicles and artillery supplied by the Soviet Union. For years, the T-34 medium tank of World War II fame served as the backbone of a relatively small armoured corps. However, during the late 1950s, the Chinese military establishment came to the realization that armoured capability must be a component of its future armed forces.

China intervened in the Korean War, supplied weapons to North Vietnam during the 1960s, and during that time began to produce some of its own armoured vehicles, although the preponderance of these were clones or modifications of existing Soviet designs. For example, the Type 59 tank, armed with a 100mm (3.9in) main cannon, was a direct copy of the Soviet T-54A. The Type 62 light tank was another adaptation of the T-54A, which was then based on the Type 59. The Type 63 amphibious tank, which entered service in 1963, bore a striking similarity to the Soviet PT-76.

During the three decades from 1960 to 1990, the People's Liberation Army armoured force grew to roughly 10,000 tanks in 11 armoured brigades. Although efforts had been under way to develop indigenous Chinese tank designs, the bulk of Chinese armour, at least two-thirds, consisted of the clone Type 59 and Type 62 tanks. As these vehicles began to age, many were retired. Others, however, were continually upgraded as new technology became available. Likewise, approximately 2000 Type 63s remain in service, the recipients of numerous modernization packages.

Strained relations with both the Soviet Union and North Vietnam resulted in brief but sharp armed clashes in 1969 and 1979 respectively. Although the Chinese used tanks as mobile artillery support during these border clashes, the value of the armoured fighting vehicle on the battlefield was clarified. In

▲ **Show of strength**
Chinese Type 69 tanks parade at a military review outside of Beijing. The Type 69 was essentially an improved Type 59 with upgraded fire control systems and a more powerful gun.

addition, the Chinese military establishment became concerned that the survivability of its frontline tanks was substantially inferior to newer Soviet designs. The Tank Research Institute was created to begin work on new Chinese armoured vehicles. In 1977, the Communist Party Central Committee adopted a statement asserting that self-reliance in weapons design and production was a goal to be achieved during the sixth five-year plan for national defence.

Mechanized and modern

The People's Liberation Army of the 1980s received the Type 69 and Type 79 tanks, both of which were still based on the Soviet T-54A. Each did include some imported Western technology and an improved 100mm (3.9in) or 105mm (4.1in) rifled gun. They were, however, the first independently developed tanks in China's arsenal. Second generation tanks included the Type 80, which was revealed to Western journalists in 1987; the export Type 85, which was sold to Pakistan; and the Type 88. The experimental Type 90 was not adopted by the People's Liberation

Army; however, it was also sold to Pakistan and served as the basis for the MBT 2000 Al-Khalid, a joint venture between China and Pakistan.

In the 1980s, the People's Liberation Army also grew to 118 infantry divisions and 13 armoured divisions. Each armoured division included three regiments and fielded about 240 main battle tanks. However, mechanized transport and reconnaissance capabilities for accompanying infantry formations were still woefully lacking.

Modern Chinese armoured development since 1980 has been largely funded by China North Industries Corporation, NORINCO, a major defence contractor, heavy equipment manufacturer and producer of chemicals and other commodities. NORINCO has continued to produce copies of

Specifications

Crew: 7

Weight: 15.4 tonnes (34,000lb)

Length: 5.65m (18ft 6in)

Width: 3.06m (10ft)

Height: 2.68m (8ft 9in)

Engine: 192kW (257hp) Deutz 6150L 6-cylinder diesel

Speed: 56km/h (35mph)

Range: 500km (310 miles)

Armament: 1 x 122mm (4.8in) howitzer

▲ **Type 54-1 SP 122mm gun**

People's Liberation Army / 6th Armoured Division, 1965

One of China's first internally designed self-propelled artillery pieces, the Type 54-1 mounts a 122mm (4.8in) howitzer similar to the Soviet M1938, which sits in an open-top turret. The chassis is a variant of the NORINCO YW 531.

▲ **Type 63 (YW 531) Armoured Personnel Carrier**

People's Liberation Army / 34th Motorized Division, 1974

Introduced by NORINCO in the late 1960s, the light armoured YW 531 carries a 12.7mm (0.5in) machine gun for defence against aircraft and is capable of transporting 10 combat troops, who enter and exit through a large door on the right rear of the vehicle.

Specifications

Crew: 2 + 10

Weight: 12.5 tonnes (27,600lb)

Length: 5.74m (18ft 10in)

Width: 2.99m (9ft 9in)

Height: 2.11m (6ft 11in)

Engine: 192kW (257hp) Deutz Type 6150L 6-cylinder diesel

Speed: 50km/h (31mph)

Range: 425km (260 miles)

Armament: 1 x 12.7mm (0.5in) MG

Radio: Type 889

Soviet weaponry while developing new designs of its own, including the later Type 96 and Type 99 main battle tanks.

Armoured doctrine

Early People's Liberation Army armoured doctrine was based generally on Soviet techniques. However,

the combined arms approach, with all elements of the ground and air forces working in concert, has become preeminent. The concept of the battle group emerged in the 1960s with emphasis on the infantry company and its subordinate platoons and squads. Each platoon would have its own artillery and armoured support. By the 1990s, the Chinese had reengineered

Specifications
Crew: 4
Weight: 36 tonnes (35.4 tons)
Length: 6.04m (19ft 10in)
Width: 3.27m (10ft 9in)
Height: 2.59m (8ft 6in)
Engine: 390kW (520hp) Model 12150L V12
   liquid-cooled diesel
Speed: 50km/h (31mph)
Range: 450km (280 miles)
Armament: 1 x 100mm (3.9in) rifled Type 69-II
   gun, plus 1 x Type 54 12.7mm (0.5in) AA MG
   and 2 x Type 59T 7.62mm (0.3in) coaxial MGs
Radio: Type 889

▲ **Type 59-I Main Battle Tank**
People's Liberation Army, 1980
A Chinese copy of the Soviet-designed T-54A tank, the Type 59 entered service with the People's Liberation Army in 1959. Originally mounting a 100mm (3.9in) rifled gun and later a 105mm (4.1in) weapon, it was produced for more than two decades. By the time the production finally stopped in the late 1980s, a total of 10,000 examples had been produced in a number of variants, with 6000 delivered to the PLA, and the rest exported to developing countries in Asia, Africa and the Middle East.

Specifications
Crew: 4
Weight: 21 tonnes (20.7 tons)
Length (including gun): 7.9m (25ft 11in)
Width: 2.9m (9ft 6in)
Height: 2.3m (7ft 6in)
Engine: 321kW (430 hp) 12150L-3 V12 liquid-
   cooled diesel
Speed: 60km/h (37mph)
Range: 500km (310 miles)
Armament: 1 x 85mm (3.4in) Type 62-85TC rifled
   main gun, plus 2 x 7.62mm (0.3in) Type 59T
   MGs (1 coaxial and 1 bow-mounted)
Radio: n/k

▲ **Type 62 Light Tank**
People's Liberation Army / 10th Armoured Division, 1965
Based on the Type 59, the Type 62 light tank entered service with the People's Liberation Army in 1963. Produced until 1989, upgraded and still an integral element of Chinese armoured forces, it mounts an 85mm (3.4in) rifled gun. It first saw combat during the Vietnam War, when China supplied Type 62 tanks to the NVA before the invasion of Kampuchea.

their battle groups to an extent, with these forces constituted in the divisional structure and facilitating the introduction of heavy armoured assets if needed. Adapting swiftly to battlefield conditions is paramount, and theoretically an armoured infantry unit could swiftly call in tank formations if enemy armour were encountered.

The Chinese government has charged the People's Liberation Army with maintaining the authority of the communist party and securing national borders. Of course, these tenets are particularly relevant today following the Tiananmen Square uprising of 1989 and the perceived continuing threat from Taiwan, the Russian Federation, Vietnam and the United States.

Specifications
Crew: 6
Weight: n/k
Length: 5.9m (19ft 7in)
Width: 3m (9ft 10in)
Height: 2.6m (8ft 6in)
Engine: 372kW (493hp) V-2 V12 diesel
Speed: 50km/h (31mph)
Range: 300km (186 miles)
Armament: 2 x 37mm (1.45in) Type 63 AA guns, plus 1 x 7.62mm (0.3in) DT MG
Radio: None

▲ **Type 63 SP Anti-aircraft Gun**
People's Liberation Army / 13th Independent Armoured Brigade, 1966
The Type 63 self-propelled anti-aircraft gun included twin 37mm (1.45in) weapons mounted in an open-topped turret atop the hull of the obsolete Soviet T-34 medium tank of the World War II era. Many of these were exported to North Vietnam during the 1960s.

Specifications
Crew: 4
Weight: 36.7 tonnes (36.1 tons)
Length: 6.24m (20ft 6in)
Width: 3.3m (10ft 9in)
Height: 2.8m (9ft 2in)
Engine: 430kW (580hp) diesel
Speed: 50km/h (31mph)
Range: 440km (273 miles)
Armament: 1 x 100mm (3.9in) Type 62-85TC rifled main gun, plus 2 x 7.62mm (0.3in) Type 59T MGs (1 coaxial and 1 bow-mounted)
Radio: Type 889

▲ **Type 69 Main Battle Tank**
People's Liberation Army / 10th Armoured Division, 1980
Although it was yet another Chinese tank based on the Soviet-designed T-54A, the Type 69 was the first tank developed solely within the Chinese arms system. Mounting a 100mm (3.9in) rifled cannon, it was followed by the Type 79 with a heavier 105mm (4.1in) weapon.

Japan
1965–95

Limited by its post-World War II constitution, Japan has developed and maintained armoured fighting vehicles for defensive purposes and entered the arena of the main battle tank.

ARTICLE 9 OF THE JAPANESE CONSTITUTION, framed during the occupation of the country by US forces after World War II, stipulates that the government is forbidden from 'settling international disputes [by the] threat or use of force'. When the Japanese deployed a contingent of armoured troops to protect a medical detachment and other specialized units in occupied Iraq in 2003, it was an historic moment. Japanese combat troops had not been deployed outside the country in more than half a century.

During the Cold War, the limited function of the Japan Ground Self-Defence Force (JGSDF) was to defend the northernmost home island of Hokkaido against attack by the Soviet Union and to provide a modicum of security against any aggressive military action by North Korea. A single Japanese armoured division, the 7th, exists today.

American cast-offs

Early Japanese post-war tanks were American M4 Sherman and M24 Chaffees. However, by 1955 the

▶ **SU 60 Armoured Personnel Carrier**

Japan Ground Self-Defence Force, 1973

A joint venture of the Mitsubishi and Komatsu companies, the SU 60 armoured personnel carrier entered service with the Japan Ground Self-Defence Force in 1959 and was produced until 1972. The SU 60 carried a complement of six infantrymen and mounted 12.7mm (0.5in) and 7.62mm (0.3in) machine guns.

Specifications
Crew: 4 + 6
Weight: 10.8 tonnes (26,000lbs)
Length: 4.85m (15ft 10in)
Width: 2.4m (7ft 9in)
Height: 1.7m (5ft 6in)
Engine: 164kW (220hp) Mitsubishi 8 HA 21 WT 8-cylinder diesel
Speed: 45km/h (28mph)
Range: 300km (190 miles)
Armament: 1 x 12.7mm (0.5in) Browning M2 MG
Radio: n/k

Specifications
Crew: 3
Weight: 8 tonnes (17,600lbs)
Length: 4.3m (14ft 1in)
Width: 2.23m (7ft 4in)
Height: 1.59m (5ft 3in)
Engine: 89kW (120hp) Komatsu 6T 120-2 6-cylinder diesel
Speed: 55km/h (34mph)
Range: 130km (80 miles)
Armament: 2 x RCL 106mm (4.17in) recoilless rifles, plus 1 x 12.7mm (0.5in) MG

▲ **Type 60 SP Recoilless Gun**

Japan Ground Self-Defence Force, 1980

For nearly 30 years, the Type 60 self-propelled recoilless gun served in a tank destroyer role with the Japan Ground Self-Defence Force. Mounting a 106mm (4.17in) recoilless rifle, it was produced from 1960 to 1977 and withdrawn from service in 2008. More than 250 were built.

Mitsubishi Company had begun design work on a main battle tank. The result was the Type 61 with a 90mm (3.5in) rifled main cannon, and 560 of these were built between 1961 and 1975. It was succeeded by the Type 74, which was produced until the late 1980s and carried a 105mm (4.1in) gun. The Type 90 main battle tank debuted in 1989, following more than a decade of research and development. Mounting a 120mm (4.7in) Rheinmetall smooth-bore gun, the Type 90 is similar in profile to the German Leopard 2. During the 1990s, development

began on a new main battle tank designated the Type 10.

The first armoured personnel carrier to serve with the JGSDF was the SU 60, which was developed in the late 1950s and carried up to six infantrymen. Variants included a self-propelled artillery weapon. A modern infantry fighting vehicle, the Mitsubishi Type 89, was developed during the 1980s and entered service at the end of the decade. Its primary weapon is a 35mm (1.38in) cannon, and its troop compartment carries seven soldiers.

Specifications

Crew: 8

Weight: 13,500kg (29,800lb)

Length: 5.72m (18ft 9in)

Width: 2.48m (8ft 1.6in)

Height: 2.38m (7ft 9.7in)

Engine: 227kW (305hp) Isuzu diesel

Speed: 100km/h (62mph)

Range: 500km (310 miles)

Armament: 1 x 12.7mm (0.5in) HMG, plus
 1 x 7.62mm (0.3in) MG

Radio: n/k

▲ **Type 82 Reconnaissance Vehicle**

Japan Ground Self-Defence Force / 7th Armoured Division, 1988

The Type 82 reconnaissance vehicle was manufactured by Mitsubishi for the Japan Ground Self-Defence Force beginning in the mid-1970s. The vehicle has not been offered for export, and approximately 230 have been produced. Manned by a crew of eight, it mounts machine guns for defence.

▲ **Mitsubishi Type 89 Infantry Fighting Vehicle**

Japan Ground Self-Defence Force, 1993

Armed with a 35mm (1.38in) cannon, the Type 89 Infantry Fighting Vehicle was introduced in 1989. However, fewer than 60 had been placed in service a decade later, and only about 70 were built as of 2005. The Type 89 carries a crew of three and seven combat-ready infantrymen.

Specifications

Crew: 3 + 7	Speed: 70km/h (43mph)
Weight: 27 tonnes (26.6 tons)	Range: 400km (250 miles)
Length: 6.7m (22ft)	Armament: 1 x 35mm (1.38in) KDE cannon, plus
Width: 3.2m (10ft 6in)	2 x Type 79 Jyu-MAT missiles and 1 x 7.62mm
Height: 2.5m (8ft 2.5in)	(0.3in) coaxial MG
Engine: 450kW (600hp) 6 SY 31 WA water-cooled	Radio: n/k
6-cylinder diesel	

Chapter 5

The Middle East, 1948–90

The arid deserts of the Middle East have been
no strangers to military conflict. For centuries, wars of
empire, ethnicity and religion have wracked the region.
Modern warfare in the Middle East has been defined by the
power of the armoured fighting vehicle. In less than a
quarter of a century, the defenders of the nation of Israel
advanced from a vulnerable confederation of militia into one
of the world's most formidable advocates of armour. The
Arab states, faced with the burgeoning military might of
Israel, recognized both the offensive capabilities of the tank
and the urgent necessity of defending against it.

◀ **Show of strength**
Egyptian T-55 main battle tanks take part in a parade. A great deal of Soviet hardware was sold to countries of the
Middle East, especially Syria and Egypt.

National identity and nativism

The advent of the Jewish state spawned inevitable conflict with neighbouring Arab nations, frequently erupting in open warfare during the ensuing half-century, and with the tank serving as a primary weapon.

DESERT WARFARE has been likened to the manoeuvre of great fleets of warships across a trackless ocean, and is punctuated by sharp battles that alter the course of military and geopolitical fortune. Perhaps more than any other military venue, the vast expanse of the desert is the place where the tank is an icon of combat. The firepower, mobility and armour protection of the tank have become indispensable in efforts to control vast territories gained in battle and to secure national borders.

The tank achieved a place of preeminence among the armies of the Middle East in a relatively short period. Although the first Israeli armour consisted of a few 'armoured cars' jury-rigged by militia, the Jewish state has since achieved spectacular advances in modern technology and development of the main battle tank. Virtually from the beginning, the Israelis tinkered with what they had. The results were continuous improvements and upgrades.

Among these were the M-50/51 Super Sherman, similar to the British Sherman Firefly of World War II; the Sho't, an improved version of the British Mk 3 and Mk 5 Centurion with a 105mm (4.1in) cannon; the Tiran series of improvements to captured Soviet-made T-54/55 tanks; and the nation's own development of the Merkava – its first sole authorship in main battle tank design.

War surplus

Both Israel and the Arab nations initially remained dependent on the war surplus, abandoned or repaired equipment of the major powers that had battled in the region during World War II. Purchases were made through arms dealers, and at times the withdrawing armed forces of the former combatants simply looked the other way when their armour was appropriated.

Later, as allegiances to the superpowers became more polarized, the Arab states became dependent on the export variants of the T-54/55 and later models of main battle tanks designed and manufactured by the former Soviet Union and its client states, while Israel was supplied at first primarily by European benefactors, particularly France, and subsequently by the United States.

Throughout its existence, the Israeli military establishment has faced the challenges of maintaining a modern armoured force, including the stark reality of the political fallout that has accompanied open support of the armed forces, the relatively small population of the country and its limited technological base. During the last half-century, however, the proficiency of the Israeli Defence Forces (IDF) – the successors to the Haganah and other ad hoc militias that existed on the eve of the 1948 war – has been acknowledged worldwide.

The earliest known Israeli armoured vehicles were nothing more than fortified trucks with mounted machine guns and sheet metal protection attached in makeshift workshops. A few armoured cars of World War II vintage – especially the Marmon-Herrington, of South African design and adopted by the British – were available, and these were utilized by both the Israeli and Arab armed forces. The first true tanks in the Israeli arsenal were reported to have been about a dozen obsolescent Hotchkiss H-35 tanks, dating to the 1930s, which were located and purchased in France, according to some reports; or left to the Israelis by French colonial troops, according to others. Until the mid-1950s, France would continue as the primary supplier of armour to Israel, including the AMX-13 light tank, while the American-made Sherman and the British Cromwell – and later the Centurion – made up the majority of Israel's armour during the first decade of the nation's existence. A few American-built M3 half-tracks were also available.

During this period, the armoured cadre of the Israeli Defence Forces began to take shape; however, the majority of its equipment was ageing, and maintenance standards were low. The Suez Crisis of 1956 afforded the Israelis an opportunity to flex their limited armoured muscle and proved beneficial to future tactical operations and technological advances. In the aftermath of the Suez Crisis, France became more focused on its traditional colonial ties with the

Arab regions of the Middle East and eventually discontinued its arms shipments to Israel. Thus the sense of urgency among the Israeli leadership to cultivate new sources of arms, upgrade their existing tanks and armoured vehicles, and begin their own programme of arms production was heightened.

Prior to the Six Day War of 1967, the United States responded to an appeal from the Israeli government and began direct shipments of armoured vehicles, including those of the Patton series, to Israel. Meanwhile, the Israelis had embarked on a programme of modernization and improvement of those tanks they had to hand or could purchase, while also developing a main battle tank of their own. By the mid-1970s, Israeli designers had begun to craft the prototype of the Merkava, which today has gained a reputation as a superb armoured vehicle and one of the best tanks in the world. The Merkava has been the backbone of the IDF's armoured contingent since the early 1980s and has itself undergone numerous improvements to its powerplant, fire control and armour protection packages.

Arab armour

Like their Israeli adversaries, the armed forces of the Arab nations arrayed against the Jewish state were limited in their armoured capabilities during the immediate post-World War II period. The armoured car served as the primary fighting vehicle of the Arab armies, while a hotchpotch of tanks, half-tracks and motorized infantry carriers were utilized. British, American, French and even German armoured vehicles were present in the armies of Egypt and Syria, in the Trans-Jordanian Arab Legion, and to a

lesser extent in the armies of Iraq and Lebanon. As the complex political posturing of the Cold War began to evolve, the superpowers exerted influence in the Middle East via cash, technology and arms. In 1955, the so-called Czech Arms Deal supplied the Egyptian Army with the Soviet-designed IS-3 heavy tank, the T-34 medium tank and the SU-100 self-propelled gun. This influx of arms from the Soviet Bloc complemented approximately 450 armoured vehicles of Western design already in the Egyptian inventory. Other Arab countries, particularly Syria, were armed with tanks and armoured fighting vehicles manufactured in the Soviet Union, Czechoslovakia or other Eastern European countries.

As the Arab nations gravitated towards the Soviet sphere of influence during the 1960s and 1970s, the T54/55 and later the T-62 and T-72 main battle tanks became the standard for armoured formations in the Arab armies. Following the Camp David Accords and a degree of rapprochement between Israel, Egypt and the governments of other Arab states, modern Western armour has again become commonplace within Arab arsenals. The American M60 and the British Chieftain and Challenger, for example, have equipped frontline units of the Royal Jordanian Army, the Royal Saudi Land Force and the Egyptian Army. By the 1990s, those Arab nations which joined the coalition that expelled the army of Saddam Hussein from Kuwait were equipped, to a great extent, with Western tanks.

▼ **Upgunned Shermans**
Upgunned IDF M-50 Shermans gather in the Sinai desert, before the beginning of the Six Day War, 1967.

Arab–Israeli War
1948

Although armoured forces played a relatively minor role in the war for Israeli independence, it was readily apparent to military commanders of both sides that future confrontations in the Middle East would involve tanks on a grand scale.

ON 16 OCTOBER 1948, ISRAELI TANKS attacked Egyptian positions in the vicinity of Lod Airport near Tel Aviv. Two Cromwells were destroyed by enemy fire, 10 ancient Hotchkiss H-35s were rendered useless due to mechanical failure or fell into anti-tank ditches and a single Sherman did not engage the Egyptians at all. It was an inauspicious beginning for the armoured command of the Israeli Defence Forces. Arab armour fared little better. Outgunned and outnumbered, the Israelis faced a loose confederation of Arab opponents, whose armies failed to coordinate their offensive efforts and paid the price in lost opportunities.

Fight for survival
On 20 May 1948, Syrian forces had attacked the Israeli kibbutz at Degania near the Sea of Galilee. The militia defending the settlement were reportedly armed only with rifles and automatic weapons, a single British-made PIAT (Projector, Infantry Anti-Tank) shoulder-fired weapon and makeshift Molotov cocktails. The superior Syrian force included at least 18 tanks and armoured cars. During the action, five tanks penetrated Israeli defences but quickly ran into trouble. Two of the French-built Syrian tanks were taken out by a combination of the PIAT and Molotov cocktails. A third tank, this one a Renault R35, was stopped by a Molotov cocktail. It remains in the grounds of the kibbutz today as a monument to the fighting that took place there.

Although the Arab armies failed to press their advantage in firepower and numbers on several occasions, they had recognized the importance of armour early. On the eve of hostilities in 1948, the Egyptian Army fielded a handful of American Sherman and British Crusader and Matilda tanks, nearly 300 armoured Bren gun carriers and a few Marmon-Herrington, Staghound and Humber armoured cars. At least one light tank battalion, consisting of seven tanks, and an armoured reconnaissance battalion of 35 armoured vehicles had been formed.

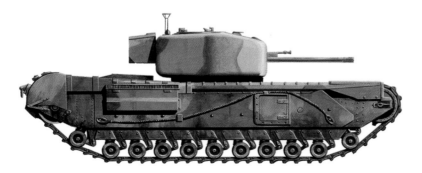

▲ **Infantry Tank Mk IV Churchill IV**

Israeli Defence Forces / 8th Armoured Brigade

The Churchill Mk IV infantry tank was the most numerous of more than a dozen variants of the versatile chassis produced by the British initially during World War II. Israel inherited, purchased or refurbished a handful of British tanks prior to 1950.

Specifications

Weight: 39.62 tonnes (39 tons)	Speed: 25km/h (15.5mph)
Length: 7.44m (24ft 5in)	Range: 193km (120 miles)
Width: 2.74m (9ft)	Armament: 1 x 57mm (2.24in) 6pdr OQF gun,
Height: 3.25m (10ft 8in)	plus 2 x 7.92mm (0.31in) Besa MGs
Engine: 261.1kW (350hp) Bedford	(1 coaxial and 1 ball-mounted in hull front)
12-cylinder petrol	Radio: n/k

Lebanese forces contributed a single armoured battalion of six tanks and four armoured cars to the war, while the Iraqi Army dispatched 47 tanks plus mechanized infantry formations. The Trans-Jordanian Arab Legion, the best trained of all the Arab forces, included motorized infantry but only about a dozen Marmon-Herrington armoured cars. Syrian forces consisted of a battalion of 45 French Renault R35 and R39 tanks along with a battalion of armoured cars.

A core of 10 Hotchkiss H-39 tanks equipped the first armoured formation of the Israeli Defence Forces. Designated the 8th Armoured Brigade, it also included jeeps and half-tracks. The Hotchkiss tanks were grouped into a single company, while the half-tracks were employed as armoured personnel carriers and the jeeps were formed into an assault company.

During the fighting around the town of Lydda and during the 'Ten Days' battles that followed, Moshe Dayan, the future commander of the Israeli Defence Forces and later the nation's defence minister, commanded one of these jeep units, which had been designated the 89th Mechanized Assault Battalion. At Lydda, Dayan reportedly led his jeeps into the town, firing rapidly. It was the 89th Battalion which formed the post-independence core of Israel's armoured forces.

By the end of the war for independence, the Israeli Defence Forces included more than 100,000 troops, the 7th and 8th Armoured Brigades (the former a new armoured formation) and several artillery regiments. The 8th had been designated as 'armoured' for morale purposes as much as anything else. At best, it lacked the training, experience and equipment to exert a decisive presence in itself on the battlefield. Its mixed bag of antiquated tanks was to be reorganized and upgraded over time; however, its contribution to the successful defence of Israel in 1948 must be described in total as limited.

Although the tank was not a decisive factor in the Arab–Israeli War of 1948, its mere presence did influence the course of events. Tanks would grow in number and importance during the years to come. Firepower and technology improved. Tactics were refined. Plans of attack and defence were formulated, discarded and redrawn. Decades of conflict were to come, and the tank would take centre stage.

HQ

Israeli Defence Forces, Tank Company, 1948

The first armoured formation fielded by the Israeli Defence Forces consisted of 10 elderly French Hotchkiss H-39 tanks dating from the 1930s. The tanks were arranged in three platoons of three each with one headquarters tank and constituted the sole tank formation of the 8th Armoured Brigade. Several of the H-39s were lost during the 1948 war due to enemy action and mechanical breakdowns.

Platoon 1 (3 x Hotchkiss H-39 light tanks)

Platoon 2 (3 x Hotchkiss H-39 light tanks)

Platoon 3 (3 x Hotchkiss H-39 light tanks)

Specifications

Crew: 3

Weight: 17.27 tonnes (17 tons)

Length: 5.89m (19ft 4in)

Width: 2.64m (8ft 8in)

Height: 2.29m (7ft 6in)

Engine: 97.73kW (131hp) AEC 6-cylinder diesel

Speed: 24km/h (15mph)

Range: 145km (90 miles)

Armament: 1 x 40mm (1.57in) 2pdr OQF gun,
  plus 1 x coaxial 7.92mm (0.31in) Besa MG

Radio: n/k

▲ **Infantry Tank Mk III Valentine I**

Israeli Defence Forces / 8th Armoured Brigade

Obsolete by the end of World War II, the British Valentine tank had equipped some frontline units of the British Army and had been abandoned after the conclusion of the war. Its assault gun variant, the Archer, was deployed by Egyptian forces during the Suez Crisis.

Suez Crisis
1956

In a joint operation with Great Britain and France to secure the Suez Canal, the Israeli Defence Forces seized the Sinai Peninsula. While its armour played an increasing role, major strategic and tactical shortcomings were revealed.

POLITICAL ACTION AND REACTION resulted in a preemptive joint military strike against Egypt by Great Britain, France and Israel in the autumn of 1956. Following the controversial arms deal with the Soviet Union in 1955, which resulted in the delivery of heavy and medium tanks and self-propelled assault guns to Egypt, the government of President Gamal Abdel Nasser recognized the communist regime of the People's Republic of China and followed quickly with a declaration that Egypt would nationalize the Suez Canal. Nasser's aggressive stance directly threatened the interests of the European powers in the Middle East and posed a military threat to Israel, which had also endured continual terrorist incursions from Arab territory.

Operation Musketeer

When British Royal Marine commandos landed at Port Said, west of the Suez Canal, and both French and British airborne troops parachuted into

IDF, 1956	
Brigades	**Strength**
Infantry	11
Para	1
Armoured	3
TOTAL	15

Egyptian territory, they were accompanied by armoured units. The Centurions of the 6th Royal Tank Regiment supported No. 40 and No. 42 Commandos, and elements of the 1st and 5th Royal Tank Regiments also participated, while a squadron of AMX-10 light tanks advanced with the 1st Parachute Regiment of the French Foreign Legion. Meanwhile, Israeli armour was to coordinate with the British and French, mounting a push into the Sinai Peninsula with approximately 200 tanks.

Operation Kadesh

At the time of the Suez Crisis, as the affair came to be known, the Israeli Defence Forces' armour consisted primarily of about 200 World War II-era M4 Sherman tanks of American manufacture, 100 French-designed AMX-13 light tanks and roughly 60 examples of the 105mm (4.1in) self-propelled *Obusier automoteur de 105 Modèle 5*, essentially the

HQ

Israeli Defence Forces, Tank Company, 1956

Through the mid-1950s, France was the primary supplier of arms to Israel. Among the armoured vehicles utilized by the Israeli Defence Forces was the AMX-13 light tank, originally equipped with a 75mm (2.9in) cannon and later upgunned to 90mm (3.5in) and 105mm (4.1in) weapons. The Israeli tank company at the time of the Suez Crisis included up to 12 AMX-13s and a headquarters tank.

Platoon 1 (3 x AMX-13 light tanks)

Platoon 2 (3 x AMX-13 light tanks)

Platoon 3 (3 x AMX-13 light tanks)

▲ AMX-13 Light Tank

Israeli Defence Forces / 27th Armoured Brigade

The oscillating turret of the French AMX-13 light tank proved a disappointment in combat conditions. The innovative design of the AMX-13, originally conceived as an air-transportable armoured vehicle, also featured an automatic loading system of revolver-type cartridges.

Specifications

Crew: 3

Weight: 15,000kg (33,000lb)

Length: 6.36m (20ft 10.3in)

Width: 2.5m (8ft 2.5in)

Height: 2.3m (7ft 6.5in)

Engine: 186kW (250hp) SOFAM 8-cylinder petrol

Speed: 60km/h (37mph

Range: 400km (250 miles)

Armament: 1 x 75mm (2.9in) gun, plus 1 x
7.62mm (0.3in) MG

Radio: n/k

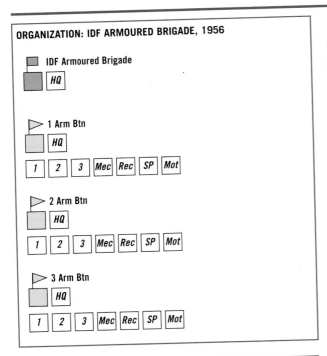

IDF Armoured Brigade
HQ

▷ 1 Arm Btn
HQ
| 1 | 2 | 3 | Mec | Rec | SP | Mot |

▷ 2 Arm Btn
HQ
| 1 | 2 | 3 | Mec | Rec | SP | Mot |

▷ 3 Arm Btn
HQ
| 1 | 2 | 3 | Mec | Rec | SP | Mot |

IDF ARMOURED BRIGADE, 1956			
Type	Number	Vehicle	Strength
Headquarters	–	–	–
Armoured Btn	3	–	–
Armoured Coy	3	Medium tank	13
Mechanized Coy	1	M3 half-track	n/k
Recce Platoon	1	Jeep	7
SP Artillery Bat	1	M7 Priest Howitzer	4
Motorized Coy	1	–	–

105mm (4.1in) weapon mounted on the AMX-13 chassis. The Egyptian Army was equipped with the Soviet T-34/85, an upgunned version of the original T-34 with an 85mm (3.4in) cannon; M4 Shermans in their original US configuration along with some that had been modified by the British; the Soviet SU-100 self-propelled gun; the Archer self-propelled variant of the British Valentine tank with a 76mm (3in/17-pounder) cannon; and at least 200 Soviet-designed BTR 152 armoured troop carriers. Total Egyptian armoured strength was estimated at more than 1000 vehicles.

The Israelis undertook Operation Kadesh to eliminate the terrorist incursions, secure their borders, lift the quarantine of the port of Eilat which had been imposed by the Egyptians and degrade the fighting capabilities of the burgeoning Egyptian Army, which had only recently accepted delivery of nearly 300 Soviet-designed tanks of Czech manufacture.

The armoured corps of the Israeli Defence Forces had been subjected to great scrutiny following the 1948 war. Its command structure was reorganized, and it was determined that armoured strength would be a key element in future military confrontations. Still, the 7th Armoured Brigade constituted the army's only standing tank force. Emphasizing speed and firepower, the evolving Israeli armoured doctrine called for tanks that were capable of rapid mobility and able to seek out and destroy enemy forces. While armour had its proponents within the Israeli military establishment, a philosophical controversy as to its

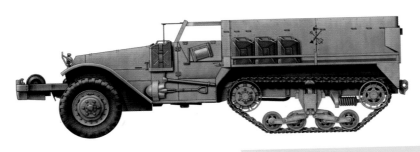

▲ M3 Mk. A Half-track

Israeli Defence Forces / 10th Infantry Brigade

Based on the M5 half-track personnel carriers built by the International Harvester Company, Israeli half-tracks were all designated M3, even M2/M9 variants. The Mk A APCs are identified as IHC M5s by the use of RED-450 engines. Israeli half-track vehicles of World War II-manufacture remained in service into the 1970s.

Specifications

Crew: 2 plus 11 passengers

Weight: 9.3 tonnes (9.15 tons)

Length: 6.34m (20ft 10in)

Width: 2.22m (7ft 3in)

Height: 2.69m (8ft 10in)

Engine: 109.5kW (147hp) IHC RED-450-B 6-cylinder

Speed: 72km/h (45mph)

Range: 320km (200 miles)

THE MIDDLE EAST, 1948-90

EGYPTIAN ARMY TANK BRIGADE, 1956			
Type	Number	Vehicle	Strength
Headquarters	–	truck	1
AA Company	1	S-60 57mm gun	3
Tank Btn	2		
Headquarters	1	T-34/85 MBT	1
Tank Company	3	T-34/85 MBT	3
Mechanized Btn HQ	1		
Headquarters	1	BTR-152	1
Mech Infantry Coy	3	BTR-152	2
Heavy Weapons Coy	1	81mm mortar	1
		57mm ATG	1
Assault Gun Btn HQ	1	truck	1
		SU-100 assault gun	4

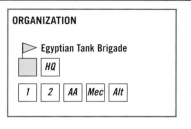

ORGANIZATION

▷ Egyptian Tank Brigade

☐ HQ

| 1 | 2 | AA | Mec | Alt |

Sherman chassis with the high-velocity French gun and produced a tank with greater firepower. The first 25 M-50s were delivered to armoured units just days before the commencement of Operation Kadesh.

actual role persisted, creating confusion among commanders in the field.

Meanwhile, the Israeli effort to upgrade its M4 Sherman medium tanks is indicative of the initiative to improve available armoured vehicles in response to the threat of Egyptian T-34 and IS-3 tanks. The M-50/51 programme resulted in a formidable tank known as the Super Sherman. The purchase of the French AMX-13 had placed in Israeli hands the powerful 75mm (2.9in) CN 75-50 cannon, which had been patterned after the German 75mm (2.9in) KwK 42 L70 as utilized in the Panther medium tank during World War II. Israeli engineers married the M4

Mobility in the desert

Operation Kadesh achieved its tactical objectives in approximately 100 hours and was fought entirely between the armies of Israel and Egypt. During the offensive of 29 October to 7 November 1956, Israeli forces occupied the entire Sinai Peninsula from the coast of the Mediterranean to Sharm el-Sheikh, took control of the Gaza Strip and halted 16km (10 miles) from the Suez Canal in accordance with a prearranged agreement with the British and French. They lost only 231 soldiers in the process.

Despite the success of Operation Kadesh, the Israeli military establishment has been criticized for failing to fully appreciate the strength of a combined arms approach to combat. Chief among those held accountable for this shortcoming was Dayan, who only late in the planning assigned any significant role to Israeli armour. Infantry had been considered primary, while tank formations were relegated to a

▲ T-34/85 Model 1953 Medium Tank

Egyptian Army / 4th Armoured Division, Port Said, Suez Canal, November 1956

An export version of the Soviet-designed T-34/85 medium tank which mounted an 85mm (3.4in) main weapon, the Model 1953 was manufactured in Czechoslovakia. Large numbers of the Model 1953 had been delivered to the Egyptian and Syrian Armies by the time of the 1956 Suez Crisis.

Specifications

Crew: 5

Weight: 32 tonnes (31.5 tons)

Length: 6m (19ft 7in)

Width: 3m (9ft 10in)

Height: 2.6m (8ft 6in)

Engine: 372 kW (493hp) V-2 V12 diesel

Speed (road): 55km/h (33mph)

Range: 360km (223 miles)

Armament: 1 x 85mm (3.4in) ZiS-S-53 cannon, plus 2 x 7.62mm (0.3in) DT MGs (1 coaxial and 1 in the bow)

Radio: R-113 Granat

support role. Armour was not fully integrated into the Israeli battle plan, and wheeled transportation for mechanized infantry was sorely lacking. During one action, Israeli tank commanders became so confused that friendly fire erupted and one formation knocked out eight of the other's nine tanks. Israeli armoured forces were deployed piecemeal and their tactics proved deficient. By the third day of Operation Kadesh, for example, the 7th Armoured Brigade had been divided into three task groups. Each of these was oriented in a different direction and unable to support the other.

No large-scale tank-versus-tank battles occurred during Operation Kadesh. However, an Israeli attack

at Umm Qatef was ordered forward without tank support. The Israeli commander on the scene had decided that an attack was too risky without armour, and the nearest tanks were several hours away. Dayan, however, insisted that an attack be carried out immediately. In the event, several Israeli half-tracks were destroyed by Egyptian Archer self-propelled guns, and the Egyptians held their ground.

The lessons learned in the Sinai would be put to good use in the years to come. The Israeli Defence Forces eventually adopted a strategy of large armoured formations attacking swiftly and achieving deep penetrations of enemy lines.

▲ **Archer 17pdr SP Gun**

Egyptian Army / 4th Armoured Division, Port Said, Suez Canal, November 1956

The self-propelled, open turret variant of the British Valentine tank, the Archer tank destroyer was deployed by the Egyptian Army during the Suez Crisis. Its 76mm (3in/17-pounder) gun was effective against Israeli armoured vehicles in the Sinai.

Specifications

Crew: 4
Weight: 18.79 tonnes (18.5 tons)
Length: 6.68m (21ft 11in)
Width: 2.64m (8ft 8in)
Height: 2.24m (7ft 4in)
Engine: 123kW (165hp) GMC M10 diesel
Speed: 24km/h (15mph)
Range: 145km (90 miles)
Armament: 1 x 76mm (3in) 17pdr OQF,
    plus 1 x 7.7mm (0.303in) Bren MG
Radio: n/k

▲ **SU-100 SP Gun**

Egyptian Army / 4th Armoured Division, Port Said, Suez Canal,
November 1956

The SU-100 self-propelled gun was developed by the Soviet Union during World War II and remained in service with Arab armies in the Middle East until the 1970s. Modifications for service in the desert resulted in the SU-100M variant.

Specifications

Crew: 4
Weight: 31.6 tonnes (69,665lbs)
Length: 9.45m (31ft)
Width: 3m (10ft)
Height: 2.25m (7.38ft)

Engine: 370kW (500hp) V-2-34 12-cylinder
    4-stroke diesel
Speed: 48km/h (30mph)
Range: 320km (200 miles)
Armament: 100mm (3.9in) D-10S gun
Radio: R-113 Granat

Six Day War
1967

Following a series of preemptive air strikes, Israeli tanks and warplanes devastated Arab armour and altered the perceived balance of power in the Middle East.

BY THE MID-1960S, yet another armed confrontation between Israel and its Arab neighbours appeared inevitable. Egyptian president Nasser had closed the Strait of Tiran, compelled United Nations peacekeepers to vacate the Sinai Peninsula and remilitarized the region. An apparent build-up of Egyptian forces on the Israeli frontier had been accompanied by bellicose public statements as well.

In the meantime, Israeli military leaders had continued to revise their plans for battle. The air force would provide a primary means of offensive operations, while the armoured corps would become the foremost element of Israeli Defence Forces ground operations. Although little is known of the specifics of Egyptian armoured doctrine, or of that of

SYRIAN ARMOURED BRIGADE, 1967			
Type	Number	Vehicle	Strength
Armoured Btn	3		
Headquarters	1	T-54/T-55 MBT	1
Tank Company	3	T-54/T-55 MBT	3
Mechanized Btn	1		
Headquarters	1	BTR-152	1
Mechanized Coy	3	BTR-152	2
Heavy Weapons Coy	1	HMG in BTR-152	2
		82mm mortar	1

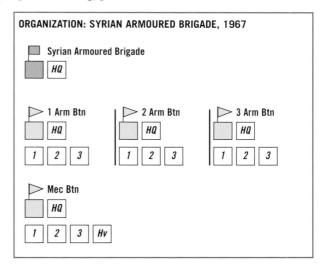

ORGANIZATION: SYRIAN ARMOURED BRIGADE, 1967

Syrian Armoured Brigade — HQ

1 Arm Btn — HQ — 1 2 3
2 Arm Btn — HQ — 1 2 3
3 Arm Btn — HQ — 1 2 3

Mec Btn — HQ — 1 2 3 Hv

▲ **T34/85 Model 1953 Medium Tank**
Syrian Army / 44th Armoured Brigade, Golan Heights, 1967
Made in Czechoslovakia, this Model 1953 T-34/85 includes a Soviet-manufactured DShK 12.7mm (0.5in) heavy anti-aircraft machine gun mounted on the turret ring. During the Six Day War, Syrian armour took serious losses from Israeli aircraft. The inscription reads, 'Al Shaheed Hormuz Yunis Butris'.

Specifications
Crew: 5
Weight: 32 tonnes (31.5 tons)
Length: 6m (19ft 7in)
Width: 3m (9ft 10in)
Height: 2.6m (8ft 6in)
Engine: 372 kW (493hp) V-2 V12 diesel
Speed (road): 55km/h (33mph)
Range: 360km (223 miles)
Armament: 1 x 85mm (3.4in) ZiS-S-53 cannon,
  plus 1 x DShK 12.7mm (0.5in) turret-mounted
  anti-aircraft HMG and 2 x 7.62mm (0.3in) DT
  MGs (1 coaxial and 1 in the bow)
Radio: R-113 Granat

▲ ASU-57 SP Gun

Egyptian Army / 7th Infantry Division, Sinai, Rafah, 1967

Lightly armed and armoured, the ASU-57 assault gun was originally intended as a support weapon for Soviet airborne formations. Its low silhouette and high speed improved survivability on the battlefield. The 57mm (2.24in) high-velocity gun offered a high rate of fire and excellent armour-penetration capabilities.

Specifications

Crew: 3	Engine: 41kW (55hp) M-20E four-cylinder petrol
Weight: 3300kg (7260lb)	Speed: 45km/h (28mph)
Length: 4.995m (16ft 4.7in)	Range: 250km (155 miles)
Width: 2.086m (6ft 10in)	Armament: 1 x 57mm (2.24in) CH-51M gun, plus
Height: 1.18m (3ft 10.5in)	1 x 7.62mm (0.3in) anti-aircraft MG
	Radio: n/k

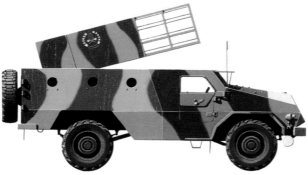

Specifications

Crew: 2
Weight: Not available
Length: 6.12m (20ft)
Width: 2.57m (8ft 5in)
Height: 2.3m (7ft 6in)
Engine: 125kW (168hp) diesel
Speed: 86km/h (54mph)
Range: 800km (500 miles)
Armament: 12 x 80mm (3.15in)
   rocket-launcher tubes
Radio: n/k

▲ Walid APC rocket launcher

Egyptian Army / 2nd Infantry Division / 10th Brigade, Sinai, Abu Ageila, 1967

A variant of the Soviet-produced BTR-152 armoured personnel carrier, the Walid was manufactured in Egypt and exported to other Arab countries. The Walid carried a crew of two and a complement of up to 10 combat infantrymen. Some were fitted with 80mm (3.15in) rocket launchers.

other Arab states such as Syria and Lebanon, it is reasonable to assume that battlefield tactics followed those of the Soviet armoured doctrine developed for potential combat against NATO forces in Western Europe.

Preemptive strike

The Israelis, on the other hand, rationalized that the preemptive strike, an offensive blow as a defensive measure, offered the best chance for victory. Thus on 5 June 1967, Israel launched a series of major air strikes against the air forces of Egypt, Syria and Jordan, destroying most of the Arab aircraft on the

ground. In practice, the strikes were instrumental in the ensuing success of Israeli ground operations.

Without adequate air cover, Arab armour was battered from above. In turn, Israeli tanks destroyed hundreds of enemy armoured vehicles, although the theory of armoured prominence was resisted in some command circles. In less than a week of fighting, more than 300 Egyptian tanks, one-third of the entire Egyptian armoured force, were captured. The remainder was virtually wiped out. The Royal Jordanian Army lost 179 tanks, and the Syrian Army suffered 118 tanks destroyed. In total, it is estimated that the Israelis destroyed 600 Arab tanks. Fewer than

700 Israeli soldiers were killed, and Israeli armoured losses were minimal.

Tank power

More than 2500 tanks took part in the Six Day War, with the Israelis deploying their ageing Super Shermans, the French AMX-13s and those British Centurions which were still operational. However, in addition to improvising and maintaining their older tanks, the Israelis had obtained some new armoured fighting vehicles. An historic arms deal with West Germany had resulted in the delivery of the American M48A2 Patton tank, armed with a 90mm (3.5in) main gun. Later known as the Magach series, the American M48s and successor M60s that entered service with the Israelis were modernized on a continual basis, fitted with heavier weapons, better engines and improved armour.

Israeli forces also captured a large number of Jordanian M48s during the Six Day War, and many of these were incorporated into the ranks of the Israeli Armoured Corps.

▲ IS-3 Heavy Tank

Egyptian Army / 7th Infantry Division, Sinai, Rafah, 1967

With its 122mm (4.8in) cannon, the Soviet-designed IS-3 heavy tank proved formidable in desert action. At Rafah during the Six Day War, IS-3s destroyed several M48A2 Patton tanks of the Israeli Defence Forces' 7th Armoured Brigade.

Specifications

Crew: 4	Speed: 40km/h (25mph)
Weight: 45.77 tonnes (45.05 tons)	Range: 185km (115 miles)
Length: 9.85m (32ft 4in)	Armament: 1 x 122mm (4.8in) D-25T gun,
Width: 3.09m (10ft 2in)	plus 1 x 12.7mm (0.5in) DShK HMG on AA
Height: 2.45m (8ft)	mount and 1 x coaxial 7.62mm (0.3in) DT MG
Engine: 447kW (600hp) V-2-JS V12 diesel	Radio: 10R (when fitted)

Specifications

Crew: 5	Speed: 37km/h (23mph)
Weight: 46 tonnes (45.27 tons)	Range: (road) 220km (136.7 miles),
Length: 9.18m (30ft 1in)	(terrain) 80km (49.7 miles)
Width: 3.07m (10ft 1in)	Armament: 1 x 152mm (6in) ML-20S howitzer;
Height: 2.48m (8ft 1in)	1 x 12.7mm (0.5in) DShK HMG on AA mount
Engine: 447kW (600hp) V-2 diesel	Radio: 10RF (when fitted)

▲ ISU-152 Heavy SP Assault Gun

Egyptian Army / 6th Mechanized Division, Sinai, 1967

The Soviet-designed ISU-152 heavy assault gun was available in relatively small numbers during the Six Day War and often deployed with the anti-tank companies that were organic to the armoured brigades of the Egyptian Army.

ISRAELI ARMOURED BRGIGADE, 1967			
Type	Number	Vehicle	Strength
Headquarters	–		
Armoured Btn	2	Centurion/M48A1	50
Reconnaissance Coy	1	jeeps with 106mm recoilless rifles	6
Mechanized Btn	1	M3/5 half-track	n/k
SP Artillery Btn	1	M3 120mm mortar on half-tracks	12

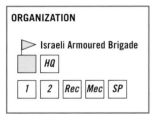

ORGANIZATION

▷ Israeli Armoured Brigade

☐ HQ

1 | 2 | Rec | Mec | SP

During the decade following the 1948 war, the United States had rebuffed several Israeli overtures for the purchase of arms. On the eve of the Six Day War, however, a direct appeal from Israeli prime minister Golda Meir finally resulted in a continuing flow of weapons from the United States to Israel. In 1966, the British government offered Israel the opportunity to purchase obsolete Centurion tanks and to participate in the development of the new Chieftain main battle tank. Although this partnership lasted only three years and was terminated largely due to an outcry from several Arab nations, the Israelis put the Centurions to good use and gained invaluable knowledge in tank design.

When the Six Day War erupted, the Israeli Magach contingent consisted of the M48A1 and M48A2 Patton tanks, some of which had been modified by the ordnance corps of the Israeli Defence Forces with the 105mm (4.1in) L7 gun, a powerful AVDS 1790a diesel engine, and better communications equipment.

In addition to the American M48s which were deployed by the Jordanians, the Arab arsenal included a large number of the World War II-era T-34/85 tanks and SU-100 self-propelled guns. May of these were Czech-built Model 1953s supplied following the 'Czech Arms Deal' of 1955. By this time, the T-54/55 series of Soviet tanks, first developed in the late 1940s, had been incorporated into an Egyptian armoured force, which had deployed them slowly after the 1956 Sinai fighting. By 1967, the Egyptians had received nearly 300 T-54/55 tanks along with

IS-3M heavy tanks and the amphibious PT-76. A large number of the T-54/55s were allocated to the 4th Armoured Division, which had been decimated in the Sinai. The ISU-152 self-propelled gun, another Soviet World War II design, remained in service with Arab forces in limited numbers.

Enter Israel Tal

The officer to whom the revised Israeli armoured doctrine of the Six Day War is primarily attributed is General Israel Tal, who had served as chief of the Israeli Armoured Corps from 1964 to 1967. Tal was a veteran of the 1948 war, had served as a brigade commander in the Sinai in 1956 and had come to the conclusion that heavy tanks, such as the American Pattons and British Centurions, served Israel's battlefield purpose better than the light French alternatives such as the AMX-13 and AMX-30. Tal reasoned that the heavier armour of the Patton and Centurion afforded greater crew survivability; these tanks also carried larger-calibre weapons. Although they sacrificed some speed, these tanks could work in conjunction with infantry and artillery to reduce fixed fortifications and rapidly penetrate enemy lines. These same tanks would ultimately close with enemy armour and fight decisive battles on a grand scale. Tal emphasized superior training, including superb gunnery skills.

Unlike in earlier Arab–Israeli combat, tank-versus-tank battles were frequent during the Six Day War, and the weaknesses of several tanks, including the M48, were exposed. Although the 90mm (3.5in) guns of the Jordanian Pattons had greater range than the guns of the Israeli Super Shermans, the M48s proved vulnerable due to their external auxiliary fuel tanks. Once the Israelis discovered this design flaw, numerous Jordanian M48s were put out of action. On 5–6 June 1967, Generals Avraham Yoffe and Ariel Sharon led Israeli armoured forces against the Egyptians at Abu Ageila. The Israeli force consisted of dozens of Centurion and Super Sherman tanks mounting the 105mm (4.1in) French CN 105 F1 gun and a number of AMX-13s with 90mm (3.5in) cannon. Opposing them were 66 Egyptian T-34/85s and 22 SU-100s. Sharon attacked the Arab force from multiple points, destroying 40 AFVs and losing 19 in the fighting.

During the brief but decisive action of the Six Day War, the Israeli Defence Forces occupied 109,000 square kilometres (42,000 square miles) of territory, including the Sinai Peninsula, the West Bank of the Jordan River and, in the north, the Golan Heights. The Old City of Jerusalem had come into Jewish possession for the first time in 2000 years. The Israelis also controlled the strategically vital Suez Canal.

Although armoured forces had contributed significantly to the stunning Israeli victory, the absence of Arab air power had increased the armour's

effectiveness on the ground. Combined arms still did not receive the emphasis which the Israelis' own doctrine seemed to demand. Nevertheless, the modern Israeli Defence Forces gained invaluable experience in the deployment of tanks on the battlefield, knowledge of the shortcomings of Arab tanks and an understanding of enhancements which would make their own armoured force one of the finest of its kind in the world.

Specifications

Crew: 5

Weight (without blade): 31.6 tonnes (67,000lb)

Length: 6.06m (19ft 9in)

Width: 2.62m (8ft 7in)

Height: 2.74m (9ft)

Engine: 312kW (425hp) Chrysler A57 30-
cylinder petrol

Speed: 40km/h (25mph)

Range: 161km (100 miles)

Armament: 1 x 105mm (4.1in) howitzer M4,
plus 1 x coaxial 12.7mm (0.5in) Browning
M2HB MG

Radio: n/k

🔺 **Sherman M4 Dozer**

Israeli Defence Forces / 7th Armoured Brigade, Sinai, 1967

The Israeli Defence Forces upgunned many of its M4A3 Sherman tanks with the 105mm (4.1in) howitzer M4 and fitted a few with the M1 bulldozer blade. The M4 also incorporated an improved horizontal volute spring suspension.

🔺 **M-51 Isherman**

Israeli Defence Forces / 7th Armoured Brigade / 2nd Battalion / 4th Company

A joint development of French and Israeli engineers, the M-51 Isherman incorporated the superb French 105mm (4.1in) CN 105 F1 gun into the original turret of the M4A1 Sherman tank, which had originally mounted a 75mm (2.9in) cannon. The tank also had installed a US-made Cummins diesel engine and wide-track HVSS suspension. The M-51 was capable of knocking out the T-34 variants and T-55 MBTs employed by Syria and Egypt.

Specifications

Crew: 5	Engine: 338kW (460hp) Cummins V8 diesel
Weight: 39 tonnes (42 tons)	Speed: n/k
Length (hull): 5.84m (19ft 2in)	Range: 270km (168 miles)
Width: n/k	Armament: 1 x 105mm (4.1in) CN 105 F1 gun,
Height: n/k	plus 2 x 7.62mm (0.3in) MG (1 coaxial and
	1 hull-mounted)
	Radio: n/k

Yom Kippur War
1973

Intent on reclaiming prestige and territory lost during the Six Day War, Egypt and Syria attacked Israel on two fronts. Following initial successes, however, they were driven back.

THE SURURISE ASSAULT by the Egyptians across the Suez Canal on 6 October 1973 was in concert with a Syrian strike against Israeli defences in the north on the Golan Heights. Taking the Israelis completely by surprise, Egyptian troops crossed the canal in small boats, their tanks and armoured vehicles following behind on ferries and pontoon bridges, and pierced the Bar-Lev Line. Israeli commanders had relied on the fixed fortifications of the Bar-Lev Line to repel Egyptian attacks against the Suez Canal and the Sinai Peninsula. They had also counted on armoured formations to hold the Golan Heights with minimal infantry support. Meanwhile, the Egyptians had deployed large numbers of Soviet-made mobile surface-to-air (SAM) missiles. The immediate result was a heavy toll in Israeli aircraft, which had decimated the Arab armoured ranks in the Six Day War of 1967. The Egyptian troops also carried Soviet-made Sagger anti-tank missiles and the RPG-7 shoulder-fired anti-tank weapon, which proved lethal against Israeli tanks. For their part, the Israelis, although they were unprepared for the sudden onslaught on two fronts, quickly recovered. Armed with US-made wire-guided TOW missiles, Israeli troops countered with the destruction of scores of Egyptian and Syrian tanks.

Still, the Yom Kippur War saw major clashes between the main battle tanks of the Israeli Defence Forces and the Egyptian and Syrian Armies. On the eve of the war, the Israelis had indeed intended to mobilize their entire air force along with four armoured divisions and had contemplated a preemptive strike against the Syrians. They were confident that their armoured forces, including the 401st Armoured Brigade, stationed along the Suez Canal and the first unit equipped with the modern American M60 Patton tank, could hold against an Arab thrust.

In 1973, the Israeli Armoured Corps consisted of at least 2300 tanks and up to 3000 other armoured vehicles. Israeli armoured formations had been battle-

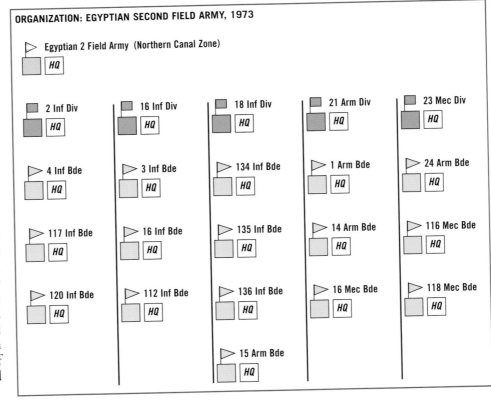

tested during the Six Day War. Their veteran units included the 7th and 188th Armoured Brigades along the Golan Heights. Israeli tanks in the field included the M48s and M60s of the Magach series, the M-50 and M-51 Super Shermans, the modified British Centurion, which the Israelis called the Sho't, and a large number of T-54/55s that had been captured during the Six Day War and redeployed with Israeli units. Many of the Israeli Magachs and Super Shermans had been upgraded with the British 105mm (4.1in) L7 cannon. An array of self-propelled weapons included the American-made M-109 155mm (6.1in) howitzer.

Egyptian forces totalled nearly 1700 tanks, and more than 1000 of these actually crossed the Suez Canal and battled the Israelis in the Sinai in 1973.

Specifications

Crew: 4	Engine: 210kW (280hp) V-6R diesel
Weight: 19,000kg (41,800lb)	Speed: 44km/h (27mph)
Length: 6.54m (21ft 5in)	Range: 260km (162 miles)
Width: 2.95m (9ft 8in)	Armament: 4 x 23mm (0.9in) AZP-23
Height (without radar): 2.25m (7ft 4in)	anti-aircraft cannon
	Radio: n/k

▲ ZSU-23-4 SPAAG

Egyptian Army / 2nd Infantry Division / 51st Artillery Brigade

With radar directed, quad-mounted 23mm (0.9in) autocannon, the ZSU-23-4 self-propelled anti-aircraft vehicle, commonly called the Shilka, was attached to numerous Egyptian armoured brigades during the Yom Kippur War. Along with surface-to-air missiles, they accounted for a number of low-flying Israeli aircraft.

▲ T-34/100 Tank Destroyer

Egyptian Army / 23rd Mechanized Infantry Division / 24th Armoured Brigade

Armed with a 100mm (3.9in) BS-3 anti-tank gun, the T-34/100 was an Egyptian tank destroyer variant of the Soviet T-34 medium tank. Utilizing the T-34 chassis, the Egyptians modified the turret with armour plate extensions and added a recoil mechanism. Lacking the heavier armour protection of more recent tanks, the T-34/100 was mainly used in a defensive role.

Specifications

Crew: 4	Engine: 372 kW (493hp) V-2 V12 diesel
Weight: n/k	Speed (road): 55km/h (33mph)
Length (hull): 6m (19ft 7in)	Range: 360km (223 miles)
Width: 3m (9ft 9in)	Armament: 1 x 100mm (3.9in) BS-3
Height: n/k	anti-tank gun
	Radio: n/k

Armoured personnel carriers of Soviet and Czech manufacture, and self-propelled guns of World War II vintage were also deployed. The Syrian Army contained more than 1200 tanks. Many of the Arab armoured vehicles were the ageing T-34/85s delivered during the late 1950s; however, the T-54/55 and T-62 main battle tanks (the latter with a 115mm/4.5in main gun) were present in significant numbers, having filled out the depleted Arab armoured formations in the wake of the Six Day War.

Sinai assault

Among the Egyptian units that crossed the Suez Canal on 6 October 1973 was the 2nd Infantry Division, later to be reorganized as the 7th Mechanized Division. Attacking the Bar-Lev Line, the 2nd Division and accompanying formations were supported by more than 800 tanks and took control of the canal, destroying Israeli strongpoints and armoured vehicles in great numbers while losing only 20 of their own tanks.

When the Israelis finally stabilized the front and counterattacked, heavy clashes of armour ensued. On 14 October, the Egyptians committed six of their 26 armoured brigades available in an attempt to claim strategically vital high ground. More than 1000 Egyptian and 800 Israeli tanks engaged in the largest armoured battle since World War II. The Israelis fought in company formation and from prepared positions with the added support of combined arms – artillery, infantry and air support. In a single day, the Egyptians lost 264 tanks, while the Israelis lost only 40. The Israelis seized the momentum and actually crossed the Suez Canal from the east, trapping the Egyptian Third Army.

Golan Heights

The 800 tanks of the Syrian 5th, 7th and 9th Mechanized Infantry Divisions included a large number of T-55 and T-62 models. These hit the Israeli positions along the Golan Heights simultaneously with the Egyptian attack in the Sinai. Only 176 tanks of the Israeli Barak and 7th Armoured Brigades stood between the Syrians and Tel Aviv. At the end of the first day of fighting, the Barak Brigade reported only 15 remaining serviceable

ISRAELI ARMY COMMANDERS, OCTOBER 1973	
Name	Command
Maj-Gen David Elazar	CoS General Headquarters
Maj-Gen Israel Tal	Deputy CoS General Headquarters
Maj-Gen Yitzhak Hoffi	GoC Northern Command
Brig-Gen Rafael Eytan	36 Mechanized Division
Maj-Gen Dan Lanner	240 Armoured Division
Maj-Gen Musa Peled	146 Armoured Division
Maj-Gen Yona Ephrat	GoC Central Command
Maj-Gen Shuel Gonen	GoC Southern Command
Brig-Gen Avraham Adan	162 Armoured Division
Maj-Gen Ariel Sharon	143 Armoured Division
Brig-Gen Kalman Magen	252 Armoured Division
Maj-Gen Yeshayahu Gavish	Sinai Command
Maj-Gen B Peled	Air Force
Maj-Gen B Telem	Navy

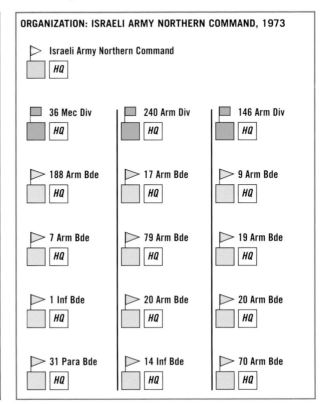

ORGANIZATION: ISRAELI ARMY NORTHERN COMMAND, 1973

tanks. Fighting raged on the heights and in the Valley of Tears. A pair of Israeli Sho't tanks were reported to have stood against 150 Syrian T-55s and T-62s, destroying dozens of them in a 30-hour fight.

In tank-versus-tank combat on the Golan Heights, the Centurion Sho't and other tanks in the Israeli forces were eventually deemed superior to the Arab armour, and within a week the Syrians had lost as many as 1000 tanks. Again, the Israelis seized the

INSIGNIA

The Israeli Armoured Corps has utilized a series of chevrons, rings, numbers and Hebrew letters for unit designation. In the case of the chevron, a vehicle belonging to a 3rd Company is pictured. Battalion markings were determined by rings around the gun barrel, while platoon and individual tanks were identified by a combination of Hebrew letters and numbers usually painted at the turret rear.

Specifications

Crew: 4

Weight: n/k

Length: 6.95m (22ft 10in)

Width: 3.63m (11ft 11in)

Height: 3.27m (10ft 9in)

Engine: 551 kW (750hp) General Dynamics Land
  Systems AVDS-1790 series diesel

Speed: n/k

Range: n/k

Armament: 1 x 105mm (4.1in) L7 gun, plus
  3 x 7.62mm (0.3in) MGs

Radio: n/k

▲ **Magach 3 M48 Medium Tank**
Israeli Defence Forces / 401st Armoured Brigade / 3rd Battalion / 3rd Company
The Israelis improved the M48 Patton tanks received initially from West Germany and later from the United States with 105mm (4.1in) guns and better diesel engines. M48s lost in the Yom Kippur War were often replaced by M60s.

▲ **Sho't Centurion Mk 5**
Israeli Defence Forces / 7th Armoured Brigade / 2nd Battalion / 1st Company
Entering service with the Israeli Armoured Corps in 1970, the Sho't was an Israeli variant of the British Centurion tank which had been upgunned with the 105mm (4.1in) L7 gun. Both the Centurion Mk 3 and Mk 5 were upgraded with improved fire control systems and armour as well.

Specifications

Crew: 4

Weight: 5.18 tonnes (4.7 tons)

Length: 7.82m (25ft 8in)

Width: 3.39m (11ft9in)

Height: 3.01m (9ft 10in)

Engine: 480kW (643hp) Continental AVDS-1790-
  2A diesel

Speed: 43km/h (27mph)

Range: 205km (127 miles)

Armament: 1 x 105mm (4.1in) L7 gun, plus
  1 x 12.7mm (0.5in) ranging MG and
  2 x 7.62mm (0.3in) MGs (1 coaxial and 1 on
  commander's cupola)

Radio: n/k

initiative and invaded Syria, halting less than 48km (30 miles) from Damascus, the Syrian capital.

They had initially reeled before the Arab onslaught, but during the Yom Kippur War the Israelis demonstrated their ability to adapt older tanks to modern conditions with improved weapons, powerplants and armour protection. Still, their losses in terms of armour were grievous, estimated at well over 1000 tanks. At the end of the Yom Kippur War, the Israeli military establishment was shaken.

IDF, Armoured Reconnaissance Battalion, 1973

Packing substantial firepower, an Israeli armoured reconnaissance battalion during the Yom Kippur War of 1973 consisted of three reconnaissance companies. Each of these included a pair of modified Centurion Sho't tanks with 105mm (4.1in) cannon and three M113 Zelda armoured personnel carriers, with a total capacity of about 100 combat infantrymen.

1 Company (2 x Sho't MBTs; 3 x Zelda M113 APCs)

2 Company (2 x Sho't MBTs; 3 x Zelda M113 APCs)

3 Company (2 x Sho't MBTs; 3 x Zelda M113 APCs)

▲ Zelda M113 APC

Israeli Defence Forces / 87th Armoured Reconnaissance Battalion / 3rd Company

Incorporating the Toga armour package of perforated steel plates on its front and sides, the Zelda M113 armoured personnel carrier was an Israeli improvement to the basic design of the ubiquitous US M113 APC. A command version of the Zelda was also produced.

Specifications

Crew: 2 + 11	Engine: 158kW (212hp) Detroit Diesel
Weight: 12,500kg (27,600lb)	6V-53T 6-cylinder diesel
Length: 5.23m (17ft 2in)	Speed: 61km/h (38mph)
Width: 3.08m (10ft 1in)	Range: 480km (300 miles)
Height: 1.85m (6ft .8in)	Armament: 1 x 12.7mm (0.5in) MG (2 x 7.62mm/
	0.3in) in some configurations

▲ **Soltam Systems L33 155mm SP Howitzer**

Israeli Defence Forces / 188th Armoured Brigade

Distinguished by its large, boxlike turret structure and based on the chassis of the M4A3E8 Sherman tank, the Soltam Systems L33 mounted a 155mm (6.1in) cannon. After trials in 1968, the L33 entered production in 1970. The vehicle was deployed shortly before the Yom Kippur War.

Specifications	
Crew: 8	Engine: 331kW (450hp) Ford GAA V8 petrol
Weight: 41.5 tonnes (40.8 tons)	Speed: 38km/h (24mph)
Length (hull): 5.92m (19ft 5in)	Range: 260km (162 miles)
Width: 2.68m (8ft 9in)	Armament: 1 x 155mm (6.1in) L33 howitzer, plus
Height: n/k	1 x 7.62mm (0.3in) MG
	Radio: n/k

Lebanese Civil War
1975–90

War-torn Lebanon suffered not only internal strife during 15 years of civil war but also the intervention of its Arab and Israeli neighbours as well as the terrorism of local insurgent groups.

FOR YEARS, LEBANON has been wracked by civil war as paramilitary factions, spurred by nationalism or religious ardour, vied for control of the country. Complicating the situation was the presence of anti-Israeli groups such as the Palestine Liberation Organization (PLO) and Hezbollah. Syria and Israel intervened from time to time in the Lebanese Civil War, with the Israelis attempting to establish a secure northern border and deter PLO guerrillas from infiltrating or launching rocket attacks against settlements near the frontier. Lebanon further provided a battleground for clashes with Syria, a traditional enemy of Israel, whose resolve to fight the Jewish state had been steeled by the separate peace between Israel and Egypt following the Camp David Accords of 1978.

Attacks by the PLO and other terrorist groups, along with concern over the growing Syrian presence in Lebanon, has prompted the Israelis to launch military operations against Lebanon on several occasions, including major operations in 1978, 1982 and 2006. In each case, Israeli armour participated. Intended initially to protect Israel against the armies of neighbouring Arab states, the Israeli Defence Forces found themselves often involved in difficult urban fighting, battling militia armed with anti-tank weapons and planting improvised explosive devices (IEDs) along roadways. Counterinsurgency operations presented particular challenges to Israeli armour. Close-quarter fighting in narrow streets diminished the effectiveness of the main battle tank's manoeuvrability, while the stand-off firepower of a high-velocity gun was lessened as well.

Armoured development

Through much of the 1970s and into the 1980s, the Israeli Magach series, based on the American M48 and M60 Patton tanks, served as the backbone of the Israeli armoured forces. These vehicles included the Magach 5 and 6, upgraded with the Blazer armour protection package, the 6B with improved fire control, the 6B Batash with fourth generation passive armour and the Magach 7A and 7C with a thermal sleeve for the 105mm (4.1in) main gun and improved armour configurations.

Following the Yom Kippur War, the Israelis committed to the development of their own main battle tank, comparable to the finest armoured fighting vehicles in the world, including the American Abrams, the German Leopard, the British Chieftain and the Soviet T-72. The result was the Merkava, or Chariot in translation from the Hebrew.

The first Merkava was delivered to the Israeli Defence Forces in 1979, the product of Israeli design, engineering and manufacturing expertise as well as the integration of technology purchased from abroad when necessary.

Merkava and its adversary

General Israel Tal receives much of the credit for the design of the Merkava, which stresses the survivability of the tank's crew, employing entry and exit ports from the rear; it has modern spaced armour, a frontal engine compartment, ammunition stowage to the vehicle's rear and a protective system against nuclear, biological and chemical attack. The latest variant, the Merkava Mk 4, is powered by a

Specifications
Crew: 2 + 6
Weight: 3600kg (7900lb)
Length: 5.02m (16ft 5.6in)
Width: 2.03m (6ft 8in)
Height: 1.66m (5ft 5in)
Engine: 89kW (120hp) Chrysler 6-cylinder petrol
Speed: 100km/h (62mph)
Range: 550km (340 miles)
Armament: 1 x 7.62mm (0.3in) MG
Radio: n/k

▲ **RBY Mk 1**

Israeli Defence Forces / Golani Brigade / 51st Battalion

A light armoured reconnaissance vehicle produced by Israel Aircraft Industries, the RBY Mk 1 has been in service with the Israeli Defence Forces and the armies of other countries since 1975. A variety of machine guns and cannon can be fitted to the vehicle, including a 106mm (4.17in) recoilless rifle. The Israelis have largely replaced it with the RAM 2000.

▲ **Rascal**

Israeli Defence Forces / Southern Regional Command / 366th Division / 55th Artillery Battalion 'Draken' ('Dragon')

The light, self-propelled Rascal 155mm (6.1in) gun was designed and built by Soltam Ltd. Weighing only 20.3 tonnes (20 tons), the Rascal was the lightest of the Soltam 155mm (6.1in) self-propelled weapons. It was capable of transport by air, truck or rail.

Specifications
Crew: 4
Weight: 19,500kg (43,000lb)
Length (with gun): 7.5m (24ft 7in)
Width: 2.46m (8ft 1in)
Height: 2.3m (7ft 7in)
Engine: 261kW (350hp) diesel
Speed: 50km/h (31mph)
Range: 350km (220 miles)
Armament: 1 x 155mm (6.1in) howitzer

General Dynamics GD833 1125kW (1500hp) diesel engine. Its 120mm (4.7in) gun is second to none in firepower.

The Soviet-designed T-72 tanks in service with the Syrian Army trace their lineage to the T-62 and the T-54/55. Production of the T-72 was undertaken in 1971. The tank mounts a powerful 125mm (4.9in) 2A46M smoothbore gun, and the basic vehicle is powered by a 585kW (780hp) V12 diesel engine. Several variants of the T-72 have been produced,

including the T-72A with improved laser rangefinding equipment and better optics. The T-72M and T-72M1, export versions of the T-72A, were delivered to Syria and included heavier armour protection for the frontal hull and turret. Estimates of the number of T-72s utilized by the Syrian Army top 1500.

During the periodic fighting in Lebanon, Israeli Merkava and Syrian T-72 tanks have reportedly met on a number of occasions. While each side has claimed that its main battle tank is superior to that of

Specifications

Crew: 7

Weight: n/k

Length (hull): 6m (19ft 7in)

Width: 3m (9ft 10in)

Height: n/k

Engine: 372 kW (493hp) V-2 V12 diesel

Speed (road): 55km/h (33mph)

Range: 360km (223 miles)

Armament: 1 x 122mm (4.8in) D-30 howitzer

Radio: n/k

▲ **T-34/122 SP Howitzer**

Egyptian Army / 7th Mechanized Division, 1975

As the T-34/85 medium tank became obsolete as a main battle tank, the Egyptian Army adapted the chassis to carry a heavy 122mm (4.8in) D-30 howitzer for mobile fire support of its mechanized infantry formations. The howitzer was mounted either in a modified turret or openly. The modification consisted of cutting away the roof and rear parts of the turret, and building a new, larger turret out of sheet armour.

▲ **T-34 with 122mm D-30 SP Howitzer**

Syrian Army / 1st Armoured Division / 58th Mechanized Brigade, Lebanon, 1982

The Syrian Army adapted the heavy D-30 122mm (4.8in) howitzer to the T-34 medium tank chassis and produced a self-propelled weapon with an open platform for the crew operating the gun. When the vehicle was in motion, the platform folded.

Specifications

Crew: 7

Weight: n/k

Length (hull): 6m (19ft 7in)

Width: 3m (9ft 10in)

Height: n/k

Engine: 372 kW (493hp) V-2 V12 diesel

Speed (road): 55km/h (33mph)

Range: 360km (223 miles)

Armament: 1 x 122mm (4.8in) D-30 howitzer

the other, it is well known that Iraqi export versions of the T-72 were decimated by coalition forces during the Gulf War of 1991 and the US-led invasion of Iraq in 2003. Although the Israelis acknowledged that they did sustain the loss of some Merkavas against the Syrians, they also asserted that none of the tanks' crewmen were killed in action.

Street fighting

While direct confrontations between Israeli and Syrian tanks have been common enough in southern Lebanon, the counterinsurgency operations of the Israeli Defence Forces required modifications to existing armoured fighting vehicles. Claims that no Merkava crewmen were killed in earlier battles could not hold true during the 2006 Lebanon War.

◀ Syrian T-55

A Syrian T-55 halts beside the road in the much fought-over Golan Heights, sometime in the 1970s.

The Israeli Merkava tanks battled Hezbollah guerrillas armed with modern anti-tank missiles, such as the Russian A-14 Komet and RPG-29 Vampir. Projectiles penetrated the armour of at least five Merkavas. Improvised explosive devices also proved hazardous. The lessons learned fighting in the streets of Lebanese towns off and on for more than a decade resulted in the addition of a removable V-shaped underbelly armour package along with other improvements.

The Merkava LIC, a variant of the Mk 3 BAZ and Mk 4 tanks, is specifically designed for urban warfare, otherwise known as 'low intensity conflict'. The Merkava LIC includes a turret-mounted 12.7mm (0.5in) machine gun for close-in fire support and protection against infantry. The weapon is fired from within the tank, avoiding the exposure of the crewmen to small-arms fire. A camera facing to the tank's rear provides the driver with a more complete view of the vehicle's close surroundings, particularly valuable in an urban setting,. A strong steel mesh protects vulnerable areas of the tank, such as exhaust tubes, optical equipment and ventilation structures, against the attachment of explosives.

▲ T-34/85M Medium Tank

Palestine Liberation Army, 1980

Also known as the Model 1969, the T-34/85M actually incorporated some components of the later Soviet T-54/55 tank, including similar road wheels, external auxiliary fuel tanks, night driving and vision equipment and improved communication gear.

Specifications	
Crew: 5	38.88-l diesel
Weight: 32 tonnes (31.5 tons)	Speed (road): 55km/h (33mph)
Length: 6m (19ft 7in)	Range: 360km (223 miles)
Width: 3m (9ft 10in)	Armament: 1 x 85mm (3.4in) ZiS-S-53 cannon;
Height: 2.6m (8ft 6in)	2 x 7.62mm (0.3in) DT MGs (bow and coaxial)
Engine: 433kW (581hp) Model V-55 12-cyl.	Radio: R-123

Specifications

Crew: 4

Weight: 58,000kg (127,890lb)

Length (hull): 6.39m (21ft 10in)

Width: 3.42m (11ft 7in)

Height: 2.435m (9ft 11in)

Engine: 900kW (1200hp) Perkins Engines Condor
V12 1200 12-cylinder diesel

Speed: 48km/h (30mph)

Range: 400km (248.5 miles)

Armament: 1 x 120mm (4.7in) L11A5 gun,
plus 2 x 7.62mm (0.3in) MGs

Radio: n/k

▲ Khalid Main Battle Tank
Royal Jordanian Land Forces, 1990

The Khalid main battle tank is based on a late production model of the British Chieftain tank, which includes specifications particular to the requirements of the Jordanian military, such as a 900kW (1200hp) Condor diesel engine and fire control specialization. In November 1979, Jordan placed an order with the UK manufacturers for 274 Khalid MBTs for delivery from 1981. Alterations carried out since the Khalid entered service with the Jordanian Army have included modifications of sights and stowage to allow for the carrying and firing of the Royal Ordnance 120mm (4.7in) APFSDS-T ammunition.

Iran–Iraq War
1980–88

Border disputes and struggles to gain preeminence among the nations of the Persian Gulf spurred Saddam Hussein's Iraq to attack Iran.

During the decade from 1968 to 1978, the Baathist regime in Iraq purchased hundreds of tanks, self-propelled guns and support vehicles from the Soviet Union and France. In 1973 alone, the Iraqis ordered 400 T-55 and T-62 tanks. This was followed by an order for 600 T-62s three years later. By 1980, the Soviets had delivered.

In 1978, the French delivered 100 AMX-30B tanks and 100 VCR-6 armoured personnel carriers equipped with anti-tank missile systems to Iraq. Meanwhile, US arms shipments to the military machine of the Shah of Iran neared $1.5 billion between 1950 and 1970. Replacement parts, including engines for the latest Patton series main

battle tank, the M60, were reported to have been supplied by Israel.

When Saddam Hussein attacked Iran in 1980, the Iraqi Army numbered nearly 200,000 men and 2200 tanks. Confident of victory, his armoured spearheads attacked areas where only company-sized Iranian armoured units were available to defend. Eventually, however, the steady Iraqi advance was halted. Throughout the 1970s, Iraq had purchased large quantities of T-55, T-62 and T-72 main battle tanks from the Soviet Union as well as more than 500 BTR-50 and BTR-60 armoured personnel carriers. By 1976, more than 1000 Soviet-built tanks had been delivered to Iraq. This trend continued during the

▶ **Iranian armour**

A Soviet-built T-72 main battle tank in Iranian colours stops by the roadside during the Iran–Iraq War of the 1980s.

eight-year war with Iran, and by 1990 Iraq had made good its losses and even augmented its armoured force to 5700 tanks.

Post-revolutionary Iran, on the other hand, had isolated itself from the rest of the world, and much of the armoured force at its disposal lacked spare parts or trained maintenance personnel. In the Iranian arsenal were American-made M47 and M48 Patton tanks, British Chieftain Mk 5 main battle tanks and light armoured vehicles of US, British and Soviet manufacture. With the ascent of the Ayatollah Khomeini in 1979, an order with Britain for the Shir Iran 2 tank was cancelled. This design was subsequently developed by the British into the new Challenger tank. In 1979, the Iranian Army fielded five organized armoured divisions and several independent armoured formations attached to infantry units. Nearly 200 of its tanks were Shir Iran

1 variants of the Mk 5 Chieftain, shipped from Britain prior to the overthrow of the Shah. During the Iran–Iraq War, the People's Republic of China emerged as a major supplier of arms to both belligerents, including copies of Soviet armoured vehicles, and along with North Korea remained a primary post-war supplier to Iran.

Neither Iran nor Iraq employed sustainable armoured doctrine to any great extent during the war. Neither chose to utilize tank formations in manoeuvre, opting to dig tanks into revetments and employ them as artillery pieces. As stationary targets,

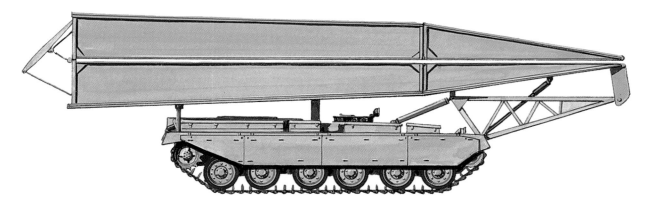

Specifications

Crew: 3	Engine: 559kW (750hp) Leyland L50 12-cylinder
Weight: 53.3 tonnes (117,500lb)	multi-fuel
Length: 13.74m (45ft 9in)	Speed: 48km/h (30mph)
Width: 4.16m (13ft 8in)	Range: 400km (250 miles)
Height:3.92m (12ft 10in)	Armament: None

▲ **Cheftain AVLB**

Iranian Army / 92nd Armoured Division

Based on the chassis of the Chieftain Mk 5 tank, the AVLB (Armoured Vehicle Launched Bridge) bridging tank was a component of a large order placed by the Imperial Iranian Army in 1971. Delivery of 707 Chieftains, including main battle tanks and several variants, was completed in early 1978.

they were often easily dispatched by anti-tank weapons. The ill-trained crewmen of both sides struggled to implement the technology of their weapons. Therefore gunnery was poor and fire control systems were underutilized. Maintenance was virtually non-existent in many cases.

Fourth largest army

An inflexible Iraqi command structure and an apparent unwillingness on the part of Saddam Hussein's generals to commit substantial armoured forces to a decisive battle hampered Iraqi combat effectiveness and contributed to the prolonged war of attrition. Iraq maintained an edge in tanks, acquiring upgraded export versions of the T-72 by 1987. In spite

of staggering losses, the Iraqi Army had swelled to 1.7 million men that year, including five armoured divisions, each with an armoured brigade and a mechanized brigade, and three fully mechanized divisions consisting of at least one armoured brigade and two brigades of mechanized infantry. The elite Presidential Guard Force included three more armoured brigades. Saddam Hussein's army had grown to the fourth largest in the world – a force with which an international coalition would soon contend.

The Iranian advantage was in sheer weight of numbers. Human wave attacks were a common Iranian offensive tactic. Each side was reported to have used chemical weapons. The estimated death toll for both combatants was well above 200,000.

Specifications
Crew: 3 + 9
Weight: 7 tonnes (15,400lb)
Length: 4.57m (14ft 11.8in)
Width: 2.49m (8ft 2in)
Height: 2.03m (6ft 8in)
Engine: 108kW (145hp) Peugeot PRV 6-cylinder
  petrol
Speed: 100km/h (62mph)
Range: 800km (500 miles)
Armament: 1 x 7.62mm (0.3in) MG
Radio: n/k

▲ **Panhard VCR Armoured Personnel Carrier**
Iraqi Army / 1st Mechanized Division
Developed in France at the request of the Iraqi government, the Panhard VCR was an armoured personnel carrier capable of transporting a complement of nine infantrymen. The vehicle was also developed as a platform for turrets capable of launching anti-tank guided missiles, following the purchase of these by Iraq.

Specifications
Crew: 1 + 12
Weight: 13 tonnes (28,600lb)
Length: 6.15m (20ft 2in)
Width: 2.59m (8ft 6in)
Height: 2.09m (6ft 10.3in)
Engine: 158kW (212hp) Detroit Diesel 6V-53N
  6-cylinder diesel
Speed: 90km/h (56mph)
Range: 850km (528 miles)
Armament: 1 x 12.7mm (0.5in) HMG, plus
  1 x 7.62mm (0.3in) MG
Radio: n/k

▲ **EE-11 Armoured Personnel Carrier**
Iraqi Army / 9th Armoured Division
Utilized by both Iraq and Iran, the EE-11 Urutu was designed, manufactured and exported by Brazil in the early 1980s. The EE-11 is capable of carrying up to 12 combat infantrymen and has proven comparable to better known, more costly designs.

Chapter 6

Post-Cold War Conflicts

The absence of Cold War has not ushered in an era of absence of conflict. On the contrary, the main battle tank, its complementary armoured fighting vehicles and the mechanized infantry who man them have maintained a preeminent role in combat operations on land. Just as control of the air and sea have long been essential for victory in war, the missions of taking and holding ground are accomplished only in the context of the defeat of an enemy army. The presence of the tank and armoured fighting vehicle projects the capability of an armed force to accomplish such a task.

◀ **Main battle tank**
A US Army M1A1 Abrams from Apache Troop, 5 Cavalry, 2nd Brigade Combat Team (BCT), 1st Cavalry Division moves out to rejoin the fight after refuelling during a combat operation in Fallujah, Iraq, during Operation Iraqi Freedom.

From Gulf War to Afghanistan

Turning their tanks against guerrilla tactics and insurgency warfare, great armed coalitions have committed to the continuing struggle for dominance in the Middle East and Central Asia.

WHILE THE THREAT of a Cold War-type confrontation between major powers has diminished sharply, the demands for military intervention to maintain an uneasy peace or to dislodge the armies of an aggressor who has unlawfully seized the territory of a neighbour have been steady during the last quarter of a century. Such has been the case with the Gulf War and in the intervention by NATO in Afghanistan, the Balkans and elsewhere. During the same period, the peacekeeping forces of the United Nations have deployed around the world, including the Middle East, the Balkans and the Horn of Africa.

Gulf War

When Saddam Hussein of Iraq sent his army into Kuwait on 2 August 1990, the civilized world met force with force. The invasion of Kuwait was the second unprovoked military offensive undertaken by Saddam Hussein in a decade. In 1980, he had taken advantage of unrest in neighbouring Iran and invaded that country, leading to a prolonged, devastating and bloody eight-year war. During that time, the Baathist dictator continued to build the capacity of his armed forces to wage war. By 1990, the Iraqi Army had grown to the fourth largest in the world. Iraq's armed forces were made up of a large contingent of infantry, Fedayeen irregular troops and an armoured capability spearheaded by the T-54/55 and T-72 tanks manufactured in the Soviet Union and the Eastern European client states of the Soviet Bloc during the 1980s.

Invasion of Iraq

More than a decade later, in 2003, a second armed coalition, led by the United States and Great Britain, invaded Iraq and toppled the repressive regime of Saddam Hussein. US Abrams and British Challenger main battle tanks were instrumental in the drive across hundreds of kilometres of desert to the Iraqi capital of Baghdad and the key port city of Basra respectively. During operations in the southern city of Nasiriyah, images of the tanks and the US Marine AAV7 amphibious infantry fighting vehicle were

▲ **Outgunned**

An Iraqi T-55 main battle tank burns after being knocked out by tanks from the British 1st Armoured Division during Operation Desert Storm, 1991. The outdated T-55 proved no match for the latest technology in the Coalition's armoury.

beamed worldwide. In Basra, the Challenger 2 tanks of the British 7th Armoured Brigade were instrumental in capturing the city and maintaining an uneasy peace in the aftermath.

Afghanistan

Meanwhile, the rise of Islamic fundamentalism has threatened to destabilize much of the Arab world and establish conservative regimes in the Middle East and Central Asia. The Taliban has fought a guerrilla war in the mountainous terrain of Afghanistan, boldly seizing large areas of the country. Financed also by the illicit drug trade, the Taliban has openly supported the terrorism of al-Qaeda.

While overwhelming military might is somewhat neutralized by the conduct of low-intensity counterinsurgency warfare, the armour protection of the main battle tank and the armoured fighting vehicle offers an offensive capability to suppress small-arms fire and advance rapidly over favourable terrain. One of the greatest hazards to armoured operations during the recent fighting in Iraq and Afghanistan has been the improvised explosive device (IED). Guerrilla fighters have engineered powerful explosives, often with discarded ordnance such as old landmines and artillery shells. Buried alongside roadways or directly in the anticipated path of an armoured vehicle or truck, the IED may be detonated by contact pressure as tyres or tracks roll forward, or

by remote control with such readily available devices as the common cell phone. In response, NATO vehicles such as the US M2/M3 Bradley fighting vehicle, the Humvee and the British Warrior have been reinforced with appliqué armour to protect crewmen and passengers. Main battle tanks have been fitted with additional armour protection and with armament and defence packages specifically designed to withstand the blast of a roadside bomb or to defeat guerrilla forces in a close-quarter, urban battle where the ability to fire and manoeuvre is limited and civilian populations may be threatened.

Global demands

During United Nations peacekeeping operations and the efforts of NATO forces to quell ethnic violence, particularly in the Balkans and East Africa, major armoured contingents from the United States, Great Britain and other nations of Europe and the Middle East have deployed to these troubled areas. These forces' armoured cars, infantry fighting vehicles and armoured fighting vehicles have proved essential for maintaining security for military and civilian areas, while providing rapid mobility in rugged terrain.

Gulf War – Coalition forces
1991

Trained and prepared for a war against the forces of the Warsaw Pact on the plains of northern Europe, major Coalition armoured assets from the United States and Great Britain entered combat in the desert.

IN RESPONSE TO THE IRAQI INVASION of Kuwait, an armed Coalition of 29 nations mounted an offensive effort on a scale not seen since World War II in an effort to liberate the tiny Arab state. A massive logistical undertaking ensued, as Coalition forces were concentrated from around the globe, many coming from bases in Europe and half a world away in the United States. Operation Desert Shield involved the movement of hundreds of thousands of personnel and millions of tonnes of equipment to staging areas in Saudi Arabia and other Middle East nations.

Primary among the engines of war brought to bear were the main battle tanks and armoured fighting vehicles of the Coalition forces. These included the American M1A1 Abrams, the British Challenger and the French AMX-30, designed and built for a confrontation against the Warsaw Pact in Europe but destined for a confrontation with the Soviet-designed T-72M main battle tanks and armoured vehicles of the Iraqi Army and its elite Republican Guard divisions.

Abrams arrival

When the US 24th Infantry Division and its mechanized units reached Saudi Arabia in the autumn of 1990, its equipment included the first Abrams tanks in theatre. Many of these were the initial configuration of the M1. Eventually, more than 1800 examples of the Abrams tank were deployed during the Gulf War, and more than 800 field modifications were made to upgrade to the M1A1, which bore the brunt of the tank-versus-tank fighting between US and Iraqi forces.

The development of the M1 Abrams may be traced to the late 1960s, more than two decades prior to the vehicle seeing its first combat in 1991. It entered service in 1980 as a replacement for the ageing M60 Patton tanks then in use with the US Army. However, some Patton upgrades, primarily the

▲ **M2 Bradley Infantry Fighting Vehicle**

US Army / 24th Mechanized Infantry Division / 3rd Armoured Cavalry Regiment
The 450kW (600hp) eight-cylinder Cummins VTA-903T diesel engine was capable of delivering road speeds of 64km/h (40mph), and the heavily armed M2 Bradley infantry fighting vehicle proved particularly adept at desert warfare.

Specifications

Crew: 3 + 6	Speed: 64km/h (40mph)
Weight: 22,940kg (50,574lb)	Range: 483km (300 miles)
Length: 6.55m (21ft 6in)	Armament: 1 x 25mm (1in) Bushmaster Chain
Width: 3.61m (11ft 9in)	Gun, plus 2 x TOW missile launchers and
Height (turret roof): 2.57m (8ft 5in)	1 x 7.62mm (0.3in) MG
Engine: 450kW (600hp) Cummins VTA-903T	Radio: n/k
turbocharged 8-cylinder diesel	

M60A1 and M60A3, were engaged during the Gulf War. The early Abrams incorporated several improvements over the M60, including better crew survivability, with ammunition stored as far from crew areas as possible and subsequently a blast door in the turret bustle, which separated ammunition from the crew compartment. Additionally, specialized blow-out armour was designed to distribute the impact of an explosion to further minimize casualties. Composite armour similar to the British Chobham was also installed. Early M1 tanks were armed with the 105mm (4.1in) M68 rifled cannon; however, as the M1 programme went into full production, the decision was made to upgun the tank with the M256

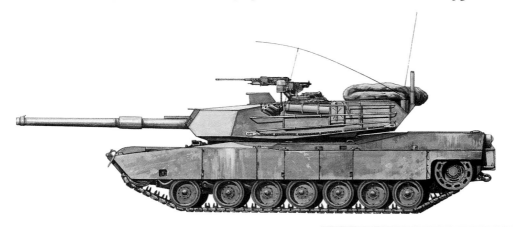

▲ M1A1 Abrams Main Battle Tank
US Army / 1st Armoured Division / 3rd Armored Brigade

The M1A1 Abrams main battle tank dominated the Gulf War battlefield and revealed the extent to which its FLIR (forward-looking infrared) sights could be effective at night. The M1A1 could fix and destroy Iraqi targets often before the opponent was aware of its presence.

Specifications

Crew: 4	AGT 1500 gas turbine
Weight: 57,154kg (126,024lb)	Speed: 67km/h (42mph)
Length (over gun): 9.77m (32ft 3in)	Range: 465km (289 miles)
Width: 3.66m (12ft)	Armament: 1 x 120mm (4.7in) M256 gun; 1 x
Height: 2.44m (8ft)	12.7mm (0.5in) MG; 2 x 7.62mm (0.3in) MGs
Engine: 1119.4kW (1500hp) Textron Lycoming	Radio: n/k

▲ M60A3 Patton Medium Tank
US Marine Expeditionary Force / 1st Tank Battalion

The M60A3 variant of the Patton tank series was deployed to the Gulf and featured improvements such as the latest in APFSDS (armour-piercing fin-stabilized discarding sabot) ammunition, laser rangefinding equipment, smoke dischargers, gun stabilization and thermal imaging night sights.

Specifications

Crew: 4	1790-2A V12 turbocharged diesel
Weight: 52,617kg (51.8 tons)	Speed: 48km/h (30mph)
Length (over gun): 9.44m (31ft)	Range: 500km (311 miles)
Width: 3.63m (11ft 11in)	Armament: 1 x 105mm (4.1in) M68 gun; 1 x
Height: 3.27m (10ft 8in)	12.7mm (0.5in) HMG; 1 x 7.62mm (0.3in) MG
Engine: 559.7kW (750hp) Continental AVDS-	Radio: n/k

120mm (4.7in) smoothbore cannon, adapted for the Abrams from the Rheinmetall gun which equipped the German Leopard 2 main battle tank.

Nearly 3300 M1s were built during the first five years of production, and by 1986 the M1A1 upgrade programme included a more sophisticated NBC (nuclear, biological and chemical) defence suite, upgraded armour protection and improvements to the tank suspension. Throughout its service life, one of the most controversial components of the Abrams has been its 1120kW (1500hp) gas turbine engine. A fierce debate as to the adoption of the gas turbine or a more traditional diesel engine had concluded with the former winning out. Its power-to-weight ratio resulted in greater power without appreciable added weight; however, the engine was a voracious consumer of fuel, presenting a logistical challenge. In numerous configurations, the M1 Abrams main battle tank has been exported to Saudi Arabia, Egypt, Australia and Kuwait.

Bradley breakthrough

Both the infantry (M2) and cavalry (M3) variants of the Bradley fighting vehicle compiled impressive combat records during the Gulf War. Having entered service in 1981, the Bradley had survived at least 15 years of controversial, scandal-ridden development. The Bradley mounted a McDonnell Douglas M242

25mm (1in) chain gun, capable of penetrating the thin skins of Iraqi BMP-1 armoured vehicles, along with the effective TOW anti-tank missile system. It had a crew of three and also transported a squad of six combat infantrymen.

British behemoth

The road to deployment for the British Challenger tank had been somewhat circuitous by the time of the Gulf War. The Challenger had been originally designed for export to Iran as the Shir Iran 2 main battle tank, but the order for delivery was promptly cancelled in 1980 after the regime of the Shah had been overthrown by the Islam-inspired Iranian revolution. The cooperative MBT-80 tank programme had failed in Britain and Germany, and the Shir Iran 2 project was adapted for use by the British Army as the Challenger, which was eventually expected to replace the Cold War-era Chieftain. The decision was made following consideration of the purchase of either the American Abrams or the German Leopard 2.

The Challenger mounted the L11A5 120mm (4.7in) gun, carried over from the Chieftain, and employed advanced composite Chobham armour, which was named for the location of the Fighting Vehicle Research and Development Establishment where the material was developed. The armour itself

▲ **Challenger 1 Main Battle Tank**

Britsh Army / 1st Armoured Division / 7th Armoured Brigade

The Challenger 1 main battle tank employed innovative Chobham armour and a powerful 120mm (4.7in) main gun during the 1991 Gulf War. Its service life was somewhat limited, and by 2000 it had been replaced by the heavily redesigned Challenger 2.

Specifications

Crew: 4	Range: 400km (250 miles)
Weight: 62,000kg (136,400lb)	Armament: 1 x 120mm (4.7in) L11A5 gun,
Length (gun forward): 11.56m (35ft 4in)	plus 2 x 7.62mm (0.3in) MGs and 2 x smoke
Width: 3.52m (10ft 8in)	dischargers
Height: 2.5m (7ft 5in)	Radio: Long range, directional communications
Engine: 895kW (1200hp) liquid-cooled diesel	system with satellite relay capabilities
Speed: 55km/h (35mph)	

▲ **Desert Storm**

A British Challenger 1 main battle tank waits by the Basra–Kuwait Highway near Kuwait City following the retreat of Iraqi forces during Operation Desert Storm. In the background are British armoured personnel carriers and a wrecked garbage truck.

had come about in an effort to improve tank survivability against a new generation of ammunition and anti-tank weapons. Offering equivalent protection to much greater thicknesses of rolled homogeneous steel, Chobham was to prove effective against the modern APFSDS (armour-piercing fin-stabilized discarding sabot) ammunition, although most of the ammunition available to Iraqi forces was of older HEAT (high-explosive anti-tank) types.

The Challenger also retained the armour side skirts of the Chieftain and much of its predecessor's suspension. The powerplant consisted of an 895kW (1200hp) V12 diesel engine. Modifications resulted in a total of four variants, or marks, being produced. The Challenger served as the primary British main battle tank during the 1991 Gulf War, and its performance was exemplary. Only with the development of the Challenger 2 did the Gulf War tank assume the designation of Challenger 1.

More than 400 Challenger 1 tanks were built; the first of them had been delivered to the British Army in 1983, initially to the Royal Hussars. By 2000, the majority of the Challenger 1 models had been retired from active service with the British Army. The Jordanian Army purchased 288 upgraded Challenger 1 tanks from Great Britain and placed them in service as the Al Hussein.

Lethal efficiency

While the 1991 Gulf War cannot firmly establish the dominance of the Coalition armoured forces over those of the Warsaw Pact, it is known that in the event the Iraqi tanks were no match for their opponents. True enough, the Iraqis utilized export variants of the Soviet main battle tanks, failed to maintain their equipment to its highest degree of efficiency and were denied the latest in ammunition and technological upgrades. Coalition tanks outranged their Iraqi opponents substantially and were regularly able to destroy targets at stand-off distances. Still, the greatest disparity between the armoured forces was determined to be the level of training and combat efficiency of the tank crews themselves. US and British tank crews had trained for endless hours, the Americans becoming quite familiar with the execution of the AirLand Battle Doctrine initially formulated for combat in Europe but equally effective in the deserts of the Middle East. Coalition tank crews worked in coordinated and effective combat teams, including mechanized infantry, armour and armoured cavalry with tactical air support.

Combined with the high level of combat-readiness exhibited by the Coalition armoured forces, the superior technology of the M1A1 Abrams and the Challenger were devastating. During the Gulf War, the Challenger was credited with the destruction of approximately 300 Iraqi tanks and armoured vehicles without a single loss to enemy fire. The M1A1 Abrams amassed a similar record. For example, during the battle of 73 Easting, the US 3rd Brigade, 1st Infantry Division destroyed 60 Iraqi tanks and 35 armoured fighting vehicles. At Medina Ridge, nearly 100 Iraqi armoured vehicles were destroyed. Only 18 Abrams tanks were lost during the Gulf War, and the majority of these were due to incidents of friendly fire.

▲ **Centurion AVRE**

British Army / Royal Armoured Corps / 2nd Royal Tank Regiment

The chassis of the Centurion main battle tank provided the platform for a number of variants. During Operation Desert Storm, the Centurion AVRE (Armoured Vehicle Royal Engineers) mounted a 165mm (6.5in) demolition gun and was often equipped with a dozer blade.

Specifications

Crew: 5
Weight: 51,809kg (113,979lb)
Length: 8.69m (28ft 6in)
Width: 3.96m (13ft)
Height: 3m (9ft 10in)
Engine: 484.7kW (650hp) Rolls-Royce Meteor Mk IVB 12-cylinder petrol

Speed: 34.6km/h (21.5mph)
Range: 177km (110 miles)
Armament: 1 x 165mm (6.5in) demolition gun, plus 2 x 7.62mm (0.3in) MGs (1 coaxial, 1 anti-aircraft)
Radio: n/k

Specifications

Crew: 1
Weight: 3050kg (6710lb)
Length: 4.67m (15ft 4in)
Width: 1.79m (5ft 11in)
Height: 2.03m (6ft 8in)
Engine: 100kW (134hp) V-8 water-cooled petrol
Speed: 105km/h (65.6mph)
Range: 748km (465 miles)
Armament: 2 x 7.62mm (0.3in) MGs

▲ **SAS Land Rover**

British Army / 22nd Special Air Service / A Squadron

The long-serving SAS Land Rover was deployed with British Special Air Service units during Operation Desert Storm, one of its primary missions being the transport of SAS teams deep behind enemy lines on search-and-destroy missions against mobile Iraqi Scud missile sites.

4th Dragoon Regiment, 1991

The standard French armoured regiment of the Gulf War included a company of AMX-10P infantry combat vehicles and a complement of 18 AMX-30 main battle tanks arranged in a headquarters detachment and three squadrons. The AMX-30 had been produced since the mid-1960s and mounted a 105mm (4.1in) main gun. It also served with the armies of Saudi Arabia, Spain, Qatar and Iraq.

HQ (3 x AMX-30 MBT)

Armoured Squadron 1 (5 x AMX-30 MBTs: 1 HQ + 4)

Armoured Squadron 2 (5 x AMX-30 MBTs: 1 HQ + 4)

Armoured Squadron 3 (5 x AMX-30 MBTs: 1 HQ + 4)

Mechanized Infantry Company (6 x AMX-10P ICV)

Specifications

Crew: 4

Weight: 35,941kg (79,072lb)

Length: 9.48m (31ft 1in)

Width: 3.1m (10ft 2in)

Height: 2.86m (9ft 4in)

Engine: 537kW (720hp) Hispano-Suiza

12-cylinder diesel

Speed: 65km/h (40mph)

Range: 600km (373 miles)

Armament: 1 x 105mm (4.1in) gun; 1 x 20mm
(0.79in) cannon; 1 x 7.62mm (0.3in) MG

Radio: n/k

▲ **AMX-30 Main Battle Tank**

French Army / Sixth Light Armoured Division / 4th Dragoon Regiment

In addition to its main armament, the French AMX-30, developed by GIAT, also mounted a powerful 20mm (0.79in) autocannon. Many of the French tanks deployed during Desert Storm were the AMX-30B with an improved transmission and engine performance, as well as the capability of firing updated ammunition.

Gulf War – Iraqi forces
1991

Although Saddam Hussein had built the Iraqi Army into the fourth largest in the world, its inferior equipment and inadequate training were incapable of withstanding the Coalition air and ground assaults.

B Y 1990, THE IRAQI ARMY included both infantry and armoured formations that had been hardened by eight years of costly combat with neighbouring Iran. Saddam Hussein had continued to import main battle tanks of Soviet design, particularly the T-72M and its sub-variants, manufactured in the Soviet Union and in the Warsaw Pact nations of Poland and Czechoslovakia.

Armed with the 125mm (4.9in) 2A46M smoothbore gun, the T-72M mounted formidable firepower. Its powerplant consisted of a 585kW (780hp) 12-cylinder diesel engine, and its improved models were equipped with ceramic composite and steel appliqué armour.

Early T-72 export models were specifically designed for the Middle East market, and initial deliveries of the T-72M to Iraq were undertaken in 1980 soon after the war with Iran broke out. During the subsequent decade, the Iraqi armoured force

INSIGNIA

The red triangle insignia was the emblem of the elite Republican Guards divisions of the Iraqi Army. During Operation Desert Storm, Republican Guards armoured formations were devastated by Coalition tanks during battles such as Medina Ridge on 27 February 1991.

mirrored the organizational structure of Western armies, particularly that of the British. Tactically, it was influenced by Soviet advisors who had been offered to instruct Iraqi crews in the operation of the T-72M.

During the Gulf War, the Iraqi armoured force included the mechanized *Tawakalna* Division and the *Medina* and *Hammurabi* Armoured Divisions of the elite Republican Guard, and the 3rd *Saladin* Division of the regular army. Organizationally, these

▲ **T-55 Main Battle Tank**

Iraqi Army / Tawakalna Division (Mechanized)

The Iraqis modified the T-55 with more armour plating, the addition of 160mm (6.3in) mortars and an observation mast. Some Iraqi T-55s had been fitted with a 105mm (4.1in) main gun, converting this antiquated tank into a tank killer capable of firing armour-piercing rounds. The *Tawakalna* Division suffered heavy losses of AFVs at the Battle of 73 Easting on 26 February, 1991 – the first ground defeat of a Republican Guard unit.

Specifications

Crew: 4	Speed: 48km/h (30mph)
Weight: 39.7 tonnes (39 tons)	Range: 400km (250 miles)
Length (hull): 6.45m (21ft 2in)	Armament: 1 x 100mm (3.9in) D-10T gun, plus
Width: 3.27m (10ft 9in)	1 x 12.7mm (0.5in) DShK AA MG mounted on
Height: 2.4m (7ft 10in)	turret and 2 x 7.62mm (0.3in) DT MGs
Engine: 433kW (581hp) V-55 12-cylinder	Radio: R-130

▶ **Defunct**
An abandoned Iraqi T-72 main battle tank remains on a battlefield after Coalition forces claimed the area during Operation Desert Storm.

included several hundred tanks each, and total Iraqi armoured strength during the Gulf War was estimated at more than 3500 main battle tanks with approximately one-third of them T-72 export variants. While the Republican Guard divisions received the most modern equipment, a number of older T-55s and T-62s, as well as Chinese-built Type 59 and Type 69 tanks, were fielded.

The Type 59 and Type 69 were among the first main battle tanks developed in China, and these were known to have been exported to Iraq during the early 1980s. Based upon the Soviet T-54 and components of the T-62, which had been captured during the brief Sino-Soviet border conflict of 1969, these tanks primarily mounted 105mm (4.1in) main guns, although some were reported with 160mm (6.3in) mortars and even 125mm (4.9in) cannon. Some examples that survived the Gulf War remained in service into the twenty-first century.

Air assault

Although the Iraqi armoured formations were indeed a force to be reckoned with, the Coalition air offensive that preceded the ground assault in early 1991 substantially degraded the combat efficiency of the Iraqis. When the ground phase of Operation Desert Storm commenced, estimates of the destruction wrought against Iraqi tank capability ran as high as 40 per cent.

Tactical Coalition air support from fixed-wing and rotary aircraft was also substantial, including the devastating fire of the AH-64 Apache and the AH-1 Cobra attack helicopters. In contrast, Iraqi air assets were neutralized early in the campaign, and although some Soviet-made attack helicopters may have been available for service, they played no significant role in the war.

Technological trap

Given that the T-72M deployed by the Iraqi Army during Operation Desert Storm was the export version of the main battle tank, the latest in Soviet technology was unavailable to Saddam Hussein. In fact, the bulk of the T-72 variants sold to Iraq during the mid-1980s and beyond may have been manufactured in Poland and Czechoslovakia.

Although automated to a certain extent, the tank's acquisition and destruction of targets included several manual steps. Laser rangefinding and infrared sighting equipment were installed on the most recent Iraqi T-72s; however, the most current T-72M1 was at least a decade behind its Coalition adversaries in technological capabilities. Iraqi tactics had been influenced by the war with Iran, during which enemy forces sometimes amassed human wave attacks. These were often repulsed by Iraqi artillery, which devastated large formations of exposed infantry but also resulted in a great dependence on artillery by the Iraqi Army.

The lack of adequate training further reduced the combat capabilities of the Iraqi tank crews, which often attempted to compensate for their shortcomings by fighting from prepared revetments or dug-in positions, presighting their weapons to certain distances and failing to coordinate their efforts. Total Iraqi losses in tanks and armoured vehicles during the Gulf War were staggering, including at least 3000 tanks and up to 2800 other armoured vehicles, most of which were Soviet-designed BMP-1 amphibious infantry fighting vehicles, which had been developed in the mid-1960s and carried up to eight combat infantrymen.

The Balkans independence wars

Josip Broz Tito, the communist strongman who had held Yugoslavia together since World War II, died in 1980. The fracture of the unified country ensued, with low-intensity guerrilla warfare erupting during a wave of unrest.

A S THE SIX REPUBLICS OF THE FORMER YUGOSLAVIA asserted independence, the Yugoslav People's Army attempted to maintain control of the disintegrating country. While their armoured forces might intimidate separatists in certain situations, it was apparent that guerrilla warfare would lessen the effectiveness of tanks and armoured vehicles. Therefore during fighting in Slovenia, Bosnia and Herzegovina, and Kosovo, Yugoslav and later Serbian armoured forces were utilized to varying degrees.

While the Yugoslav armed forces included a number of Cold War-era T-55 main battle tanks and other vehicles, the M-84, designed in the late 1970s and manufactured under licence in communist Yugoslavia, was also fielded. The M-84 was a variant of the Soviet-designed T-72 and entered service in 1984; more than 600 examples of the tank were built

before production ceased in 1991. The 125mm (4.9in) 2A46 smoothbore gun was identical to that of the T-72, but the Yugoslavs made some modifications of their own to the tank, including providing a more powerful 750kW (1000hp) engine, a domestically produced computerized fire control system and composite armour. During the late 1980s, a number of M-84s were also exported to Kuwait by the Yugoslav government.

Realizing that their limited resources included few tanks and armoured vehicles, the separatist leaders for the most part engaged in clandestine operations meant to discourage the central Yugoslav government in Belgrade from interfering with the formation of independent states. The few tanks available to these forces included American-built M4 Shermans and Soviet T-34s, relics of World War II vintage.

▲ **Fire practice**

Members of the 2nd Guards Brigade of the Croatian Defence Council (HVO) Army fire a 12.7mm (0.5in) machine gun mounted on a T-55 main battle tank, during a three-day exercise. Armed forces in the former Yugoslavia mainly use upgraded Soviet-era hardware, including the evergreen T-55.

However, anti-tank weapons such as the Soviet RPG-7 and the German shoulder-fired Armbrust were also employed by guerrilla forces, while landmines were sown in great quantities.

NATO air and ground forces intervened during the Kosovo War in 1999, numerous nations contributing infantry and armoured units to the operation. The German-manufactured Leopard 1 main battle tanks of Danish forces deployed during the intervention were reported to have taken part in combat for the first time against Yugoslav forces. The Leopard 1 mounted a 105mm (4.1in) L7A3 rifled gun of British origin. Its armour protection was up to 70mm (2.76in) thick on its front glacis and turret.

During the independence wars waged in the early 1990s, the Yugoslav People's Army lost scores of tanks to guerrilla activity, while many more were captured and placed in service with the armies of the newly independent states. An estimated 80 M-84s and other tanks were destroyed or captured during the fighting with Slovenian separatists, and during the Battle of Vukovar approximately 100 Serbian tanks and armoured vehicles were destroyed by mines and Croatian troops firing rocket-propelled grenades. The Croatians captured nearly 150 tanks, many of them T-55s, during a series of engagements collectively known as the Battle of the Barracks during the autumn and winter of 1991.

Peacekeeping forces
1991–99

The endeavour to maintain world peace prevailed upon the armoured forces of numerous countries across the globe as political factions vied for control, and centuries-old ethnic tensions revived armed conflict.

THE ARMOURED FORCES of numerous NATO countries have recently been called upon in several instances to effect peace, enforce the mandates of the United Nations or protect civilian populations from atrocities. During the final decade of the twentieth century, peacekeeping forces were deployed to the Balkans, Cambodia, El Salvador, Mozambique, Rwanda, Somalia and other locations across the globe. In many cases, the armoured forces deployed with United Nations peacekeepers were instrumental in accomplishing the assigned tasks.

Patrolling large security zones and areas of territory is a requisite assignment for peacekeeping forces, and armoured cars and fighting vehicles have proved well suited to such duties. A variety of armoured vehicles, including the German Marder, the British Warrior, the US M2 Bradley and

▲ **US Army intervention**
Soldiers from the US 10th Mountain Division sit atop their MG-armed Humvees in Bosnia during peacekeeping operations in 2005.

the Russian BMP-1 have this sort of service. The British Alvis FV 107 Scimitar is representative of those armoured vehicles which have served in the Balkans. One of several such vehicles developed by the Alvis company, the Scimitar mounts a 30mm (1.18in) L21 RARDEN cannon that may be fired in automatic or single-round mode, along with a coaxial 7.62mm (0.3in) machine gun or L94A1 chain gun. Its thin armour plating of up to 12.7mm (0.5in) is effective against small-arms fire and shell fragments but vulnerable to larger-calibre weapons. Other than its powerful armament, the distinctive advantage of the FV 107 Scimitar is speed. Capable of reaching 80km/h (50mph) on the road, the Scimitar is a mobile enforcer and an effective scouting and patrol vehicle.

Humvee

Another well-known vehicle deployed with peacekeeping forces is the US-made High Mobility Multipurpose Wheeled Vehicle, popularly known as the Humvee. Although it was never intended as a frontline fighting vehicle, the Humvee has evolved into a light scouting or armoured car platform, mounting such diverse weaponry as the M2 12.7mm (0.5in) heavy machine gun or the M220 TOW anti-tank missile. The Humvee has been produced in at least 17 variants and is also utilized as a towing vehicle for light artillery or as an ambulance. Its eight-cylinder diesel engine is capable of delivering speeds of up to 144km/h (90mph); up to 105km/h

(65mph) in the case of an armoured variant. During the deployment of US forces to Somalia in December 1992, the Humvee became one of the most

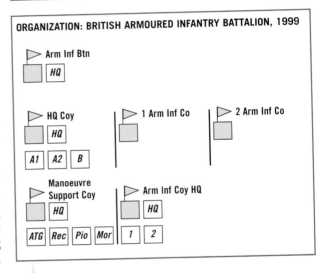

BRITISH ARMOURED INFANTRY BATTALION, 1999	
AFVS	Strength
Warrior IFV	57
Javelin ATGW	12
FV432 APC	21
Recce AFV	8
Personnel (all ranks)	741

ORGANIZATION: BRITISH ARMOURED INFANTRY BATTALION, 1999

FV510 Warrior Infantry Fighting Vehicle

British Army / 1st Armoured Division / 7th Armoured Brigade

The FV510 Warrior infantry fighting vehicle has been in service with the British Army since the 1980s, and more than 1000 units have been produced. Its troop capacity of seven combat-ready soldiers is complemented by a 30mm (1.18in) L21A1 cannon and a 7.62mm (0.3in) machine gun for close support.

Specifications

Crew: 3 + 7
Weight: 25,700kg (56,540lb)
Length: 6.34m (20ft 10in)
Width: 3.034m (10ft)
Height: 2.79m (9ft 2in)
Engine: 410kW (550hp) Perkins V8 diesel

Speed: 75km/h (46.8mph)
Range: 660km (412 miles)
Armament: 1 x 30mm (1.18in) RARDEN cannon, plus 1 x 7.62mm (0.3in) coaxial MG and 4 x smoke dischargers
Radio: Currently Bowman (originally Clansman)

recognized symbols of United Nations and NATO forces in the field. Practical experience in Somalia, particularly during the low-intensity guerrilla fighting which took place around the capital city of Mogadishu, made it readily apparent that the Humvee was vulnerable to rocket-propelled grenades, to some small arms and to powerful landmines and improvised explosive devices.

Although relatively few casualties were sustained among Humvee crewmen, an armoured upgrade

British Army, Armoured Infantry Battalion (1999)

The modern British armoured infantry battalion consists of three armoured infantry companies comprising 14 FV510 Warrior infantry fighting vehicles each, along with a battalion command Warrior vehicle. Transport capability is approximately 300 fully equipped combat troops. Lighter units, designated as mechanized infantry, are deployed in wheeled fighting vehicles such as the Saxon, manufactured since the mid-1980s by GKN Defence.

Battalion HQ

Armoured Infantry Company 1 (14 x Warrior IFV)

Armoured Infantry Company 2 (14 x Warrior IFV)

Armoured Infantry Company 3 (14 x Warrior IFV)

programme was initiated for the base vehicle. Field modification kits have been issued and installed on many of these. Since 1996, the armoured version of the Humvee, the M1114, has also been in production and has been deployed to the Balkans and the Middle East. The M1114 includes a more powerful turbocharged engine, air conditioning, an armoured passenger area and shatter-resistant glass.

Escape from Mogadishu

Perhaps the most enduring episode of the United Nations peacekeeping effort during the 1990s involved the US raid into Mogadishu to attempt the capture of a renegade Somali warlord. During the ensuing firefight, US Rangers suffered several casualties, while helicopters were shot down by rocket-propelled grenades. The incident, popularized in the book and film *Black Hawk Down*, ended with the Rangers evacuating their positions in Mogadishu following an 18-hour ordeal.

The evacuation was accomplished with the assistance of Pakistani and Malaysian peacekeeping forces stationed nearby. The Pakistanis assembled a relief column, which included the venerable M48 Patton tank and the Condor armoured personnel carrier. The Pakistani tanks provided covering fire, while troops deployed from the Malaysian Condors to assist the Rangers.

Designed by the German company Thyssen Henschel, the Rheinmetall Condor was a wheeled 4x4 vehicle with a capacity of up to 12 combat infantrymen. It was armed with a 20mm (0.79in) cannon and a secondary 7.62mm (0.3in) machine gun. During the rescue operation in Mogadishu, a Condor was struck by a round from a rocket-propelled grenade, killing one soldier.

Balkan bombardment

United Nations and NATO involvement in the Balkans included a large contingent of armoured forces opposed to tank formations of the Yugoslav People's Army and later Serbian forces. The UN and NATO forces included variants of the German Leopard 1 and 2 tanks under the flags of several nations, including Canada, Denmark and Italy; the French Leclerc main battle tank; the American M1A1 Abrams and its variants; and the British Challenger 1.

Confronting the generally inferior T-55 and M-84 tanks of the Yugoslav forces, these modern tanks provided heavy firepower and security for NATO and United Nations installations, while also safeguarding the civilian population. Another primary objective was to prevent the Yugoslav Army from redeploying its forces, particularly its armour, into secured areas.

Although the Leopard 2 has seen little combat during its service life, it has gone into harm's way in Kosovo and in Afghanistan. It continues to be regarded as one of the finest main battle tanks in the world. A considerable modernization of the Leopard 1, which had been developed during the 1960s, the Leopard 2 had a main armament upgrade with the Rheinmetall 120mm (4.7in) L55 smoothbore gun, while its 1120kW (1500hp) V12 twin turbodiesel engine is capable of delivering a respectable 72km/h (45mph) on the road. Its armour is a composite of steel, ceramic, tungsten and plastic.

▶ **Véhicule Blindé Léger (VBL) Anti-tank Vehicle**

French Army / 3rd Mechanized Brigade

Operating with the French Army since 1990, the VBL anti-tank vehicle combines mobility and firepower. Capable of a top road speed of 95km/h (59mph), it mounts a variety of weapons systems, including the medium-range MILAN anti-tank missile and the short-range ERYX missile unit.

Specifications
Crew: 2 or 3
Weight: 3550kg (7828lb)
Length: 3.87m (12ft 8in)
Width: 2.02m (6ft 7in)
Height: 1.7m (5ft 7in)
Engine: 78kW (105hp) Peugeot XD3T 4-cylinder turbo diesel
Speed: 95km/h (59mph)
Range: 600km (370 miles)
Armament: 1 x MILAN ATGM launcher, plus 1 x 7.62mm (0.3in) GPMG
Radio: VHF system with two PR4G radios, an HF System with one SSB radio for long range and a radio/intercom system for the crew

FV107 Scimitar Light Tank

British Army / Royal Horse Guards and First Dragoons

Often designated as either a light tank or an armoured fighting vehicle, the FV107 is also ideal for reconnaissance with its combination of speed and firepower. Its crew of three has provided valuable intelligence during several deployments, along with direct infantry support.

Specifications

Crew: 3
Weight: 7800kg (17,160lb)
Length: 4.8m (15ft 9in)
Width: 2.24m (7ft 4in)
Height: 2.1m (6ft 11in)
Engine: 142kW (190hp) Jaguar 4.2-litre petrol
Speed: 80km/h (50mph)
Range: 644km (402 miles)
Armament: 1 x 30mm (1.18in) RARDEN cannon,
    plus 1 x 12.7mm (0.5in) MG
Radio: Clansman VRC 353

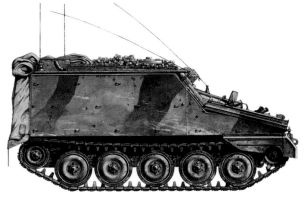

Specifications

Crew: 6
Weight: 14,300kg (31,500lb)
Length: 5.7m (18ft 8in)
Width: 2.67m (8ft 9in)
Height: 1.92m (6ft 3in)
Engine: 186kW (250hp) SOFAM 8Gxb
    8-cylinder petrol
Speed: 60km/h (37mph)
Range: 350km (220 miles)
Armament: None
Radio: 4 x radios (various)

◀ FV105 Sultan CVR(T)

British Army / 1st Mechanized Brigade / 2nd Royal Tank Regiment

A command and control vehicle deployed with British Army units, the FV105 Sultan carries a crew of up to six and provides mobile space for radio equipment as well as tactical planning. Developed in the late 1970s, it is based on the chassis of the Alvis FV101 Scorpion.

Dingo APC

German Army / 13th Mechanized Infantry Division

Developed by Krauss-Maffei Wegmann during the mid-1990s, the Dingo armoured personnel carrier is a multi-purpose vehicle deployed primarily by the German Army and capable of transporting troops, supplies and equipment, or combat casualties. The Dingo also serves in a reconnaissance and light air defence role. The Dingo has been used for patrol and transport missions by German forces during peacekeeping missions in Kosovo and Macedonia.

Specifications

Crew: 5 to 8
Weight: 8.8–11.9 tonnes (8.6–11.7 tons)
Length: 5.45m (17ft 10.56in)
Width: 2.3m (7ft 6in)
Height: 2.5m (8ft 2.4in)
Engine: 160kW (215hp) diesel
Speed: 90km/h (56mph)
Range: 1000km (621 miles)
Armament: 1 x 7.62mm (0.3in) MG
Radio: n/k

Specifications

Crew: 5

Weight: 45,000kg (99,225lb)

Length: 7.2m (23ft 8in)

Width: 3.4m (11ft 2in)

Height: 3m (9ft 10in)

Engine: 492kW (660hp) Cummins V8 diesel

Speed: 55km/h (34 mph)

Range: 240km (150 miles)

Armament: 1 x 155mm (6.1in) howitzer, plus

   1 x 12.7mm (0.5in) MG

Radio: n/k

▲ **AS-90 SP Gun**

British Army / 3rd Regiment Royal Horse Artillery

Developed during the mid-1980s and built by the Vickers company, the AS-90 self-propelled gun mounts the 155mm (6.1in) L39 gun atop its tracked chassis. Entering service in 1993, the AS-90 replaced the 105mm (4.1in) equipped Abbot and M109 self propelled guns then in service.

Former Yugoslav forces
1991–99

The break-up of the former Yugoslavia during the 1990s resulted in the formation of armed forces in those autonomous states which emerged, following a series of wars spurred largely by ancient ethnic animosity and territorial ambitions.

DURING FOUR YEARS OF FIGHTING from 1991 to 1995, the armoured vehicles of the Yugoslav People's Army, including the Soviet-made T-54/55 main battle tank and the M-84 tank, a variant of the widely produced Soviet T-72 which was manufactured in Yugoslavia, were pitted against militias, guerrilla forces and paramilitary units in the provinces of Bosnia, Slovenia and Croatia, while the central government in Belgrade came under the increasing influence of Serbia and its despotic leader Slobodan Milosevic.

On the eve of the collapse of the Socialist Federal Republic of Yugoslavia, the nation possessed a potent array of armoured vehicles, although some had certainly reached the age of functional obsolescence. With the brigade as its largest operational unit, the Yugoslav People's Army possessed several armoured and mechanized infantry formations, including more than 1600 tanks. While the number was impressive, the most advanced tank of the Yugoslav People's

Army was most likely its own licence-built M-84 clone of the Soviet T-72. Several hundred armoured personnel carriers were available for service; however, many of these were also of inferior quality due to age and poor maintenance. Regardless, these weapons found continued use in the armed forces of the independent nations that had once been part of the greater Yugoslavia.

During the Ten-Day War for Slovenian independence, few tanks were available to counter the armoured formations of the Yugoslav People's Army; however, the reality of the situation dictated that the Yugoslavs deploy their forces warily. The threat of anti-tank weapons such as the RPG-7 and German Armbrust was ever-present, while landmines and improvised explosive devices were a favoured weapon of the irregular forces. An estimated 20 Yugoslav tanks were destroyed and more than 40 captured during the brief conflict. Afterwards, the government of Slovenia, and in turn its armed forces, assumed control of all Yugoslav military equipment within Slovenian borders.

Some Croatian forces were reported to have utilized both the American M4 Sherman and the Soviet T-34, both of which traced their roots to the 1930s. The Croats executed a series of offensive actions known as the Battle of the Barracks during late 1991 and captured large stockpiles of light weapons, as well as artillery pieces and a significant number of all-important armoured vehicles. At one barracks alone, the attackers secured more than 70 T-55 tanks and nearly 90 armoured personnel carriers of various types.

During the protracted Battle of Vukovar, more than 100 Yugoslav T-55 and M-84 tanks besieged the Croatian city but suffered serious losses to anti-tank missiles, mines and the diminished effect of armoured firepower in urban conditions. A great variety of armoured personnel carriers, fighting vehicles, self-propelled guns and light tanks were utilized by both sides. Throughout more than three years of fighting in Bosnia alone, the warring factions deployed an estimated 1200 tanks of various types.

Among the most common armoured vehicles in the formations of the Yugoslav People's Army and those of the later independent states were the Soviet-

Specifications

Crew: 3 + 7	Engine: 193kW (260hp) V8 diesel
Weight: 13,600kg (23,000lb)	Speed: 90km/h (56mph)
Length: 7.65m (25ft 1in)	Range: 600km (370 miles)
Width: 2.9m (9ft 6in)	Armament: 1 x 14.5mm (0.57in) KPVT MG, plus
Height: 2.46m (8ft .8in)	1 x 7.62mm (0.3in) coaxial PKT MG

▲ BTR-80 Armoured Personnel Carrier

Yugoslav People's Army / 1st Guards Mechanized Division

The BTR-80 armoured personnel carrier entered production during the 1980s and was based on previous designs such as the BTR-70. The Soviets had modified the hull of the BTR-80 to allow greater traverse for its two machine-gun mounts.

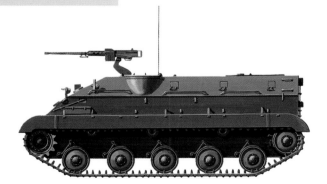

▲ M-60P Tracked Armoured Personnel Carrier

Slovenian Army / 10th Motorized Battalion

Produced in Yugoslavia, the M-60P armoured personnel carrier is fully tracked and capable of transporting up to 10 combat infantrymen. Its troop compartment is cramped due to the necessity to store ammunition, and its armament consists of a pair of machine guns.

Specifications

Crew: 3 + 10	Engine: 104kW (140hp) FAMOS 6-cylinder diesel
Weight: 11,000kg (24,300lb)	Speed: 45km/h (28mph)
Length: 5.02m (16ft 5in)	Range: 400km (250 miles)
Width: 2.77m (9ft 1in)	Armament: 1 x 7.62mm (0.31in) M53 MG
Height: 2.39m (7ft 10in)	Radio: n/k

designed BTR-80 and its predecessors. Production of the wheeled 8X8 BTR-80 was undertaken in the mid-1980s to replace the older BTR-60 and BTR-70 vehicles. However, these remained in service throughout the fighting in the Balkans, as well as the BTR-152, BTR-40 and BTR-50.

The BTR-80 had been used extensively by the armed forces of the Soviet Union and Russia. Manned by a crew of three, its troop-carrying capacity is up to seven fully loaded combat

infantrymen. Its main armament is a 14.5mm (0.57in) machine gun, which may be used for infantry support or in defence against low-flying aircraft. Its top road speed is 80km/h (50mph).

The Yugoslavs produced their own armoured personnel carrier, which they had deployed to mechanized units in large numbers by 1990. The M-60P was originally based upon the chassis of an artillery prime mover and was manned by a crew of three with capacity for up to 10 combat troops. Its

▲ M53/59 Praga SP Anti-aircraft Gun
Yugoslav People's Army / 51st Mechanized Brigade

Dating to the 1950s, the M53/59 Praga self-propelled anti-aircraft gun fielded twin 30mm (1.18in) cannon atop the Praga six-wheeled truck chassis. The gun could also be removed from the truck and operated independently. The crew of four was protected during relocation by an armoured compartment.

Specifications

Crew: 2 + 4	Engine: 82kW (110hp) Tatra T912-2
Weight: 10,300kg (22,660lb)	6-cylinder diesel
Length: 6.92m (22ft 8in)	Speed: 60km/h (37mph)
Width: 2.35m (7ft 9in)	Range: 500km (311 miles)
Height: 2.585m (8ft 6in)	Armament: 2 x 30mm (1.18in) guns

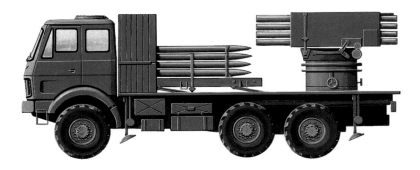

Specifications

Crew: 5	Engine: 191kW (256hp) 8-cylinder diesel
Weight: 22,400kg (49,400lb)	Speed: 80km/h (50mph)
Length: 11.5m (37ft 7in)	Range: 600km (370 miles)
Width: 2.49m (8ft 2in)	Armament: 32 + 32 x M-77 or M-91 rockets, plus
Height: 3.1m (10ft 2in)	1 x 12.7mm (0.5in) HMG
	Radio: None

▲ LVRS M-77 Oganj MLRS
Serbian Army / 2nd Land Force Brigade

Mounting 32 tubes for launching 128mm (5in) rockets, the LVRS M-77 Oganj proved a devastating weapons system during the Yugoslav Wars. Introduced in 1975 following several years of development in Yugoslavia, it is still in use today with the Serbian armed forces.

defence against attacking infantry was provided by the M53 7.92mm (0.31in) machine gun, a Yugoslav version of the venerable German MG 42. A variant of the vehicle, the M-60PB, mounted a pair of 82mm (3.2in) recoilless rifles.

Another armoured personnel carrier, built in Yugoslavia during the 1970s, was available in large numbers to all contending forces. At the beginning of hostilities, the Yugoslav People's Army possessed more than 400 examples of the M-980, which transported eight infantrymen and mounted either the Soviet AT-3 anti-tank missile or a 20mm (0.79in) cannon.

In addition to the elderly M4 Sherman, M47 Patton and T-34 tanks, and even some 100 American M3 half-tracks, pressed into service during the Balkan Wars, the Czech-manufactured M53/59 Praga anti-aircraft gun, mounted on a wheeled vehicle and first manufactured in the 1950s, was deployed by the Yugoslavs. The LVRS M-77 Oganj was a multiple-launch rocket system first developed in Yugoslavia during the late 1960s. The Cold War veteran PT-76 light amphibious tank, once seen in great numbers in the Soviet Red Army, was also utilized in the Balkans.

▲ M-80 Mechanized Infantry Combat Vehicle (MICV)

Serbian Land Forces / 17th Mechanized Battalion

Conceived as an improvement to the M-980 armoured vehicle, which had been produced in large numbers, the M-80 mounts anti-tank missiles or a 30mm (1.18in) cannon. It entered production in 1980 and has been produced in several variants.

Specifications

Crew: 3 + 7	turbo diesel
Weight: 13,700kg (30,200lb)	Speed: 60km/h (37mph)
Length: 6.4m (20ft 11in)	Range: 500km (310 miles)
Width: 2.59m (8ft 5in)	Armament: 2 x Yugoslav Sagger ATGWs or 1 x
Height: 2.3m (7ft 6in)	30mm (1.18in) cannon; 1 x 7.62mm (0.3in) MG
Engine: 194kW (260hp) HS-115-2 8-cylinder	Radio: n/k

Specifications

Crew: 2 + 17	Engine: 82kW (110hp) ZIL-123 6-cylinder
Weight: 8950kg (19,690lb)	Speed (road): 75km/h (47mph)
Length: 6.83m (22ft 4.9in)	Range: 780km (485 miles)
Width: 2.32m (7ft 7.3in)	Armament: 1 x 7.62mm (0.3in) MG
Height: 2.05m (6ft 8.7in)	

▲ BTR-152 Wheeled APC

Yugoslav People's Army

More than 200 Soviet-made BTR-152, BTR-40 and BTR-50 armored personnel carriers were available to the Yugoslav People's Army when the civil war broke out in the early 1990s. All of these had been purchased from the Soviet Army in the 1960s and 1970s.

The Caucasus
1991–PRESENT

Following the demise of the Soviet Union, the region of the Caucasus has been the focus of armed conflict involving the military forces of Russia and the former Soviet republic of Georgia, as well as counterinsurgency operations in Chechnya.

THE DEMANDS OF MODERN COMBAT have required that the Russian military continue to develop and modernize its armoured fighting vehicles during the last 20 years. The continuing unrest in Chechnya and its low-intensity counterinsurgency war, as well as the need for upgraded weapons systems to maintain some semblance of parity with the West, have given rise to the T-90 main battle tank.

In production since the mid-1990s, the T-90 is based on the design of the T-72, one of the most widely produced tanks in history. The survivor of a challenge from the Soviet-era holdover T-80U, the T-90 incorporates a 125mm (4.9in) smoothbore gun that is also capable of firing anti-tank guided missiles. Its main armament and some of its target acquisition equipment were borrowed from the T-80U. Powered by a 12-cylinder, 630kW (840hp) engine, the T-90 is capable of a top road speed of 65km/h (40mph), comparable to Western main battle tanks. Its armour protection consists of steel, aluminum and plastic composite, reinforced by Kontakt explosive reactive armour that diminishes the penetrating capability of modern ammunition, and electronic counter-measures that include jamming equipment to ward off anti-tank guided missiles.

Infantry support

Numerous weapons systems that originated in the former Soviet Union have been retained or improved by Russian engineers. Among these are the BMP-2 and BMP-3 infantry fighting vehicles. By the mid-1970s, Soviet designers had become aware of the deficiencies of their BMP-1 infantry fighting vehicle, which had proved vulnerable to even 12.7mm (0.5in) machine-gun fire during service with Egyptian forces during the Yom Kippur War of 1973. The BMP-2 entered production in the Soviet Union after 1980 with improved armour protection and is armed with the 9M113 Konkurs anti-tank missile system and a 30mm (1.18in) 2A42 autocannon, complemented by a 7.62mm (0.3in) machine gun for close defence. Its troop-carrying capacity is up to seven combat infantrymen.

▲ **M1974 SP Howitzer**

Russian Ground Forces / 5th Guards Tank Division

Mounting a 122mm (4.8in) main gun, the 2S1 Gvozdika (Carnation) self-propelled howitzer has been known in the West as the M1974, referencing the year in which it was first observed in public. Several former Soviet republics maintain the M1974 in their inventories today.

Specifications

Crew: 4	Engine: 179kW (240hp) YaMZ-238V V8
Weight: 15,700kg (34,540lb)	water-cooled diesel
Length: 7.3m (23ft 11.5in)	Speed: 60km/h (37mph)
Width: 2.85m (9ft 4in)	Range: 500km (310 miles)
Height: 2.4m (7ft 10.5in)	Armament:1 x 122mm (4.8in) howitzer, plus
	1 x 7.62mm (0.3in) anti-aircraft MG

Specifications

Crew: 3 + 7

Weight: 14,600kg (32,120lb)

Length: 6.71m (22ft)

Width: 3.15m (10ft 4in)

Height: 2m (6ft 7in)

Engine: 1 x 223kW (300hp) Model UTD-20 6-
  cylinder diesel

Speed: 65km/h (40.6mph)

Range: 600km (375 miles)

Armament: 1 x 9M113 AT-missile launcher, plus
  1 x 30mm (1.18in) cannon and 1 x 7.62mm
  (0.3in) coaxial MG

Radio: R-173, R-126 and R-10

▲ BMP-2 Infantry Fighting Vehicle

Russian Ground Forces / 131st Motor Rifle Brigade

The amphibious BMP-2 infantry fighting vehicle was developed in the Soviet Union during the 1980s and is armed with anti-tank missiles and a 30mm (1.18in) autocannon. It carries up to seven soldiers in its troop compartment.

▲ BTR-90 Infanty Fighting Vehicle

Russian Ground Forces / 201st Motor Rifle Division

In use only with the Russian armed forces, the BTR-90 infantry fighting vehicle was seen publicly for the first time in 1994. Carrying a troop complement of nine soldiers, the vehicle is armed with a 30mm (1.18in) autocannon, a 30mm (1.18in) grenade launcher, anti-tank guided missiles and a 7.62mm (0.3in) machine gun.

Specifications

Crew: 3 + 9

Weight: 17,000kg (37,500lb)

Length: 7.64m (25ft)

Width: 3.2m (10ft 6in)

Height: 2.97m (9ft 9in)

Engine: 157kW (210hp) V8 diesel

Speed: 80km/h (50mph)

Range: 600km (370 miles)

Armament: 1 x 30mm (1.18in) 2A42 cannon,
  plus 1 x automatic grenade launcher, 4 x AT-5
  Spandrel ATGWs, 1 x 7.62mm (0.3in) coaxial
  PKT MG

Radio: n/k

▲ BMP-3 Infanty Fighting Vehicle

Russian Ground Forces / 2nd Guards Tamanskaya Motor Rifle Division

The latest generation of the Soviet and Russian BMP series of infantry fighting vehicles, the BMP-3 debuted in 1987. Its 100mm (3.9in) gun doubles as an anti-tank missile launcher, and the vehicle also mounts a 30mm (1.18in) autocannon for close infantry support.

Specifications

Crew: 3 + 7

Weight: 18,700kg (18.4 tons)

Length: 7.2m (23ft 7in)

Width: 3.23m (10ft 7in)

Height: 2.3m (7ft 7in)

Engine: 373kW (500bhp) UTD-29 6-cylinder
  diesel

Speed: 70km/h (43mph)

Range: 600km (373 km)

Armament: 1 x 100mm (3.9in) 2A70 rifled gun,
  plus 1 x 30mm (1.18in) 2A72 autocannon and
  3 x 7.62mm (0.3in) PKT MGs

Radio: R-173

Although the BMP-2 has remained on active duty, a successor, the BMP-3 amphibious infantry fighting vehicle, entered service with the Red Army in 1987. Equipped with the 30mm (1.18in) autocannon, the 2A70 100mm (3.9in) gun/missile launcher system and three 7.62mm (0.3in) machine guns for added protection against infantry or tank killer squads employing shoulder-fired missiles, the BMP-3 is one of the most heavily armed infantry fighting vehicles in the world.

In addition to fighting terrorists and separatists in Chechnya, the Russian Federation's armed forces have fought with neighbouring Georgia as recently as 2008. During the South Ossetia War, the Georgian Army was reported to have lost at least 70 T-72 tanks and more than a dozen armoured personnel carriers, many of which were captured by the Russians and remained in good working order. Both sides are known to have deployed the aged T-54/55 and variants of the T-72, while the Russians also committed the T-62.

Specifications

Crew: 4	Speed: 60km/h (37.5mph)
Weight: 38,000kg (83,600lb)	Range: 570km (356 miles)
Length: 9.33m (28ft 6in)	Armament: 1 x 105mm (4.1in) gun, plus 1 x
Width: 3.37m (10ft 4in)	12.7mm (0.5in) coaxial HMG and 1 x 7.62mm
Height: 2.3m (7ft)	(0.3in) coaxial MG
Engine: 544kW (730hp) V12 diesel	

▲ T-80 Main Battle Tank
Russian Ground Forces / 4th Guards Kantemirovskaya Tank Division

Similar in design to the preceding T-64, the T-80 was deployed to the Soviet Red Army in 1976. During the First Chechen War, the tank performed poorly due to a lack of explosive reactive armour. Numerous variants remain in service in Russia and with armies of other former Soviet republics.

▲ T-90 Main Battle Tank
Russian Ground Forces / 5th Guards Tank Division

The T-90 main battle tank combines elements of its predecessors, the T-80 and the T-72, particularly the T-72BM and T-80U variants. The T-90 main armament is a 125mm (4.9in) smoothbore gun, which is also capable of firing anti-tank guided missiles. The T-90A saw combat action during the 1999 Chechen invasion of Dagestan. According to Moscow Defence Brief, one T-90 was hit by seven RPG anti-tank rockets but remained in action.

Specifications

Crew: 3	Speed: 65km/h (40mph)
Weight: 46,500kg (102,532lb)	Range: 650km (400 miles)
Length (hull): 6.86m (22ft 6in)	Armament: 1 x 125mm (4.9in) 2A46M Rapira 3
Width: 3.37m (11ft 1in)	smoothbore gun; 1 x 12.7mm (0.5in) anti-
Height: 2.23m (7ft 4in)	aircraft HMG; 1 x 7.62mm (0.3in) co-axial MG
Engine: 630kW (840bhp) V-84MS 12-cylinder	Radio: n/k
multi-fuel	

Iraq and Afghanistan
2003–PRESENT

Toppling the repressive regime of Saddam Hussein in Iraq and battling the Taliban in Afghanistan have placed demands upon the world's most advanced armoured vehicles.

WHEN THE US-led armed Coalition invaded Iraq in the spring of 2003, the objective was to remove a bloody dictator from power and neutralize the supposed threat of weapons of mass destruction. Advancing on the Iraqi capital of Baghdad and securing the port city of Basra were major challenges, particularly when confronted with an armed enemy force of more than 500,000 army, Republican Guard and fanatical Fedayeen paramilitary personnel.

As in the Gulf War of 1991, speed and overwhelming firepower would once again dictate the progress of the war on the ground. However, this time a lengthy air campaign did not precede the commencement of land operations, and within hours Coalition troops and tanks, particularly those based in Kuwait, had crossed the frontier into Iraq.

The M1A1 and M1A2 Abrams main battle tanks made up the bulk of the US heavy armour during the Iraq War, each an improved version of the original

M1 Abrams. While a number of the early M1s were upgraded to the M1A1 in the field during the Gulf War of 1991, the M1A2 variant went into production in 1992. A number of existing tanks were also upgraded to the M1A2.

Mounting the same main gun as the M1A1, the reliable 120mm (4.7in) M256 adaptation of the Rheinmetall smoothbore originally utilized in the German Leopard 2 main battle tank, the M1A2 contained extensive upgrades, with an independent thermal viewer and weapons control for the tank commander along with enhanced navigation and radio equipment. Designated the M1A2 SEP (System Enhancement Package), a sub-variant includes FBCB2 (Force XXI Battlefield Command Brigade and Below) communications capabilities, improvements to the engine cooling system, digital maps and upgraded armour that incorporates depleted uranium.

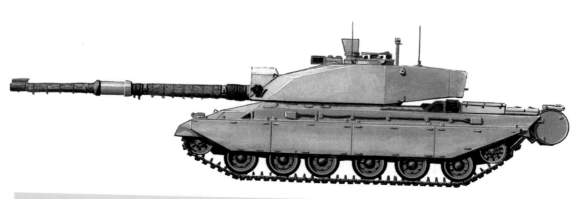

Specifications

Crew: 4

Weight: 62,500kg (137,500lb)

Length: 11.55m (35ft 4in)

Width: 3.52m (10ft 8in)

Height: 2.49m (7ft 5in)

Engine: 895kW (1200hp) liquid-cooled diesel

Speed: 57km/h (35.6mph)

Range: 400km (250 miles)

Armament: 1 x 120mm (4.7in) L30A1 gun, plus 2 x 7.62mm (0.3in) MGs and 2 x smoke rocket dischargers

Radio: Long range, directional communications system with satellite relay capabilities

▲ **Challenger 2 Main Battle Tank**

British Army / 1st Armoured Division / 7th Armoured Brigade

The Challenger 2 main battle tank entered service with the British Army in 1998 and has compiled an impressive combat record. Armed with a 120mm (4.7in) rifled gun and equipped with the latest armour protection and electronics, it is expected to serve well into the twenty-first century.

IRAQI REPUBLICAN GUARD, 2003	
Unit	**Strength**
Tank Brigade:	2
Tank Battalions	3
Mechanized Infanty Battalion	1
Motorized Special Forces Company	1
Engineering Company	1
Reconnaissance Platoon	1
Medium Rocket Launcher Battery	1
Mechanized Infantry Brigade	1
Mechanized Infantry Battalions	3
Tank Battalion	1
Anti-tank Company	1
Motorized Special Forces Company	1
Engineering Company	1
Reconnaissance Platoon	1
Medium Rocket Launcher Battery	1
Divisional Artillery Brigade	1
Self-propelled Artillery Battalions (155mm SP)	3
Self-propelled Artillery Battalions (152mm SP)	2
Self-propelled Artillery Battalions (122mm SP)	2
Divisional Units	
Motorized Special Forces Battalions	3
Reconnaissance Battalion	1
Anti-tank Battalion	1
Engineer Battalion	1

The British Challenger 2 main battle tank includes few of the components of the Challenger 1 and is armed with the 120mm (4.7in) L30A1 gun, which replaces the earlier L11 weapon of the Challenger 1. Protected by second-generation Chobham armour, the Challenger 2 fields the latest in digital fire control, thermal imaging and computerization. An armoured recovery variant and a bridging vehicle have been developed using its chassis.

Combat lethality

During the 2003 Iraq War, the T-72M and older Iraqi tanks that had survived the Gulf War once again proved no match for the modern Coalition main battle tanks. During the inter-war years, the Iraqis had been able to acquire some tanks to replace their heavy losses from 1991, including the Chinese Type 59 and Type 69, upgraded versions based on the old Soviet T-54/55 with 125mm (4.9in) guns and additional armour.

Relatively few Abrams tanks were lost to enemy action; some were disabled by mines, roadside bombs or roving anti-tank squads of Fedayeen carrying shoulder-fired missiles. Friendly-fire incidents were also reported. According to British sources, no Challenger 2s were lost to enemy action, and one tank withstood multiple hits from rocket-propelled grenades and a MILAN anti-tank missile.

Both tanks performed extremely well, and most of the losses in the field occurred during the occupation of Iraq which followed the actual invasion. Indicative of their superb tank-versus-tank performance was the

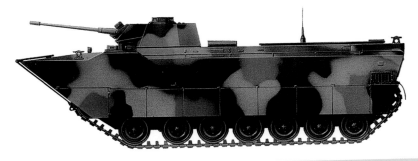

▲ **Advanced Amphibious Assault Vehicle (AAAV)**

US Marine Corps / I Marine Expeditionary Force

Designed as a replacement for the ageing AAV-7A1 amphibious assault vehicles in use by the US Marine Corps for more than 30 years, the AAAV, also known as the Expeditionary Fighting Vehicle, is scheduled for deployment by 2015 with a troop capacity of 17 Marines and a main armament of the 30mm (1.18in) or 40mm (1.57in) MK44 cannon.

Specifications

Crew: 3 + 17

Weight: 33,525kg (73,922lb)

Length: 9.01m (29ft 7in)

Width: 3.66m (12ft)

Height: 3.19m (10ft 6in)

Engine: 2015kW (2702hp) MTU MT883

12-cylinder multi-fuel

Speed: 72km/h (45mph)

Range: 480km (300 miles)

Armament: 1 x 30mm (1.18in) Bushmaster II cannon, plus 1 x 7.62mm (0.3in) MG

Radio: n/k

rapid destruction of seven T-72s by M1A2s with no losses to the Americans during a battle on the outskirts of Baghdad.

Perhaps the most highly criticized armoured vehicle deployed by the US during the Iraq War was the AAV-7A1 tracked amphibious assault vehicle. One of the fiercest battles of the invasion took place at the city of Nasiriyah as Iraqi forces contested bridges across the Euphrates River. Troops of the 1st Marine Division were heavily engaged, and several of their AAVs were destroyed by rocket-

propelled grenades while the vehicles also proved vulnerable to some small-arms fire.

The AAV was conceived to replace the prior generation of amphibious vehicles used by the US Marine Corps and entered service during the early 1980s. Its distinctive boat-shaped bow and high profile are easily recognizable, and its troop complement of 25 combat soldiers is among the largest of any similar vehicle in the world. Its armament includes the M242 25mm (1in) Bushmaster chain-fed autocannon, with a maximum rate of fire of 225 rounds per minute, as

▲ M1114 High Mobility Multipurpose Wheeled Vehicle (HMMWV)
US Army / 3rd Infantry Division
The versatile HMMWV, popularly known as the Humvee, has been in service with US forces since the mid-1980s. Its armour protection has been upgraded with field kits, while a more heavily protected production version has also been introduced.

Specifications
Crew: 1 + 3
Weight: 3870kg (8375lb)
Length: 4.457m (14ft 7in)
Width: 2.15m (7ft)
Height: 1.75m (5ft 8in)
Engine: 101kW (135hp) V8 6.21 air-cooled diesel
Speed: 105km/h (65.6mph)
Range: 563km (352 miles)
Armament: Various, including machine guns, grenade launchers and surface-to-air missile (SAM) launchers
Radio: AN/VRC-12

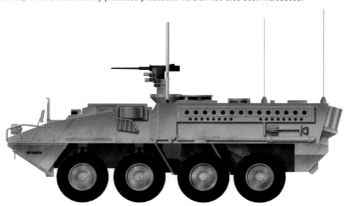

Specifications

Crew: 2 + 9	Engine: 260kW (350hp) Caterpillar C7
Weight: 16.47 tonnes (16.2 tons)	Speed: 100km/h (62mph)
Length: 6.95m (22.92ft)	Range: 500km (310 miles)
Width: 2.72m (8.97ft)	Armament: 1 x 12.7mm (0.5in) M2 MG
Height: 2.64m (8.72ft)	Radio: n/k

▲ IAV Stryker Armoured Personnel Carrier
US Army / 2nd Infantry Division / 4th Stryker Brigade
The eight-wheeled Stryker armoured fighting vehicle entered service with the US Army in 2002 and carries up to nine soldiers. Its mobility and protection have been instrumental during operations in Iraq. Its weapons systems are remotely controlled from inside the vehicle.

well as a 12.7mm (0.5in) machine gun and a 40mm (1.57in) grenade launcher.

Afghanistan intervention

Since 2001, US, British and subsequently NATO forces have been involved in the effort to end Taliban rule, quell the subsequent insurgency and destroy the al-Qaeda terror network in Afghanistan. While heavy armour has been utilized to project firepower,

particularly during heavy fighting for control of cities and urban areas, mountainous terrain has limited its mobility, often confining the main battle tank to roads and areas clear of mines and improvised explosive devices.

Light armoured vehicles such as the M2/M3 Bradley fighting vehicle, the Humvee and the Land Rover Wolf utility vehicle have proved their value as patrol and rapid response vehicles. The Land Rover

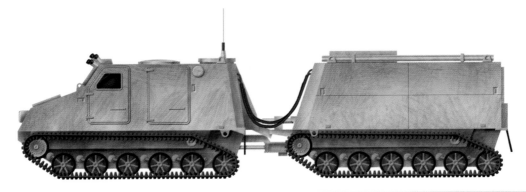

▲ BVS 10 Viking Armoured Personnel Carrier
British Army / Royal Marines / Armoured Support Group

A collaborative design effort between Britain and Sweden, the BVS 10 entered service with the Royal Marines in 2005. Fully amphibious, the vehicle carries up to four soldiers in its front vehicle and up to eight in the trailer. It is protected by specialized armour and mounts a light machine gun.

Specifications

Crew: (front car) Driver + 4 passengers; (rear car) 8 passengers
Weight: 10,600kg (23,369lb)
Length: 7.5m (24ft 7in)
Width: 2.1m (6ft 10.7in)
Height: 2.2m (7ft 2.5in)
Engine: 183kW (250bhp) Cummins 5.9l in-line
6-cylinder turbo diesel
Speed: (road) 50km/h (31mph); (cross-country) 15km/h (9.3mph); (water) 5km/h (3.1mph)
Range: 300km (186 miles)
Armament: Capacity for 1 x 12.7mm (0.5in) Browning HMG or 1 x 7.62mm (0.3in) MG
Radio: n/k

Specifications

Crew: 3
Weight: 7900kg (17,400lb)
Length: 5.72m (18ft 9in)
Width: 2.49m (8ft 2in)
Height: 2.18m (7ft 1.8in)
Engine: 179kW (240hp) Deutz diesel
Speed: 115km/h (71mph)
Range: 860km (530 miles)
Armament: 1 x 12.7mm (0.5in) MG or
1 x 7.62mm (0.3in) MG or 1 x 40mm (1.57in) grenade launcher
Radio: n/k

▲ LGS Fennek
German Army / 13th Mechanized Infantry Division

The LGS Fennek light armoured reconnaissance vehicle is currently deployed by the German and Dutch Armies and has served recently in Afghanistan. Its speed and light armour have proven optimal for scouting and patrol duties, although rocket-propelled grenades and improvised explosive devices have damaged vehicles in the field.

Wolf has been a mainstay of the British forces in both Iraq and Afghanistan, carrying up to six soldiers. The Wolf traces its lineage to the company's light truck and transport vehicles of the World War II period.

The US Army's Stryker series of infantry fighting vehicles is destined to play a greater role in Afghanistan. The vehicle was already well known for its deployment to Iraq, and the first Stryker unit arrived in Afghanistan in 2009. Developed from earlier Canadian and Swiss armoured vehicle designs, the Stryker entered service with the US Army in 2002 to complement the older M2/M3 Bradleys. Conceived as a method of introducing combat troops to the battlefield rapidly, the Stryker carries up to nine soldiers and is armed with a 12.7mm (0.5in) machine gun or 40mm (1.57in) grenade launcher mounted in the Protector M151 remote weapons station, which may be operated from the relative safety of the vehicle's interior.

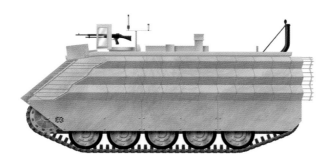

▲ FV 430 Bulldog Armoured Personnel Carrier

British Army / 1st Armoured Division / 7th Armoured Brigade

The FV 430 Bulldog entered service with British forces in Iraq and Afghanistan late in 2006 in response to the hazards posed by rocket-propelled grenades and improvised explosive devices. Equipped with an extensive reactive armour package, it also carries a remote-controlled 7.62mm (0.3in) machine gun.

Specifications

Crew: 2 + 10
Weight: 15.3 tonnes (15 tons)
Length: 5.25m (17ft 2.6in)
Width: 2.8m (9ft 2.3in)
Height: 2.28m (7ft 5.8in)
Engine: 179kW (240hp) Rolls-Royce K60 multi-fuel
Speed: 52km/h (32mph)
Range: 580km (360 miles)
Armament: 1 x 7.62mm (0.3in) MG, plus 2 x 3-barrel smoke dischargers
Radio: n/k

Specifications

Crew: 2 + 4
Weight: 17,000kg (38,000lb)
Length: 5.91m (19.41ft)
Width: 2.74m (9.0ft)
Height: 2.64m (8.67ft)
Engine: 243kW (330hp) Caterpillar C-7 diesel
Speed: 105km/h (65mph)
Range: 966km (600 miles)
Armament: Optional remote weapons station

▲ Mastiff PPV (Protected Patrol Vehicle)

British Army / 1st Armoured Division / 7th Armoured Brigade

The Mastiff PPV is the British variant of the basic Cougar armoured fighting vehicle built by Force Protection Inc. Acquired by both the British and US Armies, the Cougar is designed specifically to safeguard against mines and improvised explosive devices. The Mastiff entered service with British forces in 2007.

Chapter 7

Modern Developments

Technology has never stood still, and the development
of modern armoured vehicles is indicative of this. Indeed,
during the last decade the pace of progress may even have
quickened as both preeminent and emerging nations have
committed to the continuing modernization of their armoured
forces and to participation in the lucrative arms export
industry. The latest generation of main battle tanks and
armoured vehicles is characterized by an array of
sophisticated offensive and defensive systems, increasing
firepower while improving target acquisition, battlefield
communication and armour protection. Although technology
continues to advance, the human element remains the prime
mover for the successful employment of armoured doctrine.
A capable commander and crew combined with the basics
of speed, armour protection and firepower remain
likely to win the day.

◀ **Fording feline**
The Leopard 2 main battle tank is one of the best modern tanks in service. Besides Germany, its operators
include Austria, Denmark, the Netherlands, Spain and Sweden.

Europe

1991–PRESENT

Numerous European nations have undertaken development of armoured vehicles, or expanded their production, particularly in the areas of main battle tanks, infantry fighting vehicles and self-propelled artillery.

WHILE THE BRITISH CHALLENGER 2 and the German Leopard 2 main battle tanks remain preeminent among modern European main battle tank designs, France, Poland, Italy and others have entered their own main battle tanks into production in recent years. European nations have proved innovative in tank design since the beginning – consider the German and British machines of World War I and the speed and firepower of the *Wehrmacht* panzers of World War II. During the late 1950s, Sweden produced the turretless Stridsvagen 103, which reduced production expense and performed favourably in head-to-head testing against its contemporaries. France introduced the oscillating turret with the AMX-10.

Since its deployment during Operation Iraqi Freedom and to Bosnia and Kosovo, the Challenger 2 has continued to undergo refinement. According to the Ministry of Defence, numbers of main battle tanks and their role are changing within the military, including the consolidation of several armoured

squadrons and the allocation of one armoured regiment to focus primarily on reconnaissance. The Challenger Lethality Improvement Programme is currently in progress and includes the possible replacement of the 120mm (4.7in) L30 rifled gun with the 120mm (4.7in) Rheinmetall L55 smoothbore, which is common to the German Leopard 2. Enhanced NBC (nuclear, biological and chemical) defences are also being evaluated.

Meanwhile, the Challenger 2E emerged in response to the necessity of fighting and maintaining combat efficiency in extreme climates and is intended for the export market. Competing directly with the Leopard 2 and other main battle tanks for purchase contracts, the Challenger 2E was produced from approximately 2002 to 2005. Extensive trials took place in the deserts of the Middle East, and the Challenger 2E remains equipped with the 120mm (4.7in) L30 rifled gun. However, its combat prowess was augmented by a battlefield communications and management system that allows for the tracking of multiple targets simultaneously and

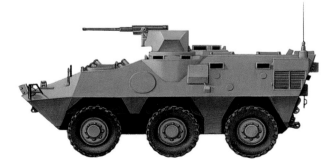

▲ **Pandur Armoured Personnel Carrier**

Austrian Army / 4th Mechanized Infantry Brigade

The Pandur armoured personnel carrier was developed in the 1980s by Steyr-Daimler-Puch Spezialfahrzeug and transports up to 12 infantrymen. Weapons systems include heavy machine guns and up to a 105mm (4.1in) cannon. A turreted version reduces troop capacity to six. The Pandur II has supplanted the Pandur I in recent years.

Specifications

Crew: 2 + 8	6-cylinder turbo diesel
Weight: 13,500kg (29,800lb)	Speed: 100km/h (60mph)
Length: 5.7m (18ft 8in)	Range: 700km (430 miles)
Width: 2.5m (8ft 2in)	Armament: 1 x 12.7mm (0.5in) HMG; 2 x 3 smoke
Height: 1.82m (5ft 11in)	grenade launchers; various other configurations
Engine: 179kW (240hp) Steyr WD 612.95	Radio: n/k

provides enhanced acquisition and ranging. Thermal sights were improved for both the commander and gunner, while the commander may also operate the turret independently. The engine was upgraded with the 1125kW (1500hp) Europack MTU 883 diesel.

Leap of the Leopard

The most recent variant of the Leopard 2, the 2A6, was the first of the German tanks to mount the longer 120mm (4.7in) L55 smoothbore gun. An auxiliary engine has been added in the 2A6 along with air

conditioning and enhanced protection against landmines, with some of these tanks designated 2A6M. The German Army began upgrading more than 200 of its frontline tanks to the 2A6 configuration in 2000, and the first deliveries of production 2A6s occurred the following year. Another variant of the 2A6, the 2E, offers greater armour protection and was developed in a cooperative effort by German and Spanish engineers. Still another variant, the Leopard PSO, includes combat survivability systems designed for urban warfare.

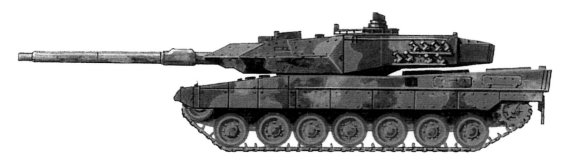

Specifications

Crew: 4

Weight: 59,700kg (131,616lb)

Length: 9.97m (32ft 8in)

Width: 3.5m (11ft 6in)

Height: 2.98m (9ft 10in)

Engine: 1119kW (1500hp) MTU MB 873

four-stroke 12-cylinder diesel

Speed: 72km/h (45mph)

Range: 500km (311 miles)

Armament: 1 x 120mm (4.7in) LSS smoothbore gun, plus 2 x 7.62mm (0.3in) MGs

Radio: SEM 80/90 digital VHF

▲ **Leopard 2A6 MBT**

German Army / 10th Armoured Division

The Leopard 2A6 main battle tank is the most recent variant of the vehicle which entered service with the German Army in 1979. The older 120mm (4.7in) main weapon in previous versions was replaced with the 120mm (4.7in) L55 smoothbore gun.

Specifications

Crew: 5

Weight: 55,000kg (121,275lb)

Length: 7.87m (25ft 10in)

Width: 3.37m (11ft)

Height: 3.4m (11ft 2in)

Engine: 745.7kW (1000hp) MTU 881 V12 diesel

Speed: 60km/h (27mph)

Range: 420km (260 miles)

Armament: 1 x 155mm (6.1in) L52 gun, plus 1 x 7.62mm (0.3in) MG

Radio: N/k

▲ **Panzerhaubitze 2000**

German Army / 1st Armoured Division

The self-propelled Panzerhaubitze 2000 provides heavy fire support to NATO troops in Afghanistan with its Rheinmetall 155mm (6.1in) L52 gun. The system has been selected by several nations to replace the ageing M109 gun. It is operated by the armed forces of Germany, Italy, the Netherlands and Greece.

Throughout its service life, the Leopard 2 has remained a popular export tank. The armies of Denmark, the Netherlands, Greece, Canada, Portugal, Spain and Switzerland are among those fielding the main battle tank today. It has been deployed in the Balkans and to Afghanistan, engaging in notable firefights with Taliban and guerrilla forces.

Leclerc and Ariete

The first production main battle tank designed and manufactured in France in more than 30 years is the Leclerc. Although the early development of a new tank had begun in the 1970s, the Leclerc did not enter production until 1990. France and the United Arab Emirates worked in partnership on the tank and share the expense of development and production.

Replacing the aged AMX-30 in French armoured formations and in the armed forces of the United Arab Emirates, the Leclerc was not intended for major export or a lengthy production run, and fewer than 1000 were built by the time production ceased in 2008. France now has over 400 Leclercs in service and the United Arab Emirates Army over 380, delivered in 2004. The Leclerc has been deployed to Kosovo and with peacekeeping forces in Lebanon; however, it has yet to see substantial combat.

With the Leclerc, French engineers initially rejected the British Chobham armour and developed their own protection package by the 1990s. Emphasis has been on armour protection with composite steel and titanium sandwiching non-explosive and non-energetic reactive armour (NERA). Active counter-measures include a top speed of 71km/h (44mph) for rapid relocation and evasion, along with the Galix defence system that utilizes infrared screening rounds, smoke grenades and anti-personnel weapons against attacking infantry.

The Italian firms Iveco Fiat and OTO Melara combined efforts to develop the C1 Ariete main battle tank, which has been deployed with the nation's armed forces since the mid-1990s. The Ariete is armed with a 120mm (4.7in) OTO Melara smoothbore cannon and protected by a classified composite armour thought to be comparable to that of contemporary main battle tanks. Its 932kW (1250hp) V12 turbocharged engine is capable of delivering a top speed of more than 65km/h (41mph). The tank is equipped with modern target acquisition and sighting equipment, allowing effective operations day or night. Active defences include smoke grenade dischargers and the RALM laser warning receiver, which sounds an alarm when the tank is 'painted' by hostile target acquisition systems. To date, the C1 Ariete has equipped only the four armoured battalions of the Italian Army, and it is scheduled for an engine upgrade as part of an

Specifications

Crew: 3

Weight: 45,300kg (99,886lb)

Length (hull): 6.95m (22ft 10in)

Width: 3.59m (11ft 9in)

Height: 2.19m (7ft 2in)

Engine: 634kW (850bhp) S-12U V12

supercharged diesel

Speed: 60km/h (38mph)

Range: 650km (405 miles)

Armament: 1 x 125mm (4.9in) gun; 1 x 12.7mm

(0.5in) HMG; 1 x 7.62mm (0.3in) MG

Radio: n/k

▲ **PT-91 Main Battle Tank**

Polish Land Forces / 1st Mechanized Division 'Warsaw'

A Polish variant of the export version of the ubiquitous T-72 main battle tank, the PT-91 Twardy (Resilient) entered service with the Polish Land Forces during the mid-1990s as both a production vehicle and an upgrade of existing tanks.

overall performance enhancement programme. Approximately 200 tanks have been produced, and the tank was deployed to Iraq in 2004.

Infantry fighting vehicles

The German Marder, which entered service in 1971 and is currently being retired in favour of the Puma, was the first infantry fighting vehicle designed and developed by a NATO country for the specific purpose of transporting troops to a combat area and providing direct fire support for their operations. It was followed by the British Warrior and the American M2/M3 Bradley. The infantry fighting vehicle has remained significant in supporting infantry operations and

▲ **Leclerc Main Battle Tank**

French Army / 6th-12th Cuirassier Regiment

The Leclerc's main armament is the GIAT CN120-26 120mm (4.7in) smoothbore cannon, which is compatible with most common NATO ammunition. The powerplant is a 1125kW (1500p) eight-cylinder engine.

Specifications

Crew: 3
Weight: 54.5 tonnes (117,000lb)
Length (gun forwards): 9.87m (30ft)
Width: 3.71m 11ft 4in)
Height: 2.46m (7ft 6in)
Engine: 1 x 1125.5kW (1500hp) SAEM UDU V8X
    1500 T9 Hyperbar 8-cylinder diesel

Speed: 71km/h (44mph)
Range: 550km (345 miles)
Armament: 1 x 120mm (4.7in) GIAT CN120-26/52
    gun; 1 x 12.7mm (0.5in) coaxial MG; 3 x 9
    smoke dischargers
Radio: 2 x frequency hopping radio sets

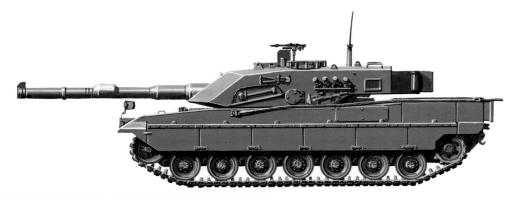

Specifications

Crew: 4
Weight: 54,000kg (118,800lb)
Length: 9.67m (29ft 6in)
Width: 3.6m (11ft)
Height: 2.5m (7ft 7in)
Engine: 932kW (1250hp) IVECO FIAT MTCA V12
    turbocharged diesel

Speed: 66km/h (41.3mph)
Range: 600km (375 miles)
Armament: 1 x 120mm (4.7in) gun, plus
    2 x 7.62mm (0.3in) MGs (1 coaxial,
    1 anti-aircraft) and 2 x 4 smoke dischargers
Radio: n/k

▲ **C1 Ariete Main Battle Tank**

Italian Army / 31st Tank Battalion

The C1 Ariete main battle tank was deployed to the Italian Army in the mid-1990s and has proved comparable in armour protection and firepower to contemporary tanks of other nations. The Ariete mounts a 120mm (4.7in) smoothbore gun and a pair of 7.62mm (0.3in) machine guns.

providing protection to troops on the ground, while the type has also performed well in a reconnaissance role. Given the need for scout, reconnaissance and patrol types, several European nations have developed their own light armoured vehicles. These have been deployed with NATO and United Nations peacekeeping forces in the Middle East and the Balkans and proved popular on the thriving export market. A new generation of self-propelled artillery has also emerged during the last decade as many NATO countries replace their ageing US-made M109 weapons systems. The German Panzerhaubitze 2000 entered production in 1998 and mounts a 155mm (6.1in) L52 gun developed by Rheinmetall, and more than 400 are in use with the armed forces of Germany, Italy, the Netherlands and Greece. A European contemporary is the British AS-90, in service since 1993 and mounting the 155mm (6.1in) L31 cannon.

▲ Centauro Tank Destroyer
Italian Army / Aosta Mechanized Brigade

The wheeled Centauro tank destroyer mounts a 105mm (4.1in) gun and two 7.62mm (0.3in) machine guns. It has seen extensive deployment to the Balkans, Somalia, Iraq and Lebanon. Combining speed and firepower, the Centauro has excelled in convoy escort and infantry support roles as well.

Specifications

Crew: 4	Speed: 108km/h (67mph)
Weight: 25,000kg (55,100lb)	Range: 800km (500 miles)
Length (with gun): 8.55m (28ft 6in)	Armament:1 x 105mm (4.1in) gun, plus
Width: 2.95m (9ft 8in)	2 x 7.62mm (0.3in) MGs (1 coaxial,
Height: 2.73m (8ft 11.5in)	1 anti-aircraft) and 2 x 4 smoke grenade
Engine: 388kW (520hp) Iveco MTCA 6-cylinder	launchers
turbo diesel	Radio: n/k

Specifications

Crew: 3 or 4	cylinder diesel
Weight: 3200kg (7100lb)	Speed: 120km/h (75mph)
Length: 4.86m (15ft 11in)	Range: 500km (300 miles)
Width: 1.78m (5ft 1in)	Armament: 1 x Oerlikon KAD-B17 20mm (0.79in)
Height: 1.55m (5ft 1in)	gun in T 20 FA-HS turret
Engine: 71kW (95hp) Fiat Model 8144.81.200 4-	

▲ OTO Melara R3 Capraia Armoured Reconnaissance Vehicle
Italian Army

The OTO Melara R3 Capraia armoured reconnaissance vehicle enables its three- or four-man crew to assess enemy strength and positions. Its armour is effective against most small arms, and the vehicle mounts a variety of weapons, including a 20mm (0.79in) Oerlikon.

▲ **Wheeled tank destroyer**
An Oto Melara Centauro tank destroyer is put through its paces somewhere in the Italian countryside.

The Middle East and Asia
1991–PRESENT

Although the emerging nations of the Middle East and Asia have utilized armoured vehicles of other nations, their development of indigenous armour has accelerated in recent years.

THE ISRAELI DEFENCE FORCES have developed into one of the most efficient and experienced fighting forces in the world, and the Merkava main battle tank has become symbolic of their prowess. From the IDF perspective, the Merkava series was born of necessity. Following the Six Day War of 1967, Great Britain and France discontinued the supply of some weapons to Israel. Therefore, the Israeli military establishment determined that the nation would become as self-reliant as possible in terms of modern military hardware. The development of a main battle tank became a priority.

Designed by Israeli Military Industries and manufactured by IDF Ordnance, the Merkava Mk 1 entered service in 1979. Since then, successive upgrades, or marks, have been introduced. Each of these has been involved in combat operations against paramilitary factions such as the Palestine Liberation Organization and Hezbollah.

Israeli armoured doctrine has long stressed the survivability of tank crews, reasoning that a confident crew, assured that its survival is likely, will assert itself more boldly in the face of an enemy. True enough, the Merkava design has reflected this philosophy and marked a radical departure from conventional configurations. The main battle tank's diesel engine and fuel tanks were located forward to provide additional protection for the crew in the event of hull penetration. Furthermore, the turret was positioned somewhat towards the rear.

Merkava MBT
The experience with the Merkava Mk 1 during the 1982 incursion into Lebanon resulted in the

upgraded Merkava Mk 2, which included improved fire control and urban warfare equipment specifically designed for low-intensity confrontations. The later Merkava Mk 3 entered service in 1989 and mounted the 120mm (4.7in) MG251 smoothbore cannon adapted from the popular Rheinmetall design, an upgrade from the original 105mm (4.1in) L7 gun.

Most recently, the Merkava Mk 4, which includes the latest in urban warfare fittings, a much improved powerplant consisting of a 1125kW (1500hp)

General Dynamics GD833 diesel engine and modular composite armour whose standards remain classified, entered service in 2004. The Merkava Mk 4 also incorporates the Trophy Active Protective System, which raises an alarm when the tank is 'painted' by enemy laser rangefinding equipment, identifies the likely point of impact and selects appropriate counter-measures.

The Merkava Mk 4 was heavily engaged against Hezbollah militia during the 2006 Lebanon War, and some critics have claimed that it proved extremely

Specifications
Crew: 4
Weight: 55,898kg (122,976lb)
Length: 8.36m (27ft 5.25in)
Width: 3.72m (12ft 2.5in)
Height: 2.64m (8ft 8in)
Engine: 671kW (900hp) Teledyne Continental AVDS-1790-6A V12 diesel
Speed: 46km/h (28.6mph)
Range: 500km (310 miles)
Armament: 1 x 120 mm (4.7in) MG253 cannon, plus 1 x 7.62mm (0.3in) MG
Radio: n/k

▲ **Merkava Mk 4 MBT**
Israeli Defence Forces / 401st Armoured Brigade, Israeli occupied territories, 2004
The Merkava main battle tank was the first armoured vehicle of its kind developed and manufactured in Israel. Since the 1980s, the Merkava has served as the frontline main battle tank of the Israeli Defence Forces, while older Magach tanks remain in service.

▲ **Arjun Main Battle Tank**
Indian Army / 67th Armoured Regiment, 2005
The development of the Arjun main battle tank was undertaken in the 1970s by India's largest defence contractor, the Defence Research and Development Organization. However, setbacks in its design and testing phases resulted in lengthy delays in Arjun production, which was not begun in earnest until early in the twenty-first century. The tank mounts a 120mm (4.7in) rifled main gun.

Specifications
Crew: 4
Weight: 58 tonnes (127,600lb)
Length: 9.8m (32ft 2in)
Width: 3.17m (10ft 5in)
Height: 2.44m (8ft)
Engine: 1044kW (1400hp) MTU MB 838 Ka 501
water-cooled diesel
Speed: 72km/h (45mph)
Range: 400km (250 miles)
Armament: 1 x 120mm (4.7in) gun, plus 1 x 7.62mm (0.3in) MG
Radio: n/k

vulnerable to anti-tank missiles. However, its combat record has validated the primary maxim of crew survivability, and more than 500 are currently in service.

Meanwhile, the government of India had embarked on the development of the Arjun main battle tank during the early 1970s; however, serious delays and political circumstances relegated the tank to a lower priority and it did not enter production

until 2004. Needless to say, numerous technological upgrades from the original version were necessary before trials with the Indian Army and acceptance into full production.

Traditionally, India had been a major arms purchaser from the Soviet Union, and this trend continued with the T-72 and later models such as the T-90. Mounting a 120mm (4.7in) rifled gun, the Arjun is being equipped with sophisticated fire

▲ Al-Khalid Main Battle Tank

Pakistani Army / 6th Armoured Division

A joint venture between Pakistan and the People's Republic of China, the Al-Khalid entered service with the Pakistani Army in 2001. The tank's design is based on the Chinese Type 90, itself an amalgamation of both Soviet and Western technology. Its main armament is a 125mm (4.9in) smoothbore gun. A current upgrade programme is under way.

Specifications

Crew: 3	Speed: 72km/h (45mph)
Weight: 47,000kg (103,617lb)	Range: 450km (992 miles)
Length: 10.07m (33ft)	Armament: 1 x 125mm (4.9in) smoothbore gun,
Width: 3.5m (11ft 6in)	plus 1 x 12.7mm (0.5in) external AA MG and
Height: 2.435m (7ft 11in)	1 x 7.72mm (0.303in) coaxial MG
Engine: 890kW (1200hp) KMDB 6TD-2	Radio: n/k
6-cylinder diesel	

Specifications

Crew: 4
Weight: 45.5 tonnes (100,327lbs)
Length: 6.89m (22ft 7in)
Width: 3.35m (11ft)
Height: 2.76m (9ft 1in)
Engine: 1 x 620kW (831hp) MTU 90 diesel
Speed: 60km/h (38mph)
Range: 600km (380 miles)
Armament: 1 x 104mm (4.1in) gun; 2 x 7.62
  (0.3in) MGs; 4 x smoke dischargers
Radio: n/k

▲ OF 40 Mk2 Main Battle Tank

Union Defence Force (United Arab Emirates), 1990

Designed for the export market during the late 1970s, the OF 40 main battle tank was a joint venture between Otobreda and Fiat. Incorporating some features of the German Leopard 1 main battle tank, its performance nevertheless proved disappointing. The United Arab Emirates has taken delivery of 36 OF-40s since 1981. These were the mainstay of the Union Defence Force until the late 1990s, when the UEA began taking delivery of Leclerc main battle tanks.

control and rangefinding equipment, while its primary APFSDS (armour-piercing fin-stabilized discarding sabot) ammunition is produced indigenously in India.

Egyptian effort

Long an arms customer of the Soviet Union, Egypt has, interestingly, pursued an upgrade of the vintage T-54/55 main battle tank. Following evaluation of an upgraded T-54, which had been modified in the United States, the T-54E, better known as the Ramses II, was accepted into Egyptian production as late as 2004. In a curious blend of once adversarial Cold War technology, the Ramses II shares a common gun,

the 105mm (4.1in) M68 rifled cannon, with the American M60A3 Patton export tanks already deployed with the Egyptian Army. Its powerplant, a 677kW (908hp) turbocharged diesel, is also quite similar to that of the M60A3. Laser fire control equipment, an improved communication system, armour skirting and updated NBC defences are in place. An estimated 400 Ramses II tanks were to be in service with the Egyptian Army when the project was completed.

Specifications

Crew: 4
Weight: 45,800kg (101,972lb)
Length: 9.9m (32ft 6in)
Width: 3.27m (10ft 8in)
Height: 2.4m (7ft 11in)
Engine: 677kW (908hp) TCM AVDS-1790-5A
  turbocharged diesel
Speed: 72km/h (45mph)
Range: 600km (373 miles)
Armament: 1 x 105mm (4.1in) M68 rifled
  gun, plus 1 x 12.7mm (0.5in) M2HB HMG
  and 1 x 7.62mm (0.3in) coaxial MG
Radio: n/k

▲ **Ramses II**

Egyptian Army / 36th Independent Armoured Brigade

A modernization of the Soviet T-54/55 main battle tank introduced a half-century ago, the Ramses II incorporates modern technology from the United States, such as an improved gun (the 105mm/4.1in M68 rifled canon), better target acquisition equipment and a high-performance engine.

▲ **Palmaria SP Howitzer**

Libyan Army, 1992

Developed solely for the export market, the OTO Melara Palmaria 155mm (6.1in) self-propelled howitzer included an automatic loading system. The heavy weapon was mounted on the chassis of the OF 40 main battle tank. The first prototypes were built in late 1970s. Production commenced in 1982 and ceased in the early 1990s.

Specifications

Crew: 5
Weight: 46,632kg (102,590lb)
Length: 11.474m (37ft 7.75in)
Width: 2.35m (7ft 8.5in)
Height: 2.874m (9ft 5.25in)
Engine: 559kW (750hp) 8-cylinder diesel
Speed: 60km/h (37mph)
Range: 400km (250 miles)
Armament: 1 x 155mm (6.1in) howitzer, plus
  1 x 7.62mm (0.3in) MG
Radio: n/k

South Africa
1980–PRESENT

During the twenty-first century, South Africa has leveraged its experience battling guerrillas across rugged terrain to develop several light armoured vehicles and a main battle tank.

FOR YEARS, THE ARMOURED FORCES of South Africa fielded the Semel main battle tank, adapted from the British Centurion of the early Cold War years. By the late 1970s, development of the Olifant was well under way, and the tank entered full production by the end of the decade. With 172 Olifant tanks in service, the South Africans have continually upgraded the vehicle. The initial upgrade, the Olifant Mk 1B of the early 1990s, was already in progress when the first production tanks were delivered. Equipped with the 105mm (4.1in) L7 gun, the Olifant Mk 1B utilized a hand-held laser rangefinder for target acquisition.

An extensive modernization programme was initiated with a contract to BAE Land Systems in 2003. The Olifant Mk 2, which entered service in 2007, features a new 675kW (900hp) turbocharged V12 diesel engine, a vastly improved turret that allows the tank to fire on the move, thermal sights

and integral laser rangefinding equipment, modular armour, and the ability to mount either a 105mm (4.1in) or 120mm (4.7in) smoothbore gun.

Safety and speed

South Africa's state-run arms manufacturer, Armscor, has embarked on a concentrated effort to increase sales, which contracted in recent years but were ironically robust during the United Nations Security Council embargo on the nation's trade during the era of apartheid. Forays into the global arms export market have been primarily characterized by the development of armoured cars and light reconnaissance vehicles.

The wheeled G6 Rhino self-propelled howitzer has been in production since 1987 and is operated by the armed forces of Oman and the United Arab Emirates as well. Mounting a powerful 155mm (6.1in) gun, the

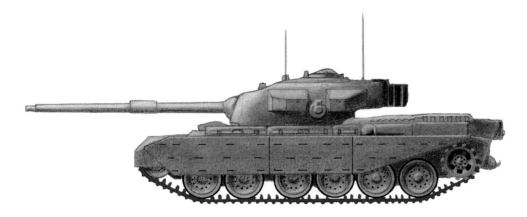

▲ **Olifant Mk 1A Main Battle Tank**

South African Army / 1st Tank Regiment

The Olifant Mk 1A main battle tank entered service with the South African armed forces during the late 1970s and was rapidly supplanted by the Mk 1B. The accuracy of its 105mm (4.1in) L7 rifled cannon was enhanced by laser rangefinding equipment which was hand operated by a crewman. Later upgrades have significantly improved the tank's performance.

Specifications	
Crew: 4	Speed: 45km/h (28.1mph)
Weight: 56,000kg (123,200lb)	Range: 500km (313 miles)
Length: 9.83m (30ft)	Armament: 1 x 105mm (4.1in) gun, plus
Width: 3.38m (10ft 4in)	2 x 7.62mm (0.3in) MGs (1 coaxial, 1 anti-
Height: 2.94m (8ft 11in)	aircraft) and 2 x 4 smoke dischargers
Engine: 559kW (750hp) V12 air-cooled	Radio: n/k
turbocharged diesel	

Rhino has been used in combat during the prolonged South African Border War and may well have inspired Iraq to develop similar heavy mobile weapons, which did not enter production but were reported to mount 210mm (8.3in) cannon. A modified G6 turret has also been fitted to the T-72 and Arjun main battle tanks.

The development of the Ratel infantry fighting vehicle arose due to difficulties in procuring replacement parts and new vehicles due to the arms embargo of the apartheid era. Since the 1970s, variants of the wheeled Ratel have mounted a variety of weapons, such as 7.62mm (0.3in) machine guns, anti-tank mines and even a 90mm (3.5in) cannon, thus expanding the capabilities of the vehicle from a basic reconnaissance type to a direct fire support platform and a 'battle taxi' carrying six infantrymen. Continuing development of armoured vehicles has proved profitable for South African manufacturers. Given the high risk of landmines and improvised explosive devices, the RG-31 Nyala 4x4 troop carrier produced by Land Systems OMC has been described as one of the finest mine-protected vehicles in the world. Capable of transporting six infantrymen, the RG-31 is in use with the armed forces of at least eight countries, including the United States, Canada and France, and is classified by the US military as an MRAP (Mine Resistant Ambush Protected) vehicle.

Specifications
Crew: 6
Weight: 47,000kg (103,600lb)
Length: (chassis) 10.2m (33ft 4.3in)
Width: 3.4m (11ft 2in)
Height: 3.5m (11ft 6in)
Engine: 391kW (525hp) diesel
Speed: 90km/h (56mph)
Range: 700km (430 miles)
Armament: 1 x 155mm (6.1in) gun
Radio: n/k

▲ **G6 Rhino 155mm SP Howitzer**
South African Army / 8th Mechanized Infantry Battalion
The wheeled G6 Rhino self-propelled howitzer has been noted for its excellent mobility and protection against anti-tank mines. It has a crew of six, and its 155mm (6.1in) L52 cannon is intended for direct mechanized infantry fire support as well as the protection of advancing tank columns.

Specifications
Crew: 3 + 6
Weight: 19,000kg (41,887lb)
Length: 7.212m (23ft 4in)
Width: 2.526m (8ft 3in)
Height: 2.915m (9ft 7in)
Engine: 210kW (282bhp) 6-cylinder
 in-line diesel
Speed: 105km/h (65mph)
Range: 860km (534 miles)
Armament: 1 x 90mm (3.5in) gun, plus
 3 x 7.62mm (0.3in) MGs
Radio: n/k

▲ **Ratel 20**
South African Army / 61st Mechanized Infantry Battalion Group
In service with the South African military for more than 30 years, the Ratel armoured fighting vehicle is slated for replacement by the Patria armoured modular vehicle of Finnish manufacture. The Ratel has proved adept at both troop transport and fire support, armed with machine guns, anti-tank missiles and cannon.

Brazil
1991–PRESENT

More than 30 Brazilian manufacturers of armoured cars and fighting vehicles have found a ready market across the globe as low-intensity conflicts are prosecuted.

WHILE SOARING SALES raised Brazil to the sixth largest exporter of arms in the world, the nation's own fleet of armoured personnel carriers is currently being upgraded by a foreign company. The Italian firm Iveco has been engaged to produce a new six-wheeled armoured personnel carrier capable of transporting up to 11 soldiers and mounting a 30mm (1.18in) cannon or 12.7mm (0.5in) machine gun, which may be incorporated into a remote turret of Israeli manufacture.

Meanwhile, the Brazilians have been recognized for their EE-3 Jararaca armoured fighting vehicle of the 1980s and the EE-9 Cascavel armoured car, which has been operated by at least 17 countries and mounts an imposing 90mm (3.5in) cannon. Both vehicles were manufactured by the now-defunct Engesa defence contractor. During the 1980s, Engesa also produced prototypes of a main battle tank, the EE-T1 Osorio, to carry either a 105mm (4.1in) or 120mm (4.7in) gun, but it never reached production.

Specifications
Crew: 3
Weight: 5500kg (12,100lb)
Length: 4.12m (13ft 6.2in)
Width: 2.13m (6ft 11in)
Height: 1.56m (5ft 1.4in)
Engine: 89kW (120hp) Mercedes-Benz OM 314A
  4-cylinder turbo diesel
Speed: 100km/h (60mph)
Range: 750km (470 miles)
Armament: 1 x 12.7mm (0.5in) Browning M2 HB
  HMG as standard

▲ **EE-3 Jararaca**
Brazilian Army / 17th Mechanized Cavalry Regiment
A light armoured reconnaissance vehicle, the EE-3 Jararaca is powered by an 89kW (120hp), four-cylinder Mercedes-Benz diesel engine and mounts a 12.7mm (0.5in) machine gun for close defence. Variants mounted 20mm (0.79in) and heavier cannon or the MILAN anti-tank missile system.

▲ **EE-9 Cascavel**
Brazilian Army / 13th Armoured Infantry Battalion
The long service life of the EE-9 Cascavel has been marked by numerous variants and upgrades, and it is expected to continue for at least another decade. The most common, the Cascavel III, mounts a 90mm (3.5in) cannon of Belgian design and manufactured under licence.

Specifications
Crew: 3
Weight: 13,400kg (29,542lb)
Length: 5.2m (17ft 1in)
Width: 2.64m (8ft 8in)
Height: 2.68m (8ft 10in)
Engine: 158kW (212hp) Detroit Diesel 6V-53N
  6-cylinder water-cooled
Speed: 100km/h (62mph)
Range: 880km (547 miles)
Armament: 1 x 90mm (3.5in) gun, plus
  2 x 7.62mm (0.3in) MGs (1 coaxial,
  1 anti-aircraft)
Radio: n/k

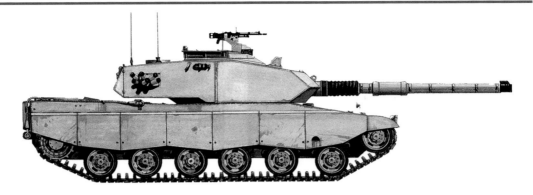

▲ **Engesa EE-T1 Osorio**

Brazilian prototype

The Osorio main battle tank project eventually led to the bankruptcy of the Engesa company, particularly after Iraq, one of its primary clients, ceased orders for armoured vheicles and Saudi Arabia opted to purchase the US M1A1 Abrams tank. The prototype Osorio mounted either a 120mm (4.7in) smoothbore or 105mm (4.1in) rifled gun.

Specifications

Crew: 4
Weight: 39,000kg (85,800lb)
Length: 9.995m (32ft 9.5in)
Width: 3.26m (10ft 8.3in)
Height: 2.371m (7ft 9.3in)

Engine: 745kW (1000hp) 12-cylinder diesel
Speed: 70km/h (43.5mph)
Range: 550km (342 miles)
Armament:1 x 105mm (4.1in) or 1 x 120mm
   (4.7in) gun, plus 1 x 7.62mm (0.3in) MG
Radio: n/k

The Far East
1995–PRESENT

The nations of the Far East have embarked on programmes of armoured vehicle development for their own armed forces and export to other nations during the twenty-first century.

ALTHOUGH ITS EARLIEST TANK designs were based solidly on Soviet technology, the People's Republic of China has begun to develop its own main battle tanks and armoured fighting vehicles, primarily funded by the manufacturing conglomerate China North Industries Corporation (NORINCO), and manufactured for the People's Liberation Army and for export purposes.

The latest generation of Chinese main battle tank, the Type 96, reached the army in the late 1990s and improved on the performance of previous main battle tanks such as the Type 88 and its predecessors, the Type 59 and 69, which were generally copies of the Soviet T-54/55. The Type 96 represents an improvement over previous Chinese designs, particularly in its powerplant, a 750kW (1000 hp) diesel with acceptable performance, outclassing previous engines whose problems had plagued Chinese engineers for decades. The Type 96 also incorporates modular explosive reactive armour and a

distinctive turret, which closely resembles those of many Western tanks rather than the rounded 'frying pan' look of older Soviet-inspired models.

The Type 96 mounts the 125mm (4.9in) smoothbore cannon, which has become standard on later model main battle tanks of Russian and Chinese manufacture. Its secondary armament consists of a pair of 7.62mm (0.3in) machine guns, and more than 1500 are currently in service with the People's Liberation Army.

In recent years, China has also entered the export market, selling a number of its Type 90 tanks to Pakistan for further joint development as the Al-Khalid. The Chinese military establishment had declined to adopt the Type 90 as its primary tank during the 1980s; however, its relative ease of manufacture and reasonable cost made it ideal for the cooperative venture. A notable 'second generation' Chinese tank is the Type 85, which was built by NORINCO and debuted in 1988.

The most advanced Chinese main battle tank is the Type 99, which was developed originally as the Type 98 during the 1990s and was seen publicly during the National Day parade in 1999. The Type 99 closely resembles Western contemporaries, utilizing sloped armour and a powerful 1125kW (1500hp) diesel engine. Through several variations, its capabilities have improved to rival those of the US Abrams, British Challenger and German Leopard tanks. It main armament includes 125mm (4.9in), 140mm (5.5in), or 155mm (6.1in) smoothbore guns, which are controlled by thermal and laser rangefinding equipment. A battlefield control system has also been installed, while the tank is protected by explosive reactive armour and a laser defence system that initiates a series of responses when the vehicle is identified by enemy targeting equipment.

Asian colossus

In recent years, the People's Liberation Army doctrine of combined arms has somewhat redefined the role of tanks and armoured fighting vehicles. In 2006, the army unveiled a reorganized mechanized infantry division equipped to fight as an independent battle group. The Type 92 wheeled infantry fighting vehicle and Type PL02 assault gun are expected to be key elements in the rapid mobility of these mechanized infantry formations. The Type 92 is armed with anti-

tank rockets, a grenade launcher or a flamethrower. The PL02 assault gun mounts a 100mm (3.9in) cannon.

The world's largest land military force, the People's Liberation Army is highly mechanized and is estimated to include nine armoured divisions, 12 independent armoured brigades and 27 mechanized or motorized infantry divisions. More than 10,000 tanks of various configurations are either deployed with active units or available in reserve.

North Korean nemesis

The secretive North Korean Chonma-ho upgrade to the Soviet-built T-62 main battle tank has produced an estimated 1200 vehicles, although their combat efficiency is somewhat questionable. It is known that the tanks mount 115mm (4.5in) or 125mm (4.9in) smoothbore cannon and are powered by a 563kW (750hp) diesel engine. The Chonma-ho debuted with North Korean forces in 1992, and a new North Korean main battle tank is reported in production. However, detail on this vehicle remains scarce.

The threat of military action by its communist neighbour to the north has prompted South Korea to remain vigilant and to develop its own main battle tank in recent years. Although the South would be confronted with overwhelming numbers of communist soldiers and armoured vehicles, it is possible that superior combat efficiency and

▲ **155/45 NORINCO SP Howitzer**

People's Liberation Army / 1st Armoured Division

The NORINCO-designed PLZ 155/45 self-propelled howitzer was conceived in the early 1990s for the Chinese armed forces and the export market. Its 155mm (6.1in) howitzer was modified by Chinese designers from an Austrian weapon. The vehicle also mounts a 12.7mm (0.5in) anti-aircraft machine gun and grenade launchers.

Specifications	
Crew: 5	Engine: 391.4kW (525hp) diesel
Weight: 32,000kg (70,560lb)	Speed: 56 km/h (35mph)
Length: 6.1m (20ft)	Range: 450km (280 miles)
Width: 3.2m (10ft 6in)	Armament: 1 x 155mm (6.1in) WAC-21 howitzer,
Height: 2.59m (8ft 6in)	plus 1 x 12.7mm (0.5in) anti-aircraft MG
	Radio: n/k

technology might bolster defences against North Korean aggression.

Although the South Korean Army has long depended on equipment manufactured in the United States and on the presence of American troops to deter North Korean military action, the South Koreans have manufactured the K1 main battle tank and its successor, the K1A1, since 1985. Based largely on the American M1 Abrams design, the tank is built in South Korea by Hyundai. The K1 was originally armed with the Korean-built KM68A1 105mm (4.1in) gun. Notable differences from the Abrams were its powerplant, the 900kW (1200hp) 10-cylinder diesel MTU-871 Ka-501 engine, and its weight of 51.8 tonnes (51 tons), making it lighter than the M1. US technology was prevalent in the K1, including thermal sights, laser rangefinding and composite armour whose characteristics remain classified.

▲ **Type 85 Main Battle Tank**

People's Liberation Army / 12th Armoured Division

The Type 85 main battle tank was introduced in 1991 and constituted an improvement over the previous Type 80, which had been based on the Soviet T-54/55. Later models included more powerful engines and modular armour. Some Type 85s were manufactured in Pakistan under licence.

Specifications

Crew: 3	Speed: 57.25km/h (35.8mph)
Weight: 41,000kg (90,200lb)	Range: 500km (312 miles)
Length: 10.28m (31ft 5in)	Armament:1 x 125mm (4.9in) gun; 1 x 12.7mm
Width: 3.45m (10ft 6in)	(0.5in) anti-aircraft HMG; 1 x 7.62mm (0.3in)
Height: 2.3m (7ft)	coaxial MG; 2 x smoke grenade launchers
Engine: 544kW (730hp) V12 diesel	Radio: Type 889B

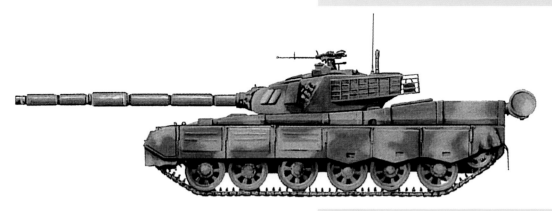

▲ **Type 90-II**

People's Liberation Army / 3rd Armoured Division

The Type 90-II main battle tank included an attempt to upgrade the powerplant of previous models with disappointing results, and the engine was replaced with a diesel of Ukrainian design. An export variant was purchased by Pakistan as the basis for the Al-Khalid main battle tank.

Specifications

Crew: 3	Speed: 62.3km/h (39mph)
Weight: 48,000kg (105,822lb)	Range: 450km (249 miles)
Length: 10.1m (33ft 1in)	Armament: 1 x 125mm (4.9in) smoothbore gun,
Width: 3.5m (11ft 6in);	plus 1 x 12.7mm (0.5in) external anti-aircraft
Height: 2.2m (7ft 2in)	MG and 1 x 7.62mm (0.3in) coaxial MG
Engine: 895kW (1200hp) Perkins CV12-1200 TCA	Radio: n/k
12-cylinder diesel	

Illustrating the globalization of arms technology, the K1A1, deployed to the South Korean Army in 2001, mounts the 120mm (4.7in) KM256 smoothbore, a licensed version of the US M256, which, in turn, is a licensed production model of a German Rheinmetall weapon. The K1A1 includes a reconfigured turret and upgraded target acquisition systems. Its armour protection is enhanced with a composite designated as KSAP (Korean Special Armour Plate).

Black Panther

While the K1 and K1A1 main battle tanks may be sufficient to oppose the technology fielded by the North Koreans, the South Korean military establishment is producing a complementary tank, the K2 Black Panther, which is intended to supplement the existing modern tanks in the armed forces while replacing those elderly tanks of the US Patton series, which have been in service for decades. Nearly 400 examples of the new tank are scheduled for production. The Black Panther implements a substantial amount of South Korean technology, which in part provided the impetus for the project, begun in the mid-1990s. Prohibitively expensive, the K2 has incorporated the contributions of at least 11 South Korean defence contractors and showcases some of the nation's most advanced military systems.

The primary armament of the Black Panther is a 120mm (4.7in) L55 smoothbore gun with automatic loading system, capable of firing modern APFSDS ammunition manufactured in South Korea. The tank is powered by a 1125kW (1500hp) 12-cylinder diesel engine. Its advanced technology includes global positioning equipment, sophisticated battlefield management capabilities through computerized command and control apparatus, a battlefield management and communication system that allows one tank to share real-time information with others in formation, and radar warning and jamming defences.

The army of the Republic of Korea fields nearly 6000 armoured vehicles, including approximately 3000 tanks, half of which are the modern K1 and K1A1. Its troop strength is roughly 520,000, the sixth highest in the world.

Japan's new generation

The Japanese Type 10 main battle tank is slated as the successor to the Type 74 and Type 90 main battle tanks currently in service with the nation's defence forces. As the Type 74, a contemporary of the German Leopard 1 and the US M60 Patton main battle tanks, and the Type 90, which was fielded more than 20 years ago, continue to be upgraded and their service lives extended, the Type 10 marks an

▲ **Type 87 SPAAG**

Japan Ground Self-Defense Force / 2nd Combined Brigade

The Type 87 self-propelled anti-aircraft gun mounts a pair of radar-directed 35mm (1.38in) autocannon. Developed during the 1980s as a replacement for the outmoded American M42 Duster, the Type 87 has a chassis by Mitsubishi, while its weapons, similar to the Swiss Oerlikon, were produced by Japan Steel Works.

Specifications

Crew: 3	diesel
Weight: 36,000kg (79,400lb)	Speed: 60km/h (37mph)
Length: 7.99m (26ft 2in)	Range: 500km (310 miles)
Width: 3.18m (10ft 5in)	Armament: 2 x 35mm (1.38in) autocannon
Height: 4.4m (14ft 5in)	Radio: n/k
Engine: 536kW (718hp) 10F22WT 10-cylinder	

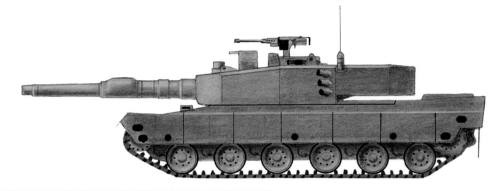

Specifications

Crew: 3	10-cylinder diesel
Weight: 50,000kg (110,250lb)	Speed: 70km/h (43mph)
Length: 9.76m (32ft)	Range: 400km (250 miles)
Width: 3.43m (11ft 4in)	Armament: 1 x 120mm (4.7in) gun; 1 x 12.7mm
Height: 2.34m (7ft 11in)	(0.5in) HMG; 1 x 7.62mm (0.3in) MG
Engine: 1118kW (1500bhp) Mitsubishi 10ZG	Radio: n/k

▲ **Type 90 Main Battle Tank**

Japan Ground Self-Defence Force / 7th Armoured Division

Mounting a licence-built version of the German Rheinmetall 120mm (4.7in) smoothbore gun with an automatic loading system, the Japanese Type 90 main battle tank entered service in 1990 and nearly 350 examples were built. Its armour protection and target acquisition equipment were comparable to Western tanks of the same generation.

impressive advance in the capabilities of Japanese land forces. Production of the Type 10 is scheduled to commence in 2010, and its design phase was undertaken during the 1990s. The tank is expected to mount a 120mm (4.7in) smoothbore main weapon manufactured by Japan Steel Works Ltd and capable of firing standard NATO ammunition. Its sloped modular armour and profile are similar to those of the German Leopard 2 or the French Leclerc main battle tanks, and its armour protection is a composite structure of ceramic, steel and other components. It

is powered by a 900kW (1200hp) 8-cylinder diesel engine, and at approximately 40.6 tonnes (40 tons) is somewhat lighter than contemporary main battle tanks of other nations.

Currently, the Japan Ground Self-Defense Force deploys approximately 1000 Type 90 and Type 74 tanks. It includes one armoured division and nine infantry divisions and totals about 150,000 troops. The primary combined arms unit is the brigade, which incorporates mechanized infantry and armoured elements.

Australian armour

The Royal Australian Armoured Corps has recently provided manpower to NATO and Coalition forces in Iraq and Afghanistan as well as during the unrest in East Timor, Rwanda and Somalia. It is equipped with the American M1A1 Abrams main battle tank and includes British

◀ **Type 90 MBT**

With its vertical front, sides and rea, the turret of the Japanese Type 90 is similar to that of the Leopard 2.

Land Rover reconnaissance vehicles and the US M113 armoured personnel carrier. The Bushmaster wheeled armoured vehicle is manufactured in Australia under licence from Timoney Technology of Ireland. The Bushmaster underwent trials with the Australian Army in the late 1990s, and more than 800 units have been built to date. Capable of transporting up to nine combat infantrymen, the vehicle mounts 5.56mm (0.22in) and 7.62mm (0.3in) machine guns for close defence. Lightly armoured, the Bushmaster is nevertheless considered effective against mines and improvised explosive devices. Several armoured cavalry regiments deploy the Bushmaster, as does the Royal Australian Air Force and the armies of Great Britain and the Netherlands.

Besides the major powers of Asia–Pacific, other regional players maintain modern armoured forces. The Malaysian Army has purchased a number of Polish PT-91M main battle tanks and fields infantry vehicles and tank destroyers of Turkish, South African and Brazilian manufacture. The Royal Thai Army includes an armoured division, a cavalry division and five independent tank battalions equipped with the British-made Scorpion light tank. The army of Myanmar has more than 100 T-55 and T-72 tanks and at least 1000 armoured infantry vehicles.

▲ Bionix 25

Singapore Armed Forces / 5th Infantry Brigade

The first production model of the Bionix armoured personnel carrier, the Bionix 25 has been manufactured since 1996. Developed in Singapore to replace the M113 vehicle of US design, it is capable of transporting up to seven infantrymen. The Bionix 25 is armed with the M242 Bushmaster 25mm (1in) cannon.

Specifications

Crew: 3 + 7
Weight: 23,000kg (50,700lb)
Length: 5.92m (19ft 5in)
Width: 2.7m (8ft 10in)
Height: 2.53m (8ft 4in)
Engine: 354kW (475hp) Detroit Diesel
    Model 6V-92TA
Speed: 70km/h (43mph)
Range: 415km (260 miles)
Armament: 1 x 25mm (1in) Boeing M242
    cannon; 2 x 7.62mm (0.3in) MGs
    (1 coaxial, 1 turret-mounted);
    2 x 3 smoke grenade launchers
Radio: n/k

▲ Warthog

Singapore Armed Forces / UK Ministry of Defence, delivery 2010

The Warthog variant of the Bronco all-terrain tracked carrier was jointly developed by Singapore Technologies Kinetics and the Defence Science & Technology Agency for the Singapore Armed Forces. The fulfilment of an order for the Warthog by the British Ministry of Defence is under way. Slated to replace the Viking carrier, the Warthog transports up to 10 infantrymen and features slat armour and anti-mine reinforcement.

Specifications

Crew: (front car) 4; (rear car) 8
Weight: 18 tonnes (17.7 tons)
Length: 8.6m (28ft 2.5in)
Width: 2.3m (8ft 2.4in)
Height: 2.2m (7ft 2.5in)

Engine: 261kW (350hp) Caterpillar 3126B
Speed: (road) 65km/h (40mph);
    (water) 5km/h (3.1mph)
Range: n/k
Armament: 1 x 7.62mm (0.3in) MG or
    1 x 5.56mm (0.22in) MG

Bibliography

Clancy, Tom. *Armored Cav: A Guided Tour of an Armored Cavalry Regiment*. Berkley Books: New York, 1994.

Crismon, Fred W. *U.S. Military Tracked Vehicles*. Motorbooks International: Osceola, Wisconsin, 1992.

Crismon, Fred W. *U.S. Military Wheeled Vehicles*. Motorbooks International: Osceola, Wisconsin, 1994.

Department of the Army, United States Army Intelligence and Security Command, United States Army Intelligence and Threat Analysis Center. *Soviet Army Operations*. U.S. Army: Arlington, Virginia, 1978.

Green, Michael & James D. Brown. *M2/M3 Bradley at War*. Zenith Press: Minneapolis, Minnesota, 2007.

Hogg, Ian. *Tank Killing: Anti-Tank Warfare by Men and Machines*. Sarpedon: New York, 1996.

Jackson, Robert. *Tanks and Armoured Fighting Vehicles Visual Encyclopedia*. Amber Books Ltd: London, 2009.

Leyden, Andrew. *An After Action Report: Gulf War Debriefing Book*. Hellgate Press: Grants Pass, Oregon, 1997.

Macksey, Kenneth & John H. Batchelor. *Tank: A History of the Armoured Fighting Vehicle*. Charles Scribner's Sons: New York, 1970.

Mossman, Billy C. *United States Army in the Korean War: Ebb and Flow November 1950–July 1951*. Center of Military History United States Army. Washington, D.C., 1990.

Zaloga, Steven. *M1 Abrams vs T-72 Ural: Operation Desert Storm 1991*. Osprey Publishing Ltd.: Oxford, United Kingdom, 2009.

Useful Websites

armchairgeneral.com
army-technology.com
defenseindustrydaily.com
eliteforces.info
enemyforces.net
globalsecurity.org

history.army.mil
historyofwar.org
israelnewsagency.com
janes.com
militaryfactory.com
militaryphotos.net

nationmaster.com
olive-drab.com
orbat.com
sinodefence.com
turretsandtracks.co.uk
wikipedia.org

Index

Page numbers in *italics* refer to illustrations and photographs.